10 9 8 7 6 5 4 3 2 1

Permissions:
University of North Texas Press
1155 Union Circle #311336
Denton, TX 76203-5017

The paper used in this book meets the minimum requirements
of the American National Standard for Permanence of Paper for
Printed Library Materials, z39.48.1984. Binding materials have
been chosen for durability.

Library of Congress Cataloging-in-Publication Data

Thorsen, Terry L., 1943- author.
  Phantom in the sky : a Marine's back seat view of the Vietnam
War / by Terry L. Thorsen.
     pages cm.
  Includes bibliographical references and index.
  ISBN-13 978-1-57441-754-8 (cloth : alk. paper)
  ISBN-13 978-1-57441-762-3 (ebook)
  1. Thorsen, Terry L., 1943- 2. Vietnam War, 1961–1975—Personal
narratives, American. 3. Vietnam War, 1961–1975—Aerial operations,
American. 4. United States. Marine Corps—Officers—Biography.
5. Fighter pilots—United States—Biography. 6. Phantom II
(Jet fighter plane) 7. Biographies.

  DS559.5 .T538 2019
  959.704/34092 [B] –dc23
                    2018054084

Phantom in the Sky: A Marine's Back Seat View of the Vietnam War is
Number 15 in the North Texas Military Biography and Memoir Series

The electronic edition of this book was made possible by the support
of the Vick Family Foundation.
Typeset by vPrompt eServices.

This book is dedicated to my wife, Audrina. Without her assistance, support, and encouragement it would have never been completed.

The book is in praise of those who didn't pass through the Vietnam combat zone over the ground at speeds often in excess of 500 miles per hour, but instead met the enemy face to face. It is especially dedicated to those whose encounter became their destiny. Their stories cannot be told nor their praises uttered often enough. Semper Fi.

I extend my sincerest appreciation to Ron Chrisman, Director, University of North Texas Press, for his insight and guidance on this memoir.

My heartfelt thanks go to Dr. Earl H. Tilford, professor and Air Force veteran, for his expert counsel and insight into Vietnam War history.

Contents

Preface

Phantom in the Sky chronicles my active duty Marine Corps experience from August 1966 through September 1970, as the Vietnam War raged. While my last semester of college was coming to an end, I decided to avoid being drafted by voluntarily enlisting. I wanted to be an officer instead of enlisted and an aviator, eliminating the possibility of becoming a ground combatant. I ended up in the Naval Flight Officer (NFO) program. It is an understatement to say qualifying for and attaining flight status is difficult. The turbulent years I was in the Marine Corps coincided with my aviation training as I had airsickness issues. Despite the odds of failure, in spite of physiological adversity and often being reproved, I earned my wings and joined the oldest and most decorated squadron in the Corps, the Red Devils of VMFA-232. It required a Herculean effort with tumultuous highs and lows, tragedies and triumphs, moments of stark terror and instances of total dejection and helplessness. Ultimately I became a proficient Radar Intercept Officer ("R-I-O") and had a successful tour in Vietnam garnering ten Air Medals, one Bronze Star Award, and two Navy Unit Commendations in addition to the usual Vietnam accolades.

I began writing this book over thirty years ago and had to wait for retirement to complete it. The source materials are many and varied: my flight logbook, all the letters I wrote home while in combat (which my mother saved), stuff gleaned from peers and reunion discussions, combat flight schedules saved by one of my RIO acquaintances, USMC history, the F-4J flight manual, current event publications at the time, and my recollection (which was much better when I first started but there are some things you never forget). Being a photojournalist in college and many years a Public Affairs Officer in a Marine Aircraft Group (in the Reserves) enhanced my abilities to author this book.

Phantom in the Sky is a back-seat perspective, a unique insight into tactical military aviation. The "GIB," the "Guy in Back," has often been overlooked or ignored. During the time of my service, the Radar Intercept Officer played an integral part in enemy aircraft intercept and ordnance delivery. That billet no longer exists due to technological avionics advances. In Navy and Marine F-4 Phantom jets, however, the RIO was a second pair of eyes for the pilot, in charge of communications and navigation and great to have during emergencies. He (there were no women then) was an immeasurable asset to the flight in an environment where minor faux pas created permanent nicknames and major ones caused fatalities.

The title stems from the Phantom jet, which was a twin-engine, tandem seat, supersonic (Mach 2+) jet aircraft and had a numerical designation of F-4. RIOs in the back seat became experts at finding bogeys (enemy aircraft targets) with radar equipment. Since Marine aviation mainly exists for our ground forces, the majority of our Vietnam missions were close air support.

This book is infused with aviation humor, jargon, procedures, actualities (including airborne emergencies), and combat lingo and happenstances.

Some names have been changed and some individuals have been assigned names because their name was never known or could not be recalled.

Prologue

As we circled our target, all hell was breaking loose on the ground. This was not going to be a routine flight but an emergency close air support mission. The whole area was hostile, crawling with an enemy that had one of our recon teams trapped on top of a hill in the A Shau Valley, a hill near the soon to be infamous Hamburger Hill. When I checked in with aerial controller "Cowboy and Indian," my pilot and I could see that the marines were totally surrounded. Their survival appeared hopeless. Muzzle flashes showing both uphill and downhill trajectories were visible even from our altitude of 14,000 feet. Though the team was putting up a great fight, they were vastly outnumbered and about to be overrun by "Charlie" (Viet Cong combatants). It was organized chaos and the sight was surreal.

The team's situation was critical and I instantly prayed they wouldn't die. Their only hope was a helicopter I observed hovering in an adjacent valley ready to pick them up if the pilot could get into position. A heavily armed Huey Cobra helicopter and our controller's OV-10 Bronco observer plane began making live fire low altitude dives, in concert, to kill the enemy or suppress their fire with a devastating effect. In the midst of the barrage, the "friendlies" (recon team) popped a purple smoke to accurately pinpoint their location and the helicopter in the valley maneuvered over them. Charlie instantly directed their fire at the chopper while the Marine team members rapidly climbed aboard. I was certain they were taking hits.

The chopper quickly departed through the valley below. My fixation with this scene was interrupted by controller Cowboy and Indian who had marked our target with a white phosphorous flare and cleared us in hot. The spectacle was over; it was time for us to go to work. As we set up on target, our controller said, "Hit my mark at 6 o'clock at thirty meters. No, make that 50 meters, they're running down hill like scared rabbits!" I radioed back, "Roger, one's in hot" and my pilot and I and our wingman blew the hell out of the side of the hill with clusters of 500-pound fragmentary bombs and 2.75-inch rockets. As we cleared the area, our two Phantom jets joined up and flew back to the relative safety of Chu Lai Air Base south of Da Nang. In a moment of reflection, I commented to my pilot, "Those guys nearly got their asses blown off." He replied, "We don't know that they didn't."

At debrief, we were informed the recon team, miraculously, was extracted without casualties, that our flight had received enemy fire and that we were credited with twenty-two KBMA (enemy killed by Marine air). I was elated for the team but in the heat of the moment, being shot at never entered my mind. Two thoughts did: our Marine Red Devil squadron, VMFA-232, was a force the enemy had to reckon with and there was nothing routine about combat. This sortie was just my third in Country. A hundred and twenty more combat missions lay ahead, containing things I could not begin to imagine at that time.

Chapter 1

Screwed

houghts raced through my mind faster than the Boeing airliner winged its way to Washington D.C. taking me to Marine Officer Candidates School (OCS). It was a cold, dismal, winter day overshadowed with misgivings and anxiety. More events began to unfold than memory could retain and it was just the beginning of my Marine Corps experience. I was nervous, almost scared, and the only thing certain was there was no turning back.

I was headed to the Marine Corps Base at Quantico, Virginia, for three months. Horror stories I had heard about OCS I would soon experience firsthand. My anxiety heightened as the distance increased from Amon Carter Airport in Fort Worth and a myriad of questions bombarded my cranium: Could I hack it and get commissioned? What happens if I wash out? Was OCS everything everyone said? Little did I know it was infinitely more; hell was waiting for me. I wondered if I could earn aviator wings but nothing prepared me for the events that began with that plane ride January 7, 1967.

In a plane full of people I never felt more alone. I was missing college graduation two days hence. Sadly, there was no pomp and circumstance for me after five years' cost and effort. Earning a degree was the first major accomplishment of my adult life; this embarkation was my second. Courtesy of the United States Marine Corps (USMC), that ceremony was the first of many events I would miss. Soon, I would rely heavily on the fortitude and perseverance it took to earn my Bachelor of Science, biology over chemistry, degree.

Early in the summer of 1966, the Vietnam War was escalating and the draft was dutifully garnering young men to meet quotas, even married ones. At the end of that summer, while finishing the last course for my degree, making a decision regarding military service was imminent. I married my fiancée Jan during my senior year and she was dead set against me serving at all. I quit my low-paying photojournalism job, though I loved the news business and had met and photographed many prominent people, including two future U.S. presidents: George H. W. Bush and then-Governor Ronald Reagan. I regrettably missed John F. Kennedy's early press conference in Fort Worth the day of his assassination due to a chemistry exam.

I acquired a higher-paying job as a chemist at a paint manufacturing company. They made commercial paints of all types, including those of military specifications. Their ugly olive drab color was on the bombs that I would ultimately drop for practice in the States and for real in Vietnam. The technical director, my boss, had been a Navy pilot in the Korean era. He swayed me towards naval aviation while I wrestled with the decision to continue my education (deferring military obligation), or joining one of the branches of the service. I preferred not to serve but it was unlikely I could avoid it with the war in Vietnam raging. Skipping the country for Canada was an emphatic no. I refused to shirk my responsibility and resented those who did.

Upon inquiring, my draft board indicated I could be called up in October that year. What knowledge I had of the armed forces convinced me that I didn't want to be drafted into the Army and possibly end up in the infantry and in Vietnam. No one in my family ever served in the military and I'd never talked to a recruiter. My father and chief advisor, an aircraft design engineer, became somewhat silent on the subject. Apparently he didn't want to guide me on this one. Eventually I decided that all I had heard made me want to be a Naval Aviator and use my degree to my best advantage by getting a commission and wings and all the glory that goes with it.

Though I got airsick on a flight in an Army observer plane while working for the newspaper, I hadn't had motion sickness issues since my childhood.

I was ignorant, uninformed, and naïve the day I walked into the Dallas Naval Air Station (NAS) and took their aviator exam. Once into the exam I wondered what form of egomania I suffered from that convinced me I had one iota of a chance to qualify for their program. Without aviation experience, I failed that category but surprisingly not by much. At this point, I hadn't a clue what to do next.

My life was on an even keel but the military service issue was front and center. I needed to resolve my quandary or face the draft. While I considered all the weighty alternatives, Jan refused to discuss the matter. Perhaps she thought ignoring it would make it go away. I wanted to fulfill my obligation but did not want to go to war. I abhorred people like Muhammad Ali who used religious or other reasons to weasel out of their patriotic duty. I felt no one demonstrated greater hypocrisy than Ali who pummeled his opponents to a pulp in a boxing ring, yet refused to serve.[1]

By this time, the Texas summer heat had cooked my brain. Between my boss and Marine Corps propaganda, I determined that the Marines were the best-trained fighting force in the world—a few good men, elite, crème de la crème, jar heads, leathernecks, devil dogs, first to fight, time-honored, esprit de corps and all that. So I visited a Marine recruiter knowing I was raw meat!

As the jet continued to Dulles International Airport, I recounted that decision and other recent ones that were shaping my future and determining my fate for the next several years. The recruiter had welcomed me with open arms. I asked about Marine Corps programs. After some minutes of elaboration, with generalities and overtures, he talked in more definitive terms, giving specifics about time frames, training, duties, and contracts. While trying to discern between bullshit and just plain shit, I quickly brushed off all the grunt stuff and informed him of my desire to be in aviation. That's when he got excited and said, "Have I got a deal for you!" He gleefully said that the Marine Corps had planes. He said I needed to take the aviation exam issued at NAS Dallas. I told him I had taken the exam and failed the aviation section. After making a phone call, the recruiter told me that my score was 6/4 and that a score of 5/5 was the minimum for pilot training.

The recruiter asked me if I had heard of the naval flight officer program. He informed me naval flight officers earned wings just like pilots did, earned the same flight pay and their training was similar but shorter. He also stated an NFO's obligation of service was less than that for pilots. It didn't take college trigonometry to conclude that I could spend less time for the same pay. It all sounded very inviting. Then he put the icing on the cake. He said nearly all NFOs got jets, whereas only the upper 10 percent of pilots did since jets were so highly sought after. I was sold, yet asked, "What's the catch?" "There is none," responded the recruiter. He told me I qualified with my test score and that the next requirement was to pass a flight physical at NAS Dallas. So, I signed an aviation officer candidate contract. What does candidate mean? It means you ain't nothin' until completion! My signature launched an extraordinary journey.

Jan and I had a huge fight that night when I told her I had signed a contract with the Marine Corps. I tried to explain that not serving was not an option and that I was going to have to join the military in one capacity or another and that at least this way I had some control over the outcome. She just didn't get it and thus began a rift that would never be patched. There was no "making the best of the situation" with her. It would always be discontent and sometimes hate. My parents took the news with ambivalence. They understood and reluctantly supported me. As miserable as it was, it got lots worse.

As the jet continued its course to D.C., I recalled that physical. At 7:00 AM on a hot August day, I joined a group of men to participate in what can only be described as a cattle herding event. About twenty-five of us stood in a lineup to be embarrassed and humiliated. While being poked and prodded by all the doctors there, my first lesson about military life was learned: there was no such thing as modesty. I passed every test with flying colors until it came to the dental exam. An old short military dentist came over, stood in front of me and informed me that I was disqualified because my teeth didn't meet in the front.

Others had been disqualified quickly, easily, or quietly. I conjectured the gap resulted from fillings. He said in a loud voice so the room full of remaining applicants couldn't help but hear, "See here, your teeth don't meet in the front." With this proclamation the dentist came up on his tiptoes, right in my face with his lips well parted, to show me a set of semi-green teeth that clearly met in the front. He hollered, "You couldn't bite a damn piece of lettuce in two." His breath was so terrible I nearly passed out from the stench. Humiliated, embarrassed, dejected, and confused I, who considered myself to be the picture of health, flunked the physical. I felt my chances slipping away. I was given a copy of my paperwork and dismissed. I'd never noticed the miniscule gap between my upper and lower teeth nor had it never affected my eating. I headed home deflated, wondering how something so small could upset the apple cart. The news elated Jan. My parents, especially my mom, tried to keep things positive.

Despondent and thinking things were hopeless I contacted the recruiter who surprisingly wasn't dashed by the news. "What do we do next?" I asked. He said he would submit my package with a waiver for my teeth and it would interrupt any draft board action unless I wasn't accepted. I had no idea what my chances of being accepted were or why my teeth not meeting in the front had anything pertinent to do with military aviation. Surprisingly, word came back about as fast as bureaucracies work stating that I needed to furnish the Marine Corps with a plaster cast of my teeth at my expense. It instantly pissed me off and exposed for me some of the character and workings of the Marine Corps. I contemplated telling them what they could do with their cast but acquiesced and furnished one. I was tired of putting forth all the effort and didn't wait for a reply.

Hoping for one viable option, I went to Carswell Air Force Base (AFB) in Fort Worth and took their officers' entrance exam. The next day, an excited Air Force recruiter called and informed me that I had knocked the top off their test. I qualified for whatever kind of officer program I wanted—supply, aviation, maintenance, or administration. I could pick! Then the recruiter asked, "When can you come to sign a contract?" I told him I was conditionally under contract with the Marine Corps. He was disappointed but said he was available if things didn't work out. That's as close as I ever got to an Air Force career but not the Air Force itself. There would be times I wished I'd chosen the Air Force instead.

My acceptance from the Commandant of the Marine Corps came in November with a notice that I would attend the 43rd Officer Candidates School in January. Though I started jogging to tone up, I was wrong in thinking I was physically fit for the Corps. The 43rd OCS class wouldn't just be historic for me; it would assure its place in history for being the USMC's class with the highest attrition rate ever and a congressional investigation would convene to try to determine why. As the plane began getting close to its destination, I thought about the war and then the protesters.

Nervously, I engaged in some casual conversation about education reform with a schoolteacher sitting next to me. We agreed that protesting dissidents should change things from the inside rather than with civil disobedience and neither of us could fathom why protesters blamed military personnel instead of politicians who set policy. I'd never rebelled against or protested anything and had little patience or understanding for those who did. We both felt our country was entering a period of moral and political uncertainty—utter turmoil. The impetus of my service and the fact that I was now inexorably connected to, yet diametrically opposed to this movement, hit home as the plane landed. I was now one of those they were protesting against. I felt the United States and I had begun a new era. Little did I know, things wouldn't be smooth for some time to come.

Chapter 2

Maggot Candidate

After emerging from the baggage claim, I looked for the Marine Corps representative who was supposed to meet and escort me to Quantico. He was nowhere to be found. I was alone, on edge and feeling lost. I quit looking for this nonexistent representative, when five other stranded aviation candidates and I found each other and thought we'd been stood up. Unbeknownst to us, our bus at Dulles was already en route to the Base while, unbelievably, we were in the Baltimore International Airport in Maryland. Being in the company of others in the same situation brought little comfort. We were all apprehensive: me, Dennis Peek, Terry Ewing, Jerry Leist, and two others.

After brainstorming, we called a Quantico contact number obtained from a local recruiter. A base representative said it was some sort of SNAFU (Situation Normal, All Fucked Up) and told us to get our asses down to Quantico any way we could and we'd be reimbursed; just get there before midnight. Agitated, the rep asked, "What the hell are you doing in Baltimore?" Our response was, "That's where our plane tickets brought us." The rep barked, "Get your asses down here, ASAP!" The full meaning and impact of "before midnight" (written on all our orders) was apparent: absent without leave. It would have been humorous if it hadn't been pathetic.

We were getting our asses chewed out for something that wasn't our fault and hadn't even checked in yet. More SNAFUs awaited us!

We pooled our money and moral support and flew to Dulles in a new Boeing 737 airliner, which my father had helped design, and chartered a limo-type taxi that drove us down to Quantico. En route to the base, the taxi driver prophetically commented, "You boys are in for a treat." We arrived at 2340 hours Military Time, 11:40 PM, and pissed off nearly everyone with whom we came in contact. Checking in was neither fun nor a "treat." The enlisted personnel shouted obscenities at us while throwing our issued goods in our faces—a crappy welcoming into the Corps. Our recruiters hadn't mentioned this! While I was receiving clothing, one of them asked where I was from. Though from a suburb, I said Dallas because it was so recognizable. "President killer," he responded. Most of the Marines issuing our goods were officer candidate washouts and resented us. While marching to our barracks loaded down with luggage, equipment, and clothing, I contemplated how lousy things were already. For many, it became temporary hell on earth. Upon arriving at E (Echo) Company barracks, our time at Quantico austerely began.

Our platoon sergeant told us all to strip down to our underwear and stand at attention at the end of the racks. He issued some pertinent instructions, mostly no, no's. While he talked, a drill sergeant walked over to me, faced me and screamed at the top of his lungs, "Where's your undershirt candidate?" I didn't like wearing undershirts and timidly replied, "I don't wear them." He screamed back at me, "I can't hear you." I knew he could because he was six inches from my face. Suddenly I realized I was supposed to be sounding off. I yelled, "I don't wear them sergeant!" The drill sergeant walked off. It was nearly 0100 hours (1:00 AM) and the platoon sergeant allowed us 30 minutes to write letters home. Strangely, this seemed important to me. I found paper but no pencil and gave up. I hadn't closed my eyes on my first day in the Marine Corps and I already felt like a piece of shit. I crawled into my rack with my eyes wide open and finally fell asleep.

Wham, clang, clank, clank, clunk. We all jolted out of bed like we'd been shot. The light was on but it was dark outside. "Fall in," our platoon sergeant loudly ordered. "Look alive candidates." We all stood at attention at the end of our racks awake, looking alive, and scared as hell. It was "O Dark

Thirty," 0430 hours, 4:30 AM. My first full day in the Corps was starting off with a bang. As we stood at attention, Captain Bennett, the Echo Company commander, came into the squad bay. He told us our group comprised his third platoon. There was no Delta Company in this OCS class, only Alpha, Bravo, Charlie, and Echo. Each company had four platoons, and each platoon ultimately had about fifty candidates. We spent a great deal of time over the next three months in that room.

Home sweet home? Not hardly, but we learned to respect those hallowed halls, not to mention scrub them and the "head" (Navy for latrine, or restroom), mop and wax the floors and keep them spotless. The tidiest wife had nothing on us. The captain said he would see us only on certain occasions and that our platoon sergeant was in charge, AND HE WAS. What followed next was more of the "I can't hear you game." We were being molded through compliance, a brainwashing of sorts. We learned to outfit ourselves, organize our foot and wall lockers, and marched everywhere as a group.

The next thing we knew the sun was up and we were marched to the chow hall. Outside, the platoon sergeant issued a series of commands with disdain. "No talking, line up candidates, assholes to belly buttons! Make the candidate in front of you smile! Move it, candidates," speaking the word "candidate" with contempt as if we were diseased. We were herded like cattle into the chow hall, a cafeteria-style arrangement, to be served food by other OCS washouts who indignantly rushed and harassed us. The food wasn't bad; everything associated with it was. The servers piled on huge amounts of food because we didn't know we had control over the selections and quantity of portions. Grace was posted and next to it, in big bold letters, was the quote: "Take all you want, but eat all you take." Once we were seated, we were rushed to get finished. I hated rushed meals. Immediately after chow, a medic administered inoculations (seven at once in the arm) and then we engaged in strenuous physical training (PT) for an hour. Not all of us threw up our breakfasts, but our inoculated arm felt like it was going to fall off.

The barbershop was also degrading. We all took turns in the chair and after being asked about bumps or moles to avoid, were shaved absolutely bald. I wasn't aware of any bumps or moles, just a scar from a bicycle accident in the sixth grade and then felt defiled as my hair hit the floor. It was another shred of the outside civilization taken away. Slowly we became acclimated, looking like candidates with cold pates in the Virginia winter. Eventually all "clingings" to outside civilization were erased. Candidates who found this unacceptable dropped out. Those of us remaining adapted in our own way. At lunch, it was more of the same, servers piling it on and dishing it out with fewer problems now that we knew how the game was played. The frequency and magnitude of physical exertion did make us hungry and OCS was seemingly 50 percent physical to me. The gist of OCS logic was "comply or die." I had to accept, like it or not.

That afternoon at the lecture hall, I entered the classroom with my utility cover (cap) on, one of the many no-no's. The platoon sergeant told me to drop and give him twenty. I immediately dropped to the floor and started cranking out push-ups. After about fifteen, he said, "I can't hear you." He couldn't because I wasn't counting out loud. I sounded off sixteen and seventeen when the platoon sergeant screamed at me to start with one! I did twenty more, calling each one out loudly, as hatred welled up inside me.

Various lectures consisted of Marine Corps propaganda and general information like first aid and hygiene. It would have been easy to go to sleep if it hadn't been for the lecturers' occasionally projecting a slide of a nude woman on the screen. The photo only shown briefly but was very effective. Various noncommissioned officers (NCOs) took the lectern to break the boredom and monotony, but not nearly as effectively as nudes. When we were given our personal copy of Marine Officer's School regulations and guidebook for Marines (the Marine Corps Manual), I wished I'd had them months earlier. My feet ached because of my new boots and my clothes itched, as lectures continued through the afternoon. We didn't dare socialize during lectures. After viewing a portion of a John Wayne movie depicting the Marines in action at Iwo Jima, I was impressed. The Marine Corps did have quite a heritage. In truth, it is a very distinguished and decorated branch of service and I began to think I made a good choice.[2] United States Marines are patterned after the British Marines. The United States Marine Corps (USMC) had its beginnings as Continental Marines on November 10, 1775, before the Declaration of Independence, and the Marine Corps that exists today, by enactment on July 11, 1798.[3] For expanded history and mission see Appendix A.

Our 43rd OCS class had a lot to live up to. My credo: I will do my best. After chow we were allowed some free time. While briefly fraternizing, the platoon sergeant and Captain Bennett came into the squad bay. No one hollered attention on deck (a serious no, no), so the platoon sergeant did and all of us snapped to attention. Captain Bennett put us at ease and "passed the word," outlining activities, etc. After the captain left, we got our asses chewed off by the platoon sergeant who told us "You fucking maggots will acknowledge any officer who comes into this room with, 'Attention on Deck'." He gave us free time until 2200 hours at which time it was lights out and that meant LIGHTS OUT, PERIOD. There were no exceptions to lights out except for the captain. The platoon sergeant warned us to use our time wisely as he left. I wrote a letter home, candy coating everything. At lights out and saturated with the day's events, I had difficulty going to sleep. This continued for days to come but as OCS progressed, I lay spread eagle, went to sleep quickly and probably snored as loud as a logger's chainsaw just like other candidates.

Aviation officer candidates reported to OCS a week earlier than ground officer candidates for expressly one purpose: an aviation physical, a four-hour physical that took all day. I passed with flying colors and the minuscule gap in my teeth wasn't mentioned. After the physical there was nothing else for us to do until the remaining candidates reported in by Sunday midnight. So, we had orientation, PT, or other instruction. Occasionally there were opportunities to ask questions, but they didn't like them even if pertinent. I felt knowledge was better than a verbal bashing or push-ups. After physical training that day, I asked how to respond to a person who addressed me from outside my field of vision. It was a legitimate question but after PT with snow on the ground and icicles hanging off the roofs was not a good time to ask. Aggravated, the platoon sergeant answered, "Either answer Sir (appropriate for an officer but not if he or she wasn't) or take a quick look at the individual, snap back to attention facing forward and respond with the appropriate rank that was just visually ascertained." This answer was a no-win, two-edged sword.

After chow the next morning, in freezing cold, windy, drizzly weather, our platoon assembled in front of one of the centrally located buildings in the

OCS complex. The platoon sergeant put our group at ease and asked all the college graduates to step forward. Most of this group did. Then the platoon sergeant told those remaining in formation to watch how college graduates policed cigarette butts scattered around the area. It was a demeaning lesson. Next, we all used razor blades to scrape paint from the glass windows of various buildings where we were located, including the headquarters. It was an asinine act that exposed us all to the elements without even supplying us with gloves. I complied without complaining.

I had cut one of my fingers a couple days before flying to Quantico. I reopened that cut every day we scraped paint. After three more days of putting our "educations" to work with pointless, mundane physical labor, the first week of OCS ended and fantastic news came out of the blue. Our group of aviation candidates would be allowed liberty our first weekend in OCS. This had never been done before. We were warned if we screwed up, it would never happen again. Elated, a bunch of us went to Washington D.C. for the weekend. I would be able to see the first Super Bowl football game after all. Having been born in Wisconsin, I was naturally a Green Bay Packers fan. Ultimately, just getting out of quarters and off the base as often as I could for as long as I could, helped me keep my sanity. The historic football game was a bonus. OCS was living up to its reputation.

In the D.C. environs, our shaved heads screamed we were officer candidates from the Marine base. The weekend diversion was nice, albeit short and sweet. I related all I dared in my lengthy and emotional phone call with Jan. I maintained an air of optimism even though apprehension consumed me thoroughly and ominously. Jan's sadness was obvious. I promised to call and write every weekend since I was totally entrenched during the week and unavailable except for emergencies. I watched the Super Bowl game in the lobby of the Ambassador Hotel where many of us stayed. The emotional high of the Packers win quickly faded at 2100 hours Sunday night as the "grunts," the ground officer candidates representing the bulk of the school, arrived.

As I stared at the new faces in our E Company squad bay, I saw the same fear I had exhibited one week prior. My week's advantage totally disappeared the next morning at 0430 hours when the trash can once again careened across the squad bay. Bright eyed, bushytailed and standing sharply at attention, the 43rd OCS officially began. The Delta Company barracks building next to ours was used for storage of our personal belongings, which included my camera. I wouldn't need nor have the opportunity to use it. (Over twenty years later, while attending Command and Staff College as a reservist, I photographed those buildings just before they were torn down.)

There was absolutely no privacy at OCS. The three S's prevailed: shit, shower, and shave. All the shitters and showers had open stalls. Anatomical differences and oddities had no significance. The showers had no constant temperature, something I found to exist at nearly every old Navy and Marine base. No comfortable temperature could be maintained. Was it intentional? The staff apparently found it comic. Then there was the shitting part. If a candidate was on the toilet crapping and any member of the command leadership entered the squad bay, they hollered into the head, "squeeze it off candidate, front and center." I believed this game was one of their favorites. All personally degrading things had to be tolerated. Non-tolerance or adverse reactions were exploited.

Once we all had our permanent lockers and racks (no one was in my upper bunk), we settled in for the duration. Our racks were assigned alphabetically; candidates Rusk and Wenniger were my immediate neighbors. Except for a few empty racks near us, the rest of the squad bay was full. Training and instruction now began in earnest. Everything counted. We were meat to be tenderized and virgins to be raped. Things we learned within those walls we applied for years as part of Marine Corps tradition. We had a tirade from the captain, then the company gunnery sergeant and then our platoon sergeant and drill instructor. We maggots would eat and breathe the Marine Corps. Mail call, instruction, rifle cleaning, quiet time, study time, shining boots, cleaning of equipment, blocking our covers (starching our utility uniform caps), and sometimes limited PT were also conducted. It was shape up or ship out as we tried to become "mean green fighting machines." If good enough, we would get commissioned. Good enough meant excellent: physically, mentally and philosophically. I disliked the manner of training and prevailing doctrine.

Though I disagreed with the methodology (thinking there was a better way), I had twelve more weeks to endure it commencing right then. After the platoon sergeant demonstrated how to make up the racks and organize wall lockers, he hollered out, "Candidate Steele's lockers and hospital folds are perfect. Use his for an example." I resented him for being "A. J. squared away" on the first day. Turns out, Steele had the benefit of boot camp and years of prior enlisted service. It was fallout time for all the companies of the 43rd OCS. The assembly of over 800 skinheads was quite a sight. In this class would be some of the finest officers in the modern Marine Corps and, sadly, a great many of them would lose their lives. We marched to the classroom en masse. During this instruction, we learned the hierarchy of things. We were Marines first, then rank structured, and then military occupational specialty (MOS) categorized. That was the individual Marine. Collectively, the Marine Corps was organized as Fleet Marine Force, Division, Battalion, Company, Platoon, Squad, and Fire Team. We had to learn Navy and Marine Corps rank quickly.

During PT, I exhausted myself early and waned towards the end of the exercises. I realized right then I had to develop some endurance to meet the physical requirements. Just before noon chow the instructor talked about a forced march. We were having one every other Saturday, beginning that week. The marches sounded like something I didn't want to experience. Then the other foot hit the floor. The first one was just three miles but every two weeks, two additional miles were added making the final one a whopping fifteen miles long! This information psyched out some of the candidates before the march even started.

We were issued M-14 rifles. The U.S. 7.62mm, M-14, was a gas-operated, magazine fed, air-cooled, shoulder weapon weighing 9.1 pounds with the sling and a magazine full of twenty rounds of ammo. It had an overall length of 44.14 inches without the bayonet and a 22-inch barrel having four lands and grooves with a right twist. The muzzle velocity was 2,800-feet-per-second and the chamber pressure was 50,000 pounds per square inch.[4] In other words, it killed the enemy very well and anyone else if you weren't careful with it. We all had to become very familiar with our rifle. We marched and drilled with it and carried it everywhere, including on the forced marches. Eventually we would learn to tear it down completely and reassemble it from memory, with speed, and keep it clean and lubricated. My limited gun experience was target shooting and hunting.

That Saturday morning the platoon sergeant prepped us for the three-mile forced march. Prior to falling out, one of the candidates from the other end of the squad bay asked if we were supposed to fall out "with guns." The platoon Sergeant called him to the center of the squad bay, telling him to bring his rifle with him. The platoon sergeant asked him to repeat after him, "This is my rifle (having him hold it up in his right hand) and this is my gun (having him grip his crotch with his left); this is for fighting (holding up the rifle again) and this is for fun (gripping his crotch again)." Then the platoon sergeant said, "I can't hear you" and the candidate did it all over again. The platoon sergeant then said, "Your instruction on the M-14 is not complete. Do not carry it on this march. You will on all the others." And then he barked, "Put your rifles in your wall lockers and fall out, maggots!"

As we fell out, apprehension gripped me, but not as much as the nine-degrees-above zero temperature. Forced march meant rapid paced. The entire E Company of four platoons, approximately two hundred candidates, lined up outside the barracks in the road wearing utilities (uniforms) and covers (caps) but no jackets. We were freezing our nuts off while waiting with fully loaded packs on our backs for the Company Commander. I was doing everything I could to stave off the cold without success. I began to flex muscles without moving but was still shivering. I began wiggling my toes, hoping I might not be noticed. That partially worked and I thought I was okay until the platoon sergeant's voice quietly asked near my left ear, "Are you cold candidate?" I loudly replied, "No Platoon Sergeant!" The platoon sergeant came back louder, "I can see you shivering. Tell me the truth candidate; you are a little cold, aren't you?" Being used to warmer climes, I admitted, "Yes platoon sergeant!" "You stand at attention like everyone else, you maggot piece of shit," he yelled. "You won't be cold once we get started." Finally, Captain Bennett arrived.

I thought I heard the platoon sergeant call him "skipper." The skipper addressed the entire company of candidates. He outlined the procedure and the course of the forced march. Then he said, "We aren't stopping for anything or anybody." I thought it couldn't be that bad since the captain and sergeant both had packs too. It was only near the end of OCS that we discovered that the drill sergeant's and skipper's backpacks were filled with foam rubber.

We were all pissed off about that. About the time I thought we were ready to go, our captain put us at ease. Typical military I thought: hurry up and wait.

While we were waiting, a little snow began to fall. When a jeep with a corpsman and one troop carrier with a stretcher arrived, we were off in sequence of platoons, one through four. The sequence changed on each subsequent march by moving the platoon in first position to the rear. As the march progressed, the reason became immediately clear. Each platoon was coached by their sergeant. He attempted to keep pace with the skipper, keeping all of us motivated and moving, and above all, keeping it tight. The "accordion effect" instantly came into play. Keeping it tight was extremely important because the distances between candidates would lengthen and shorten during the march. The size of the group magnified the effect, with the last platoon always playing catch up. Being first was best.

Amazingly, not long after the march began, I was no longer cold and soon began to sweat. Nine degrees and sweating was totally alien to me. Once the marches got longer, some candidates quickly lagged. The screams to "keep it tight" that we learned that day would begin at the rear almost immediately. Had the marches been on level ground they wouldn't have posed near the problems they did. The marches took place in the hills of Virginia, thickly wooded and formidable with steep and slippery inclines, creeks, lots of mud, sticks, stones, and branches that put whelps on your face if you didn't see them coming. Then there was the January snow. I observed as much of the landscape as possible through a photographer's eye. How beautiful it would have been if I hadn't been humping my butt off and in excruciating pain from blisters caused by my boots. I wasn't alone in my misery.

As quickly as the forced march began, after being pushed physically and mentally, it was over. There had been a few dropouts. The dropouts were issued pink slips and verbally chastised. I was glad not to be among them. A couple of heavy candidates were transported to sick bay (base hospital). Obesity was not evident in OCS, on candidates or anyone else. At 1200 hours, we were given liberty until 2100 hours Sunday night. We could be human beings and not maggots, but confined to the base and Quantico town. The day and a half was not a total "freebie." We had to do laundry, shine boots and brass, study, and organize things. I called home while doing laundry. The stress levels of OCS amplified everything. Any reprieve was welcomed.

Each Sunday was a free day, special and coveted. Nobody fucked with you. Brunch was also special. The food was all you wanted but was prepared any way you wanted it. As I stood in line waiting my turn, I pondered things. I ate leisurely, reflecting on the previous week, now anxious for the ones ahead. By now, there were already a few empty racks, all dropped on request. None of us knew our fate but the attrition rate averaged around 40 percent. I was not a quitter; they would have to flunk me out. That afternoon I studied, wrote letters home, and even memorized part of the Marine Corps manual. I read up on the M-14 rifle, preparing for the upcoming week. The weekend flew quickly, then, lights out.

Monday morning, "O Dark Thirty" came again without warning. There was more boring instruction, PT, and a whole lot about the M-14 rifle—both classroom and hands-on. We learned to respect, honor and yes, at times, hate this weapon in addition to learning about it statistically, operationally, and completely. It was an instrument of precision accurate to five hundred yards. The 1-2-3 trench, the outdoor shitter, was very important. One-foot-wide, two-feet-deep, and three-feet-long trenches were dug in an appropriate, suitable setting for bowel movements. Where would we be without a place to take a dump!?

During first aid instruction, I glanced at my cut finger. It was more of a nuisance than anything. Various ways to care for wounded and cardiopulmonary resuscitation (CPR) were taught. But medical advice on heatstroke and heat exhaustion were my favorite: I learned the old adage, "face is red, raise the head; face is pale, raise the tail." As the instructors touched upon combat theory, formation, signals, squad, fire team tactics, nuclear, biological and chemical warfare, and the five-paragraph order, nude photos kept us awake.

Cold weather added an ominous, negative element at OCS. The operative approach was to take advantage of the weather, if possible. That was difficult at that time and in that environment; yet it was realistic. The crux of it all was that we must be prepared to destroy the enemy and avoid destruction. About this time I'm thinking, "Why didn't they just say, kill the enemy before he kills you"? This day's instructional ended with military discipline and courtesy.

Every Thursday each platoon performed field day on their squad bay and head so it would pass the "white glove" treatment. Yes, they really used a white glove. After the first couple weeks we started to pass inspection. There were always inspections, including bouncing quarters off of sheets. On Saturday mornings with no forced march, personnel inspections were held and few of us passed at first. By the third week, most of us were passing, me included. Some never did, mainly those in "crud corner."

Jerry Leist, a candidate I became friends with, was one of the few in that corner who was "squared away" and did pass. The rest of the candidates in that corner earned the name from the platoon sergeant. Contraband, including "pogey bait" (Marine vernacular for candy), was dealt with severely. Anyone not squared away was referred to as "Joe Shits, the rag man." There were some in all platoons, as all oddities and weaknesses were exploited. For example, a Charlie Company staff member discovered one of his candidates could yodel. Every night for a week, just before taps and lights out, he was forced to yodel from the second-floor balcony of Delta barracks. He was very good but we still chuckled. At one time or another everyone screwed up. Not one facet of our physical, mental, or emotional stamina went untested. Every week something new was added or attempted and taught or accomplished as we began becoming Marines.

Chapter 3

A Marked Man

Interviews with the skipper began the second week. Captain Bennett probed deeper into each candidate. I made two mistakes in my interview. Both had disastrous results, one immediate, one long term. In the middle of the interview, a question was directed to me by someone in the room outside my field of view. As previously instructed, I turned, ascertained the rank of the Marine (the company gunnery sergeant), snapped back to attention with eyes forward and started to respond to his question using the appropriate rank instead of the ambiguous "sir." Very few words escaped my mouth before I was almost knocked flat on my face. The gunny's screaming was deafening as he hollered into my right ear, "Don't you ever move while at the position of attention, Candidate. You slime ball piece of shit, I'll put my size eleven boot so far up your ass your eyeballs will be black if I ever catch you doing that again! Do you hear me Candidate, you fucking maggot?"

"Yes, sir," I hollered back. I tried to explain and justify my actions to no avail.

"Shut up candidate," he responded and then muttered, "Do as you're told. Don't ever fuck up like that again you maggot dip shit asshole."

My interview was shot to hell. The exchange could be heard all over the building. It scared the crap out of me as I stood there in shock and humiliation, seething with anger.

My second mistake was worse. We had many jocks and one NFL (National Football League) running back in our class. The skipper, having reviewed my background and noting the absence of family military history or heroes, college accolades, athletic prowess, or anything else, asked, "Why do you want to be a Marine officer?"

I answered, "I thought it would be a good way to serve my country."

The skipper then asked, "Do you think you have what it takes?"

Finally, I had the opportunity to tell someone that I had the leadership, confidence, and physical and mental wherewithal to be an officer. But instead, I answered, "I don't know. I'm here to find out." My confidence had been shaken from the outset, my composure had slipped and truthfully I was no longer sure. I instantly became a marked man. They didn't pick on me outright but badgered me for several weeks. Consequently, I never was sure I would make the grade. All I could do was trudge on, hoping for the best.

I often thought of dropping out. But since I was not a quitter, it was full blown, game on. Our hard-nosed drill instructors conducted the close order drills on the parade deck (the "meat grinder"). Those drills grew longer and more complicated and any candidate who screwed up was chastised and had to pump out push-ups. The cold wasn't noticeable as long as we were exerting ourselves but a reminder of how cold it was came during a break in the drill. My canteen lid had a slight leak in it and was frozen shut with icicles on the side of its pouch.

All our activities made time fly. Saturday of the third weekend arrived and our company had the five-mile forced march. I was now having a little trouble with PT and dropped out of this race near the end, earning my first pink slip. I had given up mentally because I gave out physically. A few candidates passed out while others barfed in the ditch beside the trail. The addition of the nine-pound rifle was a huge factor and sweat, cramps, blisters, aches, pains, and fatigue couldn't be ignored. I hated candidates who made it look easy. A few did. I hated my platoon sergeant who seemed to effortlessly go forward and back along our platoon chiding us and threatening us with, "I'll put my boot up your ass if you slow down asshole, move it, move out you pussies. My mother runs faster than you scumbags." I was ashamed of my performance. We were too slow, too stupid, too weak; anything but good.

We were always wrong; we were always candidates and rarely praised. It was a mind game with physicality as a sidebar. Everything was done to discourage, embarrass, degrade, shame, confuse, or make a candidate doubt. Knowledge, acceptance, and compliance didn't guarantee anything. They were trying to get us to drop out, give up, or to defeat us mentally. Recognizing the methodology didn't make me capable of exhibiting the correct attributes. I had to demonstrate ability and worthiness. I was in control of my own destiny.

Early in February, OCS entered its fourth week and somehow the pace picked up. My academics, inspections, adaptation to the program and marching were fine, but physically I was not making the grade and the training now seemed to me to be 75 percent physical. Some candidates were maxing out on different forms of PT. My PT was adequate; forced marches were my problem even though I felt positive about the good things I was doing. Pugil stick matches were that week. After breakfast, we marched out onto the athletic field to conduct simulated hand to hand combat using pugil sticks. Pugil sticks were approximately four-foot-long poles with padded leather covering each end: essentially elongated boxing gloves. We were matched up according to relative height, size. and weight. Paired combatants faced each other about two to three feet apart, wearing a pair of gloves and a helmet for protection. When the platoon sergeant blew the whistle, the pair pummeled each other for advantage, knock down or knock out, while the rest of the platoon watched. The platoon sergeant blew the whistle a second time to end the match if neither combatant had advantage or no knock down or knock out occurred.

When it was my turn, I paired with Candidate Steele. Steele was savvy and in great shape. We doffed our helmets and gloves but my helmet was tight. It was so tight I didn't hear the whistle blow to begin the match. While I was standing there not knowing the fight had begun, Steele gave me a right cross to the head which nearly knocked me down. I saw stars but mainly saw red and a very intense fight ensued. I fought back with all of the anger and might I had. We fought a seemingly long time and I refused to let Steele get the advantage. Then the whistle blew for us to quit. My head was pounding so hard I didn't hear that whistle either and not knowing Steele dropped his guard, I got a free shot to his chin which caused him to stagger temporarily.

There was no reprisal once the platoon sergeant learned I couldn't hear either whistle. My surprise and elation were hard to hide. It was a day with a high note. That quickly vanished on Saturday when I dropped out of the seven-mile forced march in the last mile, earning another pink slip.

After I caught my breath, I felt the pulsing pain in my re-opened finger. Once back at the barracks, many candidates left on liberty. I stayed, cleaned my rifle and got everything squared away so that I had little to do on Sunday except relax. When I called home later that evening, Jan said, "Why don't you quit?" I replied that I couldn't and outlined the ramifications if I failed to get a commission. The conversation turned out to be about as depressing as the week had been. When I got back to the barracks, it was all abuzz. In the middle of the squad bay sat the garbage can full of mud and M-14 parts from all the rifles that had not been cleaned. The floor around the can was littered with the stocks. I rushed to my wall locker. My rifle was there. At lights-out the skipper entered the squad bay. He told all the candidates whose M-14's were not in their wall lockers that beginning in the morning they would each retrieve their rifle parts from the garbage can, clean them, and re-assemble their rifles. Then he added, "I hope you all learned a valuable lesson and acknowledge and prioritize your duties."

I only thought I would sleep well that night. At about 0100 hours, I was awakened by candidate Rusk. Rusk was standing at the foot of his rack and shaking it violently back and forth by the vertical bars supporting the upper bunk. Fortunately, no one slept in the upper berth. After about a minute, he lay back down in his rack. The next morning, I asked Rusk if he was aware of what he had done. He wasn't. It was a testament to our stress levels and how some candidates endured. The candidates with rifle parts in the garbage can began their arduous task. I was elated not to be one of them. We qualified with our M-14 rifles the next week. I could have done better with more practice but ended up qualifying as rifle "Sharpshooter." "Expert" was best and "Marksman" was the worst. I was proud I never got a "Maggie's Drawers," the dreaded white flag indicating a completely missed target. Problem solving came later in the week and I did well. I began feeling more confident.

Chapter 4

Humping It

Our next major event was the obstacle course, consisting of eight individual challenges to be accomplished sequentially. A maximum score was achieved by completing the course in seventy seconds or less, which was considered outstanding. Finishing in over two minutes and ten seconds was failure. The first obstacle was a high, horizontal bar that had to be negotiated over. Kipping (a gymnastics maneuver) was the quickest way if the candidate was able. Obstacle #2 was an average-height horizontal log that had to be climbed up on in order to maneuver onto one of several logs that leaned down to the ground. Another obstacle was an eight-foot wall that had to be scaled. The rest of the obstacles were variations of pits, crawls, and hurdles that had to be maneuvered over, under, or through and the last one was climbing a twenty-foot rope.

If a candidate failed an event, he had to repeat it until successful. Numerous candidates had all kinds of trouble with one obstacle or another and many failed the course, time after time. I didn't have gymnastics experience but tried a kip on the first bar after seeing other candidates do it. Amazingly, I was successful and carried my exuberance into the second obstacle where I fell off the leaning log and had to do it over. I still passed with an average score. I passed the course every time I ran it but when it came time to record

The author's photo of the obstacle course at Officer Candidates School (OCS), Quantico, Virginia, showing obstacle #2 in the foreground.

my best score, I completed it in seventy-two seconds. I had finally achieved something good athletically.

Every candidate was required to act as the platoon sergeant for a day, marching the platoon everywhere and getting it to the designated places on time. When my day came, I did not use Candidate Steele's cadence as advised; I relied on my high school marching band experience. Uncharacteristically, all the staff seemed to be absent that day. I had done very well and lamented the fact that no one noticed. The next day we learned the skipper had broken the middle finger on his right hand playing handball. The jokes and rumors were endless. His finger was in a cast until the end of OCS. It didn't affect rifle inspections one iota; he just couldn't quickly snatch a rifle away from a candidate as he preferred to do. Later that day I was summoned into the skipper's office. I stood at attention wondering what the hell I had done only to hear the skipper say, "You did a really good job with the platoon yesterday." This joyful news lasted until the next day's inspection.

Before we fell out in chrome domes (silver helmet liners that repelled rain) and raincoats, change alpha came for us to fall out in utility covers and field jackets. My thought was, screw with us all you want because it doesn't make a shit; we're going to be cold and wet in whatever we're wearing. Shortly before falling out, I drove a cotton patch down the bore of my rifle and headed out to be inspected by the skipper, cast and all, with his middle finger sticking out. It was difficult to keep a straight face. When the skipper stood in front of me, he commanded, "Inspection arms!" I brought my rifle up to present arms across my chest. I opened the chamber, glanced down and peered well into the chamber (too long) and then continued to hold it for the skipper while at attention. The gesture is supposed to be only a brief token one, a head nod, which I wasn't aware of, to verify that there is no round of ammo in the chamber. We had no ammo. The skipper called me down for the faux pas. While at inspection arms, the inspecting officer does not have to take the rifle. If he raises his left hand, it is to adjust something. If he raises his right hand, the candidate lets go of the rifle. The skipper grudgingly and gingerly took my rifle, inspected it, and commented, "The least you could have done was run a patch down the bore before you came out here."

I replied, "Yes sir," while eyeballing the skipper and knowing that is exactly what I had done. He knew it too.

The morning of the dreaded nine-mile forced march arrived. For me, much was riding on this march. As the march proceeded, the trail up and down hills was wet and treacherous in addition to the cold. I lagged and caught up, lagged and caught up over and over again, pushing myself extremely hard. There was no sense of time or distance, just the relentless urgings of the platoon sergeant to keep up. This day we were assholes, puke faces, ass wipes, scuzz buckets, dip shits, fairies, tick turds, maggots, ugly mothers, or slime balls. Humorous yes, but in some cases accurate. I felt like a bucket of worms. I was huffing and puffing as we humped up a fairly tall hill. I was not waning, but the trail was getting very slippery from use and the bitterly cold rain. At one point I stalled.

My five-foot-ten, long-waisted, fairly short legged, frame could not negotiate a tall step up. Each time I tried, I failed to get my boot over the ledge and slipped back down. There was nothing to grab hold of to help. No matter how hard I tried, I wasn't getting over it and going around was not an option. I was moving my feet, losing energy and going nowhere. Candidate

Wenniger, behind me, somehow raised me up enough on my next attempt to make the step. I vowed to thank him later. Wenniger was a big Wisconsinite, yet a very gentle man and seemed like a real nice guy. I would soon realize how nice. The platoon was heading down the hill only to begin up another. Now, I was beginning to fatigue and apparently it showed. Wenniger told me to hand him my rifle. I did and the temporary reprieve had a positive effect.

When the platoon got to the bottom of the hill, the platoon sergeant appeared beside me asking, "Candidate, where's your rifle?" I breathlessly said, "Candidate Wenniger has it," pointing behind me and hoping he wasn't in trouble. The platoon sergeant snatched it away from him and handed it to me saying, "Don't you ever do this again maggot." I did not respond as the sergeant headed off to urge on the group. I loved Wenniger for what he did.

Later I became stuck in the mud and fell behind. When I caught up to the group, they were heading back up another hill. This one did me in. It was too wet, too slippery, and too steep. I dropped out.

After catching my breath for a couple minutes, I climbed over the hill and not more than a hundred feet beyond the base was the platoon. I was that close to finishing. I got another pink slip and though furious with myself, I was somewhat pleased for coming close to completing the march and vowed to finish the next one. Neither Wenniger nor I got in trouble. I thanked him profusely during liberty and offered to make it up to him if there was any way I could. Years later, while in Quantico in the reserve officer's Command and Staff College, I visited the Vietnam Memorial in Washington, D.C. I went straight to the W's to see if his name was there. It was not. Others I knew were.

Just prior to liberty, the platoon sergeant conducted mail call in the usual, detestable way. With us gathered around him, he called the name on the envelope or package and the candidate sounded off loud and clear. No matter where the candidate was in the room, the platoon sergeant would throw the letter or package as hard as he could in the opposite direction. Candidates who received packages from home had those stomped flat before they were tossed. A lot of good cookies were smashed that way and the crumbs shared with everyone. This day candidate Dolan received a package from a friend. Dolan was a large individual, easily six-foot-two, weighing 210 pounds or more.

He was a model candidate. A friend sent him a bra and pair of panties. Dolan was required to open the package and show everyone the contents. Of course his friend knew exactly what he was doing. Dolan had to wear them everywhere on the outside of his utilities for a week. He took it in stride.

Our next weekend's liberty authorized us to go off base, within a fifty-mile radius. A lot of us went to D.C. The weekend turned out to be about as eventful as the happenings in OCS. Terry Ewing, my roommate at the Ambassador for the weekend, wanted to go bar hopping in Georgetown. Though I drank on occasion, I wasn't particularly interested and declined the offer, opting to go to a movie instead. I had an emotional and visceral reaction to The Sand Pebbles, left the movie lonely and walked back to the hotel depressed. When I got to our room, I found Terry flat on his face, buck naked, passed out on the bathroom floor with his upper torso in the shower stall. His face was in a pool of vomit. Fortunately the shower was not on or he might have drowned. Though dead weight, I managed to get him, incoherent, into the shower horizontally. I got him cleaned up, onto his bed and covered, and then cleaned up the mess. He owed me one!

The next day, while Terry slept it off, Jerry Leist and I went sightseeing, ending up at the Washington Monument. The two of us raced each other to the top of the steps. Washington was escapism for all candidates. It was emotionally refreshing and gratifying to be surrounded by so much American history, government, and memorials. Without any pressure, we were able to let down our guard and just be ourselves. My call home to Jan and my parents was uplifting. It was the middle of February. I sent Valentine's cards home, had a leisurely dinner and went back to the hotel. I met up with Terry and asked him how he felt. The response was, "Okay." I related what happened the night before and he couldn't believe it. He profusely apologized and suggested we go to church in the morning. Though underdressed, it was good to be in the house of the Lord. The minister's sermon was appropriately about being tested in order to grow. I had grown in the last six weeks and prayed for strength to overcome my deficiencies.

Back at Quantico, while doing laundry, one of the other candidates informed us that Candidate Gardino, another Wisconsinite in our platoon, was expelled. Inebriated, he had scuffled with the MPs outside a bar. That was high on our list of no, no's, even though the military at that time in some ways condoned drinking. I never got to have the conversation with him about our hometown of Beloit. Empty racks were increasing in all the platoons. Many candidates' dreams of being a Marine officer had vanished. Monday morning the skipper addressed us, "I'm sure you are all aware of what happened to Candidate Gardino. The same fate awaits any one of you who fucks up that bad while in OCS. Now, get your chrome domes and raincoats on, we're picking up the pace." Gardino was forgotten. There was no time to dwell on anything but the situation at hand.

Was it snow or sleet? Hell, it didn't matter. It was another cold wet day in Quantico but I was becoming relaxed about things. I stayed up late after lights out studying under my blanket with a flashlight while other candidates snored or talked in their sleep. I also heard the changing of the guards. We all stood fire watch (guard duty), in one- to two-hour shifts between 2200 hours and 0600 hours, once every two weeks on average. It was a bitch to stand guard in the POV, privately owned vehicle, lot. The parking lot was in the middle of nowhere surrounded by a ten-foot-high chain link fence. Nobody was stealing anything from there. It was good training in rain, snow, or sleet and below freezing, bitterly cold temperatures. The wind chill cut right through us, freezing our asses off. It was a reminder that any Marine who failed to man his post endangered the lives of other Marines, most dramatically in a combat zone. Upon returning from one of my guard duties after 0300 hours, I found Candidate Rusk shaking his rack again and muttering incoherently.

The next forced march was eleven miles. It was almost March but by Texas standards it was winter. This day there was no precipitation and our platoon was at the front of the column. I was pumped. Once the skipper joined, we headed out broken finger and all. I was so focused, I was hardly aware of my surroundings. Up and down the hills we went and I was right with them. I sweated from exertion, not nerves. I attacked hills at the base and eased off at the top. I got into a rhythm, ignored the pain and fatigue and reached down for hidden strength. I thought only of the finish; time and distance were inconsequential. While I was praying for additional strength, the march ended. I was near the back of the platoon but not close to dropping out. The skipper and sergeant noticed. I stood there gasping for breath, sucking in and out, enjoying every minute of it.

Those minutes didn't last long before disaster struck. The captain and the sergeant started back up the hill. I thought I was going to die. I couldn't believe it was happening. I'm screwed, I thought, I'll get a pink slip after all. The skipper didn't go very far, maybe a quarter of a mile or so. That was enough for me and a few others to drop out. My mood went from elation to deflation. I had stuck it out through the whole thing and then ... wham. I thought my efforts were for naught. While wondering if the extra was just for me, the skipper addressed the group with his reasoning, "You have to have something left to fight with." I waited for my pink slip. It never came. I praised God for that and my healed finger.

I called home. Jan congratulated me. The new week brought field, simulated combat exercises. I screwed up my five-paragraph order. The acronym, SMEAC, stands for situation, mission, enemy, administration, and command and signal. My field exercise went about a good as my five-paragraph order and then it was over. Neither was pretty but I passed. The next day the platoon sergeant was standing just inside our squad bay door about to have mail call as I returned from the head. I started to pass through the hatch (doorway) and out of courtesy said, "By your leave, Platoon Sergeant," military for pardon me. He unbelievably said, "No." I froze halfway through, standing next to him not knowing what to do. That's when he astonishingly said, "Suppose the enemy was near?"

I responded to this ludicrous statement with "Here in the United States?"

After a short pause, he commanded, "Give me twenty, candidate."

"Enemy my ass," I thought as I cranked out push-ups, calling them off loudly. Only a few more weeks of OCS remained but the platoon sergeant was never going to pass up an opportunity to fuck with me.

Chapter 5

Striking Gold

After one last weekend in D.C., the home stretch began. I had no problems with the week's events but the thirteen-mile forced march was that Saturday. I made it through the march lagging near the end of the platoon but encouraged others around me not to give up and gut it out. I even ran backwards part of the time to face those lagging. Some of them eventually did give up. But as a result of my urging, a couple more of them finished. I was proud of my accomplishment and making a difference to others. My lesson from this experience was that a person quits mentally before he or she quits physically. A philosophy that I would live by the rest of my life became manifest right then.

I eventually saw a published quotation, which summed it up perfectly: "The dominant force in our lives is the way we think. Each one of our beliefs is a choice. There can be no great accomplishment without great commitment. We can never be defeated, until we accept defeat in our minds." I eventually forgot the author but never the message. I finished the thirteen-mile forced march strong. I wasn't rebuked for motivating others. My refusal to accept failure was a major factor but not wanting to wash out and be an enlisted Marine was greater. I ultimately had great admiration for all grunts; I just didn't want to be one.

There were only two weeks left to OCS. Up to this point in my life, the thirteen-mile forced march was the single most agonizing physical event I had ever encountered. The ominous and infamous fifteen-mile forced march loomed on the horizon and I was psyching up for it. After days of agonizing, the time had come. I attacked it from the outset. I never thought it possible, but I managed to finish feeling good, totally surprising myself. Once again, I encouraged others and now felt I had a chance of being commissioned.

The next week was war games, an all day and overnight exercise. It quickly became a disorganized gaggle fuck. I was certain of that once night fell. It was raining sleet. We got our orders and I was part of the perimeter defense. After canned rations for dinner, we settled in for the night. We had dug our foxholes during the day, although not deep enough, and stood guard as best we could. To me, it seemed more of a test to see if we could tolerate the weather. Somehow I failed to receive the word about sleeping bags. When I went to get mine, they had all been passed out! How could there not be enough for the company? Then came the stark realization, "I was going to freeze my ass off." As unbelievable as that was, I got chewed out for not being there when they were issued. I didn't fuck up. Some bean counter miscounted! It was a colossal screw up and I was the "lucky" victim. I walked back to my foxhole in my poncho, cold, wet, and very angry.

Around 2100 hours, sleeting and pitch black, there was activity. I was busy shivering in my foxhole when flares lit up the sky and our platoon (and company) came under attack. We had a successful firefight against the "enemy" and then settled in. We alternated guarding and sleeping. Since I couldn't sleep I stood guard most of the night. Long after midnight, while I was on watch and trying not to freeze, something seemed amiss. I didn't see or hear anything for the darkness and noise of the freezing rain but sensed a "presence." It was the enemy, who said, "You're dead." So much for realism, I thought. I felt I failed, but nobody took my name. At daybreak, we terminated the exercise and returned to the barracks.

Within twenty-four hours I was sick as a dog. I went to the sick bay, was given a shot and was confined to bed rest. I lay in my rack shivering with mild pneumonia for the next twenty-four hours without eating anything or getting up, except for toilet runs. I was back to normal in two days and went with the platoon to practice for field day competition. Surprisingly, I was entered in two events: the obstacle course and the rope climb. Field day was fun, but our platoon did not fare that well. I had a good run at the obstacle course, tying my best effort of seventy-two seconds. I thought I had earned some respect and was cautiously optimistic about being commissioned.

The next day was orientation for graduation, commissioning, and beyond. That same day, candidates were to entertain the staff with skits performed by each platoon. Most of the skits dealt with poking fun at just about everything including the staff and there was even a digital display of sorts during a mock inspection. Everyone from E Company knew who that was for. General Davis addressed the group, congratulating all of us and recognizing certain individuals. I realized then, being part of this group, that I had made it and would be commissioned. No one ever told me I was. I was left guessing up to the end. Since I was never told I was going to be commissioned, it was never an option for my family to travel from Texas to attend the graduation. All of us candidates were proud, but for me it was magnanimous.

After we left the graduation ceremony wearing our new butter bars (gold Second Lieutenant insignias), our platoon sergeant was waiting for us outside the door of the auditorium. He saluted each of us individually and instantly pocketed twenty-eight silver dollars, the final tally from E Company, 3rd platoon. It was tradition to give one to whoever saluted a newly commissioned officer first. Though perturbed when I gave him one that I supposed he earned, I then gave a silver dollar to the next Marine who saluted me. This happened at the Chow Hall where we now paid for our food. After lunch, we checked in all our equipment, got our orders, got paid, processed out, and arranged for our flights home. My OCS experience was over. I was a Second Lieutenant in the Marine Corps. Ooorah!

While flying home, I had flashbacks of events and my accomplishments during officer training. I had done something truly amazing. Once home, I got a royal welcome and everyone wanted to know all about it. I related all that I could. Everyone could see I was different from the experience. I was hulked and none of my clothes fit. With thirty days' leave and orders to Pensacola, Florida, my military future lay ahead. Jan was apprehensive; her younger brother in awe.

Chapter 6

Beaches and Banana School

After several days home, I was bored. Stupidly, I took too much leave before reporting to BNAO ("banana") school. BNAO is the Navy acronym for Basic Naval Aviation Orientation, a school referred to as flight prep or, as we nuggets (neophyte aviators) called it, preflight. Since the Marine Corps is under the Department of the Navy, all naval aviators, Navy and Marine—pilots, naval flight officers, radar intercept officers, and bombardier/navigators—started with flight prep. The amount of authorized leave I took turned out to be very significant; firstly, because it was all I was going to earn per year and secondly, and most importantly, it delayed my starting date for banana school. That affected the dates of my NFO School and subsequently my entry into an active duty squadron, determining the date of my overseas tour to Vietnam.

Jan vainly hoped my orders would be canceled. I was ignorant about some workings of the Marine Corps, somewhat naïve in military ways, but I knew my orders wouldn't be canceled. Anxious about the next phase of training, I loaded up a rental trailer and headed for Pensacola alone. Jan joined me once I got a beachfront apartment. She was displeased with just about everything even though the base was a nice facility with great surroundings. I surmised she wasn't going to be happy unless she was back in Texas or with her parents. Pensacola was an old and quaint town and Jan and I explored it. But even the old and quaint escaped her. She was determined not to like anything. My military future, on the other hand, depended on embracing whatever environment I was in.

Pensacola NAS, known as the "Annapolis of the Air," is steeped with history and tradition. It began as a Naval yard in 1826. The first aviation training began in 1913, well before World War I. The Naval Cadet program was established in 1935 and its peak production of aviators occurred one year after my attendance with 2,552 graduates in 1968. Pensacola was eventually picked to be the headquarters for all Navy education and training in 1971.[5] Upon arrival and while checking out the base, I noticed a lot of vintage aircraft, some of which were still in use. But the most notable planes were the Blue Angels who used Pensacola as their home base and happened to be practicing that day. The base also had a museum, a large theater, a beautiful new chapel, and a large, beautifully landscaped, cemetery, that was reminiscent of Arlington National Cemetery.

One of my early requirements was to buy my uniforms within sixty days. Two months wasn't the problem: affording them was. While waiting for a new class to begin, one morning during roll call, I met P. J. Allen, a fellow Marine flight prep officer. P. J. had scraped the black off the western hemisphere, North and South America portion of his globe and anchor pin on his fore and aft cover (a narrow hat that is called a "piss cutter" in Marine vernacular). I thought it looked really cool. The next morning, during roll call formation, our Administrative Officer chewed him out for it. The lesson was, no matter what base we were on, we were still subject to every Marine Corps regulation. We also had to pass periodic physical training tests.

Before our classes began, we had to pass a very thorough aviation physical, starting with a night vision test, something I hadn't been tested on before. It went okay. That afternoon was a pressure chamber check out and an ejection seat ride. The chamber accommodated about a dozen persons, including an instructor and a Navy corpsman due to the gravity of the test. We wore oxygen masks as the chamber depressurized simulating ascending to 40,000-feet altitude. My ears popped many times as air escaped and my sinuses also drained. After the 40,000-foot equivalent was attained, we paired up to take off our masks and perform tasks until we became disoriented, due to the lack of oxygen. The first pair was given a deck of cards and told to play poker. After a little while they were giddy and couldn't shuffle or deal the cards. We all laughed but the seriousness of the exercise was obvious. If the aviator failed to recognize the symptoms of oxygen deprivation (hypoxia) and take immediate action, he would die and he, the plane and possibly aircrew would be lost from the Navy inventory. Oxygen deprivation resulted in the deaths of professional golfer Payne Stewart and those on his plane October 25, 1999.[6]

P. J. and I were next. With our masks removed, we were told to play patty cake. At first we were doing fine but then as we began to get light headed and our extremities tingled, we lost the sequence and quickly couldn't even pat our hands together before patting each other's. It was comic. The next thing I was aware of was the corpsman putting my mask back on. I had almost blacked out. After all the pairs had participated in the exercise, the technician began to bring the air pressure in the chamber back to sea level.

During re-pressurizing, I very early on began to experience extreme pain in my sinuses. I put out my hand to level off, as instructed. The corpsman came over and asked what the difficulty was. I explained. The corpsman showed me how to utilize the "valsalva" technique where I could force air into my ears by pinching my nose closed and then closing my mouth and blowing, pushing air into my ears through the Eustachian tubes. I used that technique often during my aviation career. It did not relieve my painful sinuses. After some minutes I felt better due to pressure equalization in my sinuses and gave a thumbs-up for the technician to resume pressurizing. Soon, I was experiencing pain again and signaled to level off. This continued throughout pressurization until the sea level equivalent was attained. I had interrupted the progression so often it delayed the next group. I failed the pressure chamber and was told to see a flight surgeon. I immediately proceeded to the base hospital. I was afraid of missing the ejection seat ride that afternoon but really feared USMC reprisal, washout, or discipline. If I washed out of the training command I would go to Tactical Basic School to be a ground officer. That scared the hell out of me.

The flight surgeon was surprisingly amiable and gave me an antihistamine prescription. I rushed on to the ejection seat briefing, making it just in time. When it came my turn, I was strapped into the seat and given a signal for an all clear. I quickly reviewed the sequence in my mind, then reached up and pulled the handle. After the boom, the next sensation was slowly descending back down the rails. It happened that quickly. I was critiqued for having my head forward somewhat instead of straight back against the seat. I acknowledged that and was given my "Omiass" card and left.

I rescheduled the pressure chamber ride and went home. Jan was on the phone with her mom. Our long-distance bills were horrendous. When she got off the phone, I related what had happened during the day. I thought she was interested but instead she said, "I wish you WOULD fail the pressure chamber; then we could go home." That's when the fight started. I told her if I washed out, she would go home when I was transferred to Quantico for months of ground officer training.

My neck was a little stiff for a couple days but a week later, after taking sinus medication daily, I successfully completed the pressure chamber checkout without any problems. I took over-the-counter antihistamines when needed and never had any pressure issues again.

Instructors at flight prep were both Navy and Marine officers. We were taught meteorology, aeronautics, aviation safety, flight rules, Federal Aviation Administration (FAA) regulations, navigation, land and sea survival, etc. We attended classes Monday through Friday and our studies were a continuous and escalating progression. It was now early summer and it was gorgeous on the Gulf Coast. With weekends off, the white sand beaches could not be ignored and everyone took advantage of them.

When Jan's parents came to visit, she was on cloud nine and showed great enthusiasm towards our location and the base facilities. One night she took her folks to a movie at the base theater. She commented that there were some great seats in the center of the audience and that the National Anthem was played prior to the show. She said the entire audience, including those in the balcony, rose and remained standing at the end of the movie until she and her parents rose, talked for a time and then left the building. She said they were the only ones seated in those really great seats, called "general seating."

I replied, "Those weren't seats for just anyone, those were reserved seats for general officers, active duty or retired. You were not supposed to be in those seats!" They apparently got away with it because Jan's dad was grey headed and partially balding. I chuckled at her faux pas and said, "Don't do it again." She was less enthusiastic when my parents came for a visit but weaseled a ride back to Texas with them to spend more time with her folks. I hoped travelling 800 miles in the back of their Karmen Ghia gave her a pain in the neck.

Meteorology was taught by Marine Captain Morrison. One of Morrison's training slides was of a high-wing Cessna aircraft that made a flight from Oklahoma City to Dallas and while en route was caught up in a frontal passage. I had seen such frontal systems numerous times, including a few tornados. The leading edge of the Cessna's wings had been beaten flat by hailstones. The pilot was lucky to have survived. Morrison got off subject at one point and compared the weather to aviation. He said, "Like meteorology, aviation is not an exact science, but will always be subject to the laws of physics, including gravity, which is sometimes unforgiving."

A lot more mention would be made about "Davey Jones locker" and the "Grim Reaper" (death) throughout our instruction and we were all reminded flight pay was hazardous duty pay. There were lots of variables to aviation, and some were potentials for disaster. One teacher said it was mostly routine flying interrupted by moments of stark terror. The idea was to be as prepared as possible for any emergency. Many things went into the making of a good pilot or naval flight officer but academics alone did not a good pilot make.

The best pilots developed a feel for the plane and most aviators develop an air of confidence that many women find attractive. The sexual exploits of the unmarried students and some married ones became the stuff of legends. Every flight prep student was under pressure from day one because of class standings but some students burned the candle at both ends.

Classroom instruction swiftly shifted from generic to tactical and military, with subjects of avionics, power plants, flight systems, hydraulics, and communications, preparing us for our first flight. Our personal life didn't matter unless it interfered with our military one. For the Marines, our instructors told us, "If we wanted you to have a wife, we'd have issued you one." We got spoiled in Pensacola because of being workweek-oriented without any additional duties. But the wives got the message. Thus far, I was doing fine with everything. Sea survival had to be completed prior to our first flight so we began spending afternoons in the swimming pool. Ultimately, we swam a mile in flight suits and boots, jumped off a high-dive platform followed by swimming twenty-five feet under water and then took a plunge in the Dilbert Dunker. The Dilbert Dunker simulated going into the "drink" off an aircraft carrier and then going inverted.

I swam like a fish and passed all the requirements but dreaded being dropped in the ocean because of my tendency toward motion sickness. Ocean hazards never entered my mind. On the day of sea survival, after a couple hours of prep, we were issued our gear and headed for the dock. We donned our helmets and boarded the World War II-vintage landing craft. The crew cranked the four diesel engines and they bellowed black exhaust as we headed out to sea. That exhaust seemed to downdraft right on the stern of the boat where we were seated. That made me nauseous before reaching our destination ten miles out. The boat slowed and dropped us off one by one about 100 feet apart. We would be "rescued" if necessary; otherwise we were on our own, "sink or swim." As the ship made a huge circle I inflated my "Mae West" vest and jumped into the ocean when directed. The refreshing cool quickly vanished as I began my sequence of survival procedures.

I yanked on the lanyard to inflate my raft and nothing happened. I yanked on it again, hard. Again, nothing happened. In the meantime, the boat pulled away to make the next drop. I yanked and yanked with my right hand until it gave out and then I started yanking with my left, all to no avail. I was desperately trying to inflate the raft but running out of strength. I put the handle between my feet and yanked thinking the combined strength would do the trick. That put my head bobbing under the water part of the time and I began sucking in sea water. No matter how hard I yanked, the cartridge would not punch, so I rested a moment. When I next looked up, the boat had returned and was only a few feet away. The Navy personnel seemed more amused than sympathetic when I related my problem. Then one of the seamen hollered "shark!" and pointed. Poof, the CO_2 cartridge started inflating the raft. Where brute strength failed, adrenaline came through. I quickly climbed into the raft once it inflated and lay there catching my breath while feeling like a drowned rat. Though the shark was probably a ruse, I was grateful nonetheless.

After practicing with my survival equipment, I got nauseous and barfed in the ocean. From then on I concentrated on watching the horizon. After about four hours, I was picked up with the others. That's when I found out another student had caught a small shark. Maybe it hadn't been a ruse.

Sea survival was over and it was now July. I was doing well but other students were not. Maybe it was booze and bikinis or sports cars and dog races, pitfalls I avoided. I wondered how the importance of the missions we would ultimately fly or being entrusted with multi-million dollar aircraft could be approached so casually?

Mandatory attendance of "Happy Hours" at the Officer's Club (O Club) didn't help the booze situation either. Students and instructors alike couldn't wait for Fridays. I liked the socializing but did not fit in well at the club and didn't care if command noticed my nonconformity. Years later the military would no longer condone drunkenness and largely quit tolerating any behavior associated with it. But in 1967, drunkenness in the military, especially among fighter pilots, was common and a lot of instructors and students got "shit faced." One of the best things at the club was the countless number of aviation sea stories told, some tragic, some funny, but all entertaining. We nuggets would soon have our own tales to tell.

Chapter 7

Launch the Nuggets

My first military flight was in a Navy UC45J twin-engine Beech-craft, on August 15, 1967. The design and manufacture dated back to 1933.[7] A quintet of us "nugget" students took turns assisting the pilot with pre-flight, navigation, and communication. We all worked up a flight plan for practice, departing from and returning to Pensacola. This flight was essentially a familiarity ("fam") hop and flown according to visual flight rules (VFR). On my turn in the copilot's seat I made small correctional and communication errors but otherwise did okay. Allen took the "hot" seat after me and we returned to the base. My Dramamine had done its job. We were critiqued, graded, and dismissed. I had six more flights in the Beechcraft and two in a jet to go, all more involved and difficult. There were no more "gimme" (simple) hops. We were nuggets but we were no longer virgins. I got home early to Jan's surprise and pulled her into the bedroom.

The next week our entire class went to Eglin AFB in the Florida panhandle for three days of land survival. We had one day of instruction. Early the next day, without any breakfast, we were divided into small groups and dropped off in a deserted, designated area. It was hot and ugly but we "survived" using our own resourcefulness and survival kit items, until we were picked up. No one got snake bit but most of us had the runs for the next several days and I never ate snake again, which did not taste like chicken.

I made the deadline for my uniforms and looked good in them. I loved my name engraved on my Mameluke sword. I was outfitted for any duty station; I just didn't know which one. Successfully completing aviation training came first. I discussed Vietnam with other students but never with Jan. Most students were leaving things to fate. I left it to fate and faith and tried to live in the moment even though the future loomed large.

My first jet flight was August 28. I went by the flight-line in advance to see the plane. It looked so old I was surprised it was still in use. It was a tandem two-seat, single-engine jet with a cigar-shaped fuselage and straight wings with tanks on the ends. It was known as the "Shooting Star" but the Navy designated it a T-33.[8] To me it was museum material. Upon arriving early for the brief, my instructor pilot talked about the flight in general, reviewed the route—a three-legged triangular flight over southern Alabama—and outlined my duties. It was a perfunctory first jet hop. I took a Dramamine tablet one hour prior to the brief hoping it was in full effect by the time we launched. This timing became my procedure for all hops from then on. We proceeded to flight equipment where I suited up in loaner equipment: oxygen mask, flight helmet, G-suit and gloves. I was a mixture of excitement and anxiety. I looked like a naval aviator, despite my anxiety.

In the maintenance hangar, one yellow sheet gripe that stood out was loss of cabin pressurization at altitude. There was a three-ring binder with yellow sheets of paper for every plane on the flight-line. The pilot would make a yellow sheet entry of the plane's performance for the flight he (and these days, she) made in the plane. Reviewing those sheets was very important and informative. We headed to the flight-line to pre-flight the plane. Pre-flighting was visually inspecting the plane's exterior, checking flight control surfaces, etc. This entire sequence of events from brief to takeoff would repeat itself for every military flight I ever flew unless the hop was canceled or the plane experienced a mechanical malfunction. The only other exception to this standard operating procedure (SOP) was during hot pad launches, primarily in combat. Hot pad launches were those where getting airborne quickly was of the essence, i.e. emergency situations or friendly forces in dire straits. Everything checked out and our plane captains (enlisted flight-line personnel) helped us get strapped in.

Launching on my first military jet flight was a proud and scary moment. I put my helmet and oxygen mask on when power was added to the plane. My pilot and I now conversed on the intercom system (ICS). He told me to sit tight while he ran up the engine and checked out the plane's systems and control surfaces. I took it all in, finding the interaction between the pilot and the plane captain very unique. I also reviewed my notes about the flight and the radio frequencies. After things checked out, my pilot lowered the canopy and declared we were ready to taxi to the duty runway. I responded, "roger."

I verified that I had the right frequency set into the radio, took a deep breath, depressed the microphone and called, "Pensacola ground control this is Navy flight 1-5-5 [one, five, five] requesting taxi instructions, over." Pensacola ground control came back, "Roger flight 155, you are cleared to runway one niner [19], your winds are one eight zero [180] degrees at 10 knots and the barometric pressure is two niner point eight-two [29.82]." I wrote all of it down and responded, "Flight 155 copies." My pilot ran up the engine's RPMs and began to taxi off the flight-line. He returned the plane captain's salute and we were on our way.

My pilot taxied the plane to the duty runway and halted short of it. He asked, "Lieutenant, are you going to make the call?"

I depressed my mic and called, "Pensacola tower, this is Navy flight 1-5-5 requesting permission to take the duty runway for takeoff, over."

Pensacola ground control came back, "Flight 155, this is ground control, we copy your transmission; switch to tower frequency 107.2."

I responded (knowing full well I had just screwed up), "Roger ground control, flight 155 switching 107.2" and then I switched. I was embarrassed but had to plow through it. I called the tower saying, "Pensacola tower, this is Navy flight 155 requesting permission to take the duty runway for engine run up, over."

The tower replied, "Roger flight 155, you are cleared, notify when ready for takeoff."

I replied, "Flight 155 copies." I'd been so busy with all the details of the flight I hadn't had time to get nervous. It was now time as I was about to boom into the sky in a tactical airplane even though it was old.

The pilot ran up the engine, read off a couple gauges and the flaps position and then notified me that he was ready for takeoff. I called the tower, "Navy 1-5-5 is ready for takeoff." Due to the large contingency of aviation students, Pensacola was a very busy airport. There was constant chatter on the radio. It was all new to me and often one aircraft's transmission covered (blocked) another. It was sometimes difficult to wait one's turn and occasionally a little tricky to know when to jump in. Even so, students with prior aviation experience or those who had their private pilot's license were very familiar with the process and quickly adapted. After no response to my call my pilot said, "Lieutenant, make the call again."

As soon as there was a lull in the traffic, I called for takeoff again. The tower responded quickly to my request, "Flight 155, you are cleared for takeoff" adding, "winds are 180 degrees at 8 knots" and with that I had no time to reflect on anything as my pilot pushed the throttle to maximum power and the plane began to roll down the runway. I called, "155, copy, cleared."

Even though the Navy T-33 jet was a small subsonic craft, its takeoff was still quite exhilarating. Within a few seconds the nose came up and we were airborne. My pilot called wheels up. I remained silent while I absorbed this new airborne sensation. Once again my pilot ordered, "Lieutenant, make the call."

I responded, "Yes, sir" and panicked about what I was supposed to call. I quickly looked at my knee pad and realized that I was supposed to contact the Air Traffic Control (ATC) and check in. I switched to the ATC frequency but was stopped by my pilot who caught the radio change.

He said to me, "No, call the tower and notify them that you are departing their frequency and switching to the ATC." I was getting deflated. I was making one mistake after another. There was so much to absorb since I had never done any of this before except for the little I had in the Beechcraft the previous week.

I acknowledged, "Yes sir." I switched back to the tower frequency and called, "Pensacola tower, flight 155 is clear your control zone and switching to Air Traffic Control."

The tower responded, "Roger 155, have a good flight."

I hoped it would get better and switched frequencies to the ATC, paused briefly, and then called, "Alabama air traffic control this is Navy flight 1-5-5, over."

The Alabama ATC came back with, "Roger Navy flight 155, steer heading 280 degrees on the Mobile TACAN (Tactical Aid to Navigation) and climb to two zero thousand feet and squawk ident," short for Identification Friend or Foe (IFF). It was actually a black box called a transponder on the plane that transmitted a specific frequency that showed up on the controller's radar-scope in graphics indicating the plane's location, identification, and altitude. All aircraft flying above 24,000 feet had to be under positive control. This was called the area of positive control, APC, in which all aircraft fly by FAA rules. It was lowered to 18,000 feet in 1971.

I responded, "Roger, squawking." The pilot accomplished the squawk. The back seat did not have, nor use, a transponder. However, there were flight controls and rudders in the back seat of this jet. NFO students were explicitly warned to "stay the hell off of the controls." I relaxed. I had a moment to absorb things and peered out the canopy at the terrain. While being totally engrossed in the view, my euphoria was interrupted by the pilot who said, "Well, Lieutenant, are you going to make the call?"

I thought, what call? Had I totally missed an ATC transmission? I never even heard them say anything to us. For novice me, when radio traffic was heavy, it was hard to sort out which call was mine. I replied to my pilot, "What call?"

"We are at 20,000 feet, Lieutenant!" I'd been so busy looking out of the canopy I hadn't noticed the altimeter. What I did notice was that flying at altitude was smooth and relatively quiet.

I apologized again and said, "Yes, sir." I notified the ATC and was wondering how many more mistakes I would make before the flight got back on the ground, when WHAM, there was a loud pop, followed by whooshing air noise and immediately my left ear ached with a piercing pain. For me the flight was over; the excruciating pain in my left ear was just beginning.

I barely heard the pilot call over the radio to the ATC, "Alabama control, this is Navy flight 1-5-5 we have lost cabin pressurization and are requesting an immediate descent with a vector back to Pensacola, over."

The ATC responded, "Roger 155, are you declaring an emergency?" Emergency!? Damn, I thought, as I fought the pain in my ear; my first flight in a military jet and I'm in an emergency.

"Negative," was the pilot's response.

"Roger 155," the controller replied, "descend to and maintain one zero thousand [10,000] feet and vector heading to one zero, zero degrees."

My pilot responded, "155 vectoring 100 degrees and descending to one zero thousand feet." At this point, the pilot turned his attention to me. "How are you doing?" he asked.

I said, "Fine except for the pain in my left ear."

At that moment I was no longer obligated to participate in the flight; my day's training was over. I repeatedly attempted to valsalva to ease the pain in my ear without success. I had a full-fledged ear block. I'd had a ruptured ear drum at age ten and hoped it wasn't a factor. We landed without incident and taxied to our flight-line. The pain in my ear was almost intolerable. The pilot excused me and I immediately went to see a flight surgeon. Unfortunately, it was the same one I had seen after my pressure chamber ride fiasco. The "doc" was amused and sympathetic. He filled a paper Dixie cup half full of water and told me to drink it. As I began to drink, the flight surgeon closed my right nostril and blew some compressed air into my left nostril.

Pow, instantly air painfully inflated my left middle ear with a pop. Then, just as quickly, all the pain was gone and I could hear in my left ear again. The flight surgeon prescribed another antihistamine and told me to never fly with a cold and congested again. I was relieved, but physiology-wise, I questioned my pursuit of a military aviation career. I re-scheduled my "first" jet hop. It went without a hitch and I performed better as a result of the "introductory" experience. With no physiological problems, airsickness, or aircraft issues and a passing score, things were good.

Except for minor mistakes, my other jet and subsequent Beechcraft hops went well. I had passed all the academics and both sea and land survival. My graduation in September was assured and it was right around the corner. The other students and I started receiving temporary additional duty orders assigning us to the advanced (jet) training in Kingsville or Beeville, Texas, for two weeks. When Jan found out, she was pissed. Then she

told me indignantly, "I will go back to my parents for the two weeks."
I said fine but informed her there was more on the horizon. I told her that
beginning in October, the majority of my class would be transferred to NAS
Glynco in Brunswick, Georgia, to complete our aviation training, hopefully
earning our wings. Jan was now seething and absolutely not keen on any
of it except going home to her parents. I accepted her frame of mind, albeit
bitchy. I had no choice with any of the orders except quitting. I viewed
Georgia as an opportunity to see more of the United States and the training
as a challenge. I dropped Jan off at her parents en route to Kingsville in
south Texas.

Chapter 8

Barf Bag Bonanza

My roommate was a very colorful Marine named Ben Yorkoff. A little smaller than me, Ben's personality was larger than life, perhaps because he was from New York. He had a great sense of humor and an uncanny philosophy. We had no down time at jet orientation. Daily classes prepared us for our FAA exam. We had to log a minimum of ten flight hours in the rear seat of the Grumman-built F9F "Panther" trainer jets,[9] with instructor pilots only. The Blue Angels aerial team flew the Panther jet back in the day. I was apprehensive about this phase of training and being in the old Panthers. Yorkoff's mannerisms and language, often crass, added some levity to ease the strain of training. The military had a penchant for profanity and Yorkoff fit right in. I wasn't given to profanity much, thinking those who did of small minds. But there were often times when an expletive was the most appropriate thing.

We were issued authentic Navy flight jackets (not needed in south Texas in September), official aviator sunglasses, and steel-toed flight boots along with temporary flight helmets, oxygen masks, G-suits, and gloves. We were all puffed up. To fulfill our ten hours, we needed to schedule both day and night flights in each category: beginner, intermediate, and advanced. I started with beginner, took a Dramamine, and the flight went without a hitch or nausea.

I threw up a few times over the next seven flights, hiding my tendency toward motion sickness as best I could. Up to this point, my compatibility with jet aviation had not been negatively observed. It was still hot as hell in south Texas but we were not far from the Gulf Coast. On the weekend, most of the students took advantage of the beach. A handful of us went to Corpus Christi based on my recommendation. We had a good time and great seafood.

I completed the necessary number of flight hours by the next Tuesday except for one additional night hop. I scheduled one for that night thinking it was the same as the previous ones I'd had. At briefing, I learned that the student pilot was an experienced aviator who had been a desk jockey for years. He was re-entering active flight status and would be joining a squadron at the completion of training. The briefing went fine and so did our pre-flights. In the air, however, the flight quickly went from beginner to advanced. My "old salt" ex-fighter pilot instructor quickly assessed the other pilot's abilities and asked him if he was ready for some "fun." The other pilot quickly replied "Roger" and the airborne chase was on. My pilot said, "Hold on to your seat, Lieutenant!" and powered the plane into a steep dive. My stomach went up into my throat and from that point on I wasn't aware of much except being all over the sky in every attitude a plane could be in and from 18,000 to 6,000 feet.

I vomited until there was nothing else to throw up and then kept on heaving for what seemed an eternity. I had never been that sick in my life and would have chosen death if it was offered. I prayed to God for relief when I wasn't with my face in the bag. I had my oxygen mask off as much as it was on and during dives my ears ached because I couldn't even take time to force air into them. Had there been an airborne emergency, I might not have noticed the ejection light. My extremities tingled and my stomach muscles began to ache from heaving. I was barely conscious. I finally mustered the courage to ask the pilot for a few moments of straight and level flight. He refused, saying, "You're not here for that" and with that he continued to try to lose the pilot on our tail. I fought back with all I had, wishing it would end. Crashing would have been a blessing.

My pilot finally told the other pilot to join up, the flight smoothed out, and we returned to the base. My prayer was answered; the planes had reached bingo fuel and the flight was over. Once the plane was on the flight-line, in chocks and shut down, I just sat there catching my breath. I was sopping wet, disoriented, and unable to move. I told the plane captain I needed a few minutes to recover and slowly took off my helmet. My pilot said he'd meet me in the ready room for debrief. I didn't give a damn about debrief. I didn't give a damn about anything at that moment. I needed to collect my thoughts and guts. After a few minutes, I slowly got out of the plane and somehow got down the ladder unto the deck. It felt unbelievably good. I could barely walk, but slowly made my way into the ready room.

My instructor pilot took one look at me and said, "You're green Lieutenant. You need to drop out of the aviation program," and walked off. My airsickness was no longer concealed. I thought, so much for debrief or empathy. I gingerly made my way into the head and threw away my two bags of vomit, washed my face and took a small swig of water, a very small swig. Then I looked at myself in the mirror. I WAS green. I looked as bad as I felt. I headed back to my quarters, wondering why I was punishing myself. While walking, I realized that I was losing weight but more ominously, my resolve. I had no idea how I could ever cope with flights like these, much less contribute to a flight's mission. It was a dilemma that was not going away. Without eating, I crashed on my bed. I slept for twelve hours. The crash after Dramamine and Actifed was huge, not to mention the trauma my body had been through. I knew I couldn't get wings without solving the problem.

Chapter 9

Roger, That's Your Bogey

orkoff woke me up just before noon and asked me what was going on. I reluctantly explained. Yorkoff came back with, "You're not the only one who has ever gotten sick or the only one getting sick here. Let's get lunch." I appreciated what he said but Yorkoff did not get sick and he was not the one who had thrown up everything but his toenails the night before. I was starving, though.

I gave Yorkoff a ride to Love Field in Dallas on my way to join Jan in Arlington. After spending a few days in Arlington, Jan and I headed back to Pensacola. I got away with the few days of unauthorized absence and gratefully accepted orders to the next phase of training at NAS Glynco to begin NFO School. Apparently the night flight pilot had not recommended I be dropped from the aviation training. Jan was not enthusiastic about the move.

Several of us students caravanned from Pensacola to Brunswick, Georgia, and rented at the same apartment complex. The curious bad smell in Brunswick turned out to be a pulp mill. In uniform, I checked into the Marine Detachment and was instantly impressed. As I entered the building heading for Administration, a Marine lance corporal, who was working on a spotless floor of the hallway, hollered out, "Officer on deck!" and several enlisted personnel immediately slammed their backs against the bulkhead (wall).

I put them at ease saying "Carry on, Marines," and smiled with pride as I walked into the Administration Office with my orders. Admin had prepared packets for us and I was out of the office in no time. Jan and I hurried to get settled in.

During our welcome aboard, we learned that three types of aviators came out of this class: BNs, the right-hand seat in A-6 Intruder jets; RIOs, the rear seat in F-4 Phantom jets; and NFOs, who would be navigators or flight technicians on large planes, transports, anti-submarine warfare aircraft, etc. Our designation was unknown until we graduated—if we graduated.

When our class convened, we were each assigned a mentor. Having a mentor was new. I was assigned Captain Castonguay. Closely monitored one-on-one training began that afternoon and quickly progressed to simulators and hops in the Lear jet-looking T-39 Sabreliner.[10] This advanced training would go well beyond just running intercepts on "enemy" aircraft in three-dimensional and, ultimately, hostile environments. Once again, everything counted.

Simulators in the late sixties were not as sophisticated as today's, but posed enough difficulty for any student who could not orient himself in the intercept scenario. I acclimated quickly and was soon scoring high on the tests. That scenario concept seemed simple enough. Our plane was vectored toward a "bogey" plane, which we were to acquire and shoot down (ferret out the enemy and pounce on him). This was easier said than done in a 360-degree arena, however. We processed the controller's information, acquired the bogey on our radarscope, and with verbal commands, directed our pilot in for a kill. The bogey's location, altitude, and direction were a constant only for training purposes; real life, combat situations were an entirely different and complicated undertaking.

Phantom jets did not have guns or a canon, only missiles (one radar-guided and one heat-seeking) to shoot down the enemy plane. This dictated only two kill-shot possibilities: the frontal radar-guided missile shot with the Raytheon brand AIM 7 Sparrow, or maneuvering behind the enemy plane for a heat-seeking AIM 9 Sidewinder shot. The latter was the more reliable for a variety of reasons but also more difficult to achieve. Our simulators were two dimensional, open (not encapsulated), and did not have any motion to add to the realism of aircraft attitude, altitude, or G-force. The T-39s did everything simulators could not, in spades. The boxes checked on our score sheets were Outstanding, Excellent, Above Average, Good, Fair, and Failure for the simulator and added airsickness on flights.

After returning home from the first day's classes, I found Jan on the couch crying. She was not homesick or depressed, but upset because our relatively nice apartment complex was roach infested. She said she was fixing herself some breakfast and when she lifted the cup towel off the countertop, several roaches scurried away. Roaches remained an issue the entire time we were there. Our efforts to enjoy the area, which included the Golden Isles scenery, were thwarted by an insect, small-town Georgia, and the training command.

Many students had trouble with intercepts. I did not until my first flight. Five of us briefed with Captain Castonguay. Four students, including me, flew with Castonguay in one plane and one flew in the copilot seat of the bogey plane. The T-39 converted passenger jet was configured with six seats in the passenger compartment of the plane, three on each side. Each seat had a console in front of it with a radarscope. There was also a scope in the copilot seat. I had no say in the seat assignments, but asked Castonguay if I could conduct my intercepts first. When Castonguay asked why, I said that I might end up getting motion sick as the flight progressed. Castonguay consented. Both planes took off and headed out over the Atlantic Ocean. Once we were in our restricted area, the controller separated our planes in opposite directions for interval and then turned us 180 degrees toward each other and the hunt was on. I contacted the controller and requested bogey information. He replied, "Your bogey is three four zero degrees at forty nautical miles." Castonguay was standing off my right shoulder waiting to interject or offer advice if I requested or needed. I glanced at my attitude, direction indicator (ADI), and altimeter. While our pilot had us heading due north, I "painted" with my radar and contacted the controller:

"I have a bogey at three four five degrees at thirty nautical miles."

"Roger 212. That is your bogey."

I locked on the target and called, "Navy 212, Judy."

The controller replied, "Roger, Judy." ("Judy" means you are taking control of the intercept.)

From the moment "Judy" is called, the controller is no longer involved unless the student loses contact with the bogey or requests help. I commanded my pilot to turn port and the pilot immediately responded, by turning the plane left. When our plane was headed directly at the bogey, I commanded the pilot to bring the plane wings level, with "Level up." Once again the pilot immediately responded and the plane's wings went level. I was wired. Everything was going pretty good. I notified the pilot of the bogey location and then called for a "Fox one." The pilot called "Fox one" (designation for a Sparrow missile shot) and immediately I commanded him to turn the plane starboard hard. The turns commanded by the NFO are port (left) or starboard (right), port or starboard hard, port or starboard hard as possible (maintaining altitude) and port or starboard wrap it up. The last one is do everything but pull the wings off, sacrificing altitude. Then there was one command that did not go in increments: break port or starboard. This command requires the pilot to immediately put the plane in the maximum amount of turn possible.

Students at NFO School wore flight boots and flame-retardant flight suits but no G-suits, so there was not going to be any "wrap it up" maneuvers. The pilot turned the plane hard to the right. My stomach went up into my throat and I got tunnel vision, as I was pulled down into my seat by the G- force. This sensation was accentuated because our seats were aft of the center of gravity of the plane. Instantly I got nauseous but kept my eye on the scope and when the bogey was once again off the left side of the nose, I called for wings level. I caught my breath. As the blip on my scope began to drift, I commanded the pilot to turn port hard and flexed my stomach muscles. The plane immediately turned left and I watched my scope to check the results of my commands. As the plane came around, I transmitted to the pilot that the bogey was in range and then, "You've got the dot." The rest was up to the pilot. I was ecstatic, thinking it was pretty much just like the simulator. The pilot called a Fox two and requested that the controller set us up for the next run. My instructor, Castonguay, had a few comments but basically said I had done a good job and then said, "Now let's see if you can do it again."

The next run was good enough and my turn was over. It was a good thing because I was starting to get sick. When the next student had his turn and began a series of maneuvers, I threw up and then again a few more times during the flight. There was a slight reprieve when our plane was bogey and we flew straight and level. During debrief, Castonguay addressed my airsickness problem. I said it hadn't previously been this bad and indicated that flying in the bogey plane might be better for me since I would be at the front of the plane with better visibility and not aft of the center of gravity. Castonguay was noncommittal. He indicated that if I didn't lick the problem I would have to drop out regardless of how well I could run an intercept and reviewed my scores for the hop. He scored me above average for my intercepts and communication and then checked the box labeled airsickness. Castonguay indicated he would be keeping his eye on me. I had no place to hide.

The next flight went pretty much the same, vomiting numerous times since Castonguay refused to let me fly in the bogey plane and made me sit at the back of the plane to run my intercepts after the others in the group. His excuse was that he wanted to observe me firsthand, something he couldn't do if I was in the bogey plane. He also scored me low, but not failing. (To my credit, I never received a failing score in the simulator or for any of my intercept flights.) At this point, I hated Castonguay's guts and went to talk to instructor/mentor, Bill Lepore. I reinforced my request to fly in the bogey plane citing my good scores and the front cockpit's better visibility. I added that planes in the squadron I got assigned to would have excellent visibility.

Lepore agreed but cautioned me that everything depended on whether or not I could adapt. My first hop in the bogey plane went well and I got two excellent scores without vomiting. The Dramamine helped but I still got nauseous from the turns and bending over the scope during my runs. It subsided once my intercepts were done and I could look out of the cockpit. The bogey plane also flew more straight and level during the flight and some of the pilots, who were often bored, allowed me some stick time. The T-39 used a yoke to control the plane rather than a control stick, but it was still fun flying the plane. I requested the bogey plane from then on. It was nearly always granted because the other students didn't want it. They wanted the instructor present for assistance.

Author, Second Lieutenant Thorsen, in Dress White uniform, ready for the Marine Corps Ball in 1967.

The day of the annual Marine Corps Ball came, November 10, 1967, and all aviation students wore dress white uniforms. Jan made us late to the formal event, just as she did nearly everywhere we went. I was pissed off big time. We were the last student couple to arrive and the only two seats left to sit in were directly across the table from the Marine Detachment Commander, Lieutenant Colonel McCool. McCool was a heavily decorated Marine officer with two rows of miniature medals on his mess dress blouse. I, like most students, had one medal, the National Defense, which we all jokingly referred to as our "fire watch ribbon."

Before I could caution Jan regarding protocol, she looked at Colonel McCool and asked, "What do you do here?" Embarrassed as hell, I wished I could have disappeared under the table. The woman had absolutely no military sense whatsoever. McCool was cool and informed her that he was in charge of the Marine detachment. My attempt to minimize her interaction was without success. We danced some and left early. I didn't like crowds or brass and preferred to have as little contact with the upper echelon as possible. I hoped Jan's small talk wasn't detrimental; I didn't need additional stress.

Thanksgiving happened without much fanfare. Most of us were not able to go home and had opted for Christmas instead. Jan and the other NFO students' wives in our apartment building prepared a wonderful feast in the apartments' social room. It was a somber but poignant affair. Most of us had never been away from home for the holidays but we were each thankful in our own way. The weekend passed quickly and it was back to training.

I kept getting Excellent and Outstanding scores in the simulator. My next airborne intercept hop was in a bogey plane and I performed flawlessly though the maneuvers made me nauseous. When it came time to contact the tower on return to the base, I threw up at the exact moment I needed to call the tower and the pilot had to make the transmission. At debrief, the pilot checked the Outstanding box, then said, "Oops, you threw up when you needed to make that tower call, I'll have to make that Excellent instead," and then he checked the airsickness box. I couldn't tell if my airsickness was getting any better but flying in the bogey plane was God sent. If that went away, I was in trouble. I was at the halfway point of the program with the outcome uncertain. In spite of airsickness, I was near the top of my class and Castonguay knew it.

Our training got more intense and the stress had a profound effect on my personality, demeanor, and libido. Great local sites and seafood only partially helped. Home for Christmas was good and passed quickly. We all put on a happy face but the entire holiday was strained. Everyone wanted to know about my training. That kept Jan from being the center of attention. Friction between us was escalating just like the Vietnam War. New Year's Day 1968 came and went without optimism or a positive outlook.

Back in the air, as the flights got tougher, my airsickness became more pronounced. The flight surgeon at Glynco was no help and tried to convince me it was all in my mind. I continued with Dramamine hoping for better effectiveness. Patches had not yet been invented. My saving grace was that I was scoring very well, even with the airsickness box checked the majority of the time. It was my problem to deal with and the hour of coping or quitting was rapidly approaching. Luckily, the focus was not entirely on me. Many class members were not faring that well and were in a marginal status.

Near the end of training, with only six hops to go, I was called before a panel of instructors for an interview. My class standing, though admirable, was quickly glossed over. The gist of the conference was my airsickness and the panel's need to arrive at a decision regarding whether I would earn my wings. I played up my class standing and my proficiency in intercept scenarios. I admitted my airsickness was a negative but felt the panel should not let it be a deterrent to receiving wings. I told the panel I felt I would adapt better once I got in a squadron. I was certain I could acclimate and not be a detriment to whatever mission was assigned. It all reeked of bullshit but I'd come too far to wash out. I knew that I could be a hell of an NFO without airsickness issues and certainly would enjoy flying a lot more. I was dismissed and went home with my emotions in a knot.

I was now in survival mode clinging to hope with every hop. I flew exclusively in the bogey plane and got very high marks on my next flights, while only vomiting once. I was desperate to hear from the panel and the suspense was killing me. With less than two weeks to go, the pressure was astronomical and not just for me. Both Navy and Marine students were hard pressed to maintain their composure. Each was vying to do his best, each attempting to score well, and some trying to just complete the course with passing marks.

Whether we made it or not would determine our military future and be life changing for us all. For many of us it would be our ultimate accomplishment, putting us in an elite class of our own. Though not pilots, we were still in a very select group. I was certain Jan didn't grasp its significance and her indifference added pressure and anxiety to my already taxed and fragile stamina. At a time when I needed to be well rested for hops, I was restless before, during, and after sleep, worrying about almost everything—marriage, training, going to war, and the country's state of unrest. The panel's silence had me in agony. But in spite of my angst, I continued my intercept mastery and honed my skills. Everything was on the line. At the time, nothing in my life seemed as tantamount as the decision of this board.

In the middle of the final thrust, I got scheduled for two flights on the same day. I didn't know if I could cope. In spite of my determination and fortitude, I threw up during the second flight but still managed to have good intercepts. I crashed hard when I got home. I had given it all I could. Two flights in one day were devastating to my system. I had completed twenty of the twenty-two required hops, having the airsickness box checked fifteen times. Before my next hop, with one week to go, Castonguay confronted me. He indicated the board decided to graduate me unless something went seriously wrong during the next week or with my last two hops. I assured him that it would not, maintaining my facade. Castonguay asked me if I thought my airsickness had improved. I told him yes and that I thought I would do much better in a squadron. He said he hoped so and walked off. I knew that it had been a squeaker and that part of the reason was the urgent need for RIOs and BNs. The Marine Corps did not want to spend this kind of time and money and not gain an aviator.

My twenty-first hop went well and I went home elated. Jan was not. She asked what that meant. I said it meant that I earned my wings and would be designated a Naval Flight Officer and I would get orders to a squadron at a new duty station. She sighed, "Does that mean we can't go home?"

I replied, "For a visit." My twenty-second hop went just as well. The airsickness box had been checked on 75 percent of my hops.

A copy of a newspaper clipping of the author having his wings pinned on by his wife Jan during the NFO graduation ceremony, February 1968, at NAS Glynco in Georgia.

In late February 1968, in a small ceremony, Jan pinned on my wings. I had come in second among Marines. Class standings were irrelevant to me as long as I got my wings, however. We were all Naval Flight Officers and I thought training was over. All eight of us Marines received orders to El Toro Marine Corps Air Station (MCAS) in southern California to join VMFA-232, a squadron of Phantom jets called the "Red Devils." We would all be Radar Intercept Officers. We were going to fly in the back seat of the fastest, most modern fighter attack plane in the free world, in the Marine Corps's oldest and most decorated squadron. Hallelujah! We celebrated at the club and never saw our Navy counterparts again. Jan actually seemed somewhat pleased with the orders. She had relatives living in southern California.

Chapter 10

Red Devil Duos

Most of my fellow RIOs beat feet to California and got stuck in a blizzard on Interstate 40 in New Mexico and Arizona. Jan and I went to Texas to visit family on the way, fortuitously avoiding the storm. Time there was brief but precious. My parents were proud but it was my mom who commented on my weight: 145 pounds. Instead of explaining why I had lost weight, I ate her home cooking like a pig. As we headed west, we saw the Grand Canyon and the tons of snow we missed and although we had lots of time to talk, meaningful conversation was sparse. I knew Jan was not pleased with our current circumstances. I was cautiously upbeat. We were on the same journey, just not on the same page. Fear about acclimating and assimilating into the squadron made it difficult to focus on the scenery but the Grand Canyon was one more beautiful place I saw courtesy of the Marine Corps. Not all things would be pretty.

I checked in at El Toro in early March and ran into P. J. Allen. As a result, Jan and I moved into the same apartment building he and his wife lived in. The following Monday, I drove past row after row of orange groves while heading to the base. El Toro was a huge sprawling base located near Irvine in Orange County at elevation 383 feet. It was established in 1942 and first occupied in 1943, the year of my birth. It doubled in size in 1944 and became the master West Coast jet air station for Fleet Marine Forces. The two 8,000-foot and two 10,000-foot runways, were big enough to handle the largest aircraft in the military inventory. While active, it had every post-World War II president land there in Air Force One. The El Toro logo depicting a flying bull was designed by the Disney Studios.[11] The principal organization there was Marine Aircraft Group (MAG) 33. Our sister squadron, VMFA-334 (a squadron of F-4Js that was rotating to Vietnam that September) was also there. Numerous other jet squadrons, one transport squadron, and various support and maintenance units called El Toro home until it was decommissioned in 1999.[12]

I saw the flying bull on the superstructure of the guard shack as I approached the gate. After a snappy salute, I headed for 232.[13] (See Appendix B for 232's history.) As I neared the 232 flight-line, the awesome-looking Phantoms came into view. Knowing I would soon be flying in the back seat gave me chills. I was overwhelmed with pride and totally awestruck. During my Admin check in, I was briefed on general things and told to read the bulletin board daily. On this board was a read-and-initial sheet of paper we called the "read and heed." Not heeding was a huge "no, no." Our initials were verification that we had read it and would comply with any instructions therein. Other pertinent info was passed during All-Officer Meetings (AOMs). I was introduced to Executive Officer Zych followed by Operations Officer Schnippel. I gave Schnippel my flight logbook. After finding out I was from Arlington, Texas, he told me that he had lived there while at NAS Dallas. Then I toured the squadron facility, hangar, and flight-line. I now was a real person in a real squadron. I was euphoric being a Red Devil and the status of naval aviator felt phenomenal!

I was fitted for all my flight equipment, including a survival vest. I was ready to fly once I completed Naval Aviation and Maintenance Orientation and NATOPS (Naval Aviation Training and Operations Procedures and Standardization) training the next week. That week we intensely trained on the J model of the Phantom jet from nose to tail and were given a NATOPS manual for study and reference. The McDonnell Douglas F-4J Phantom II aircraft was a two-place (tandem seat) supersonic, Mach 2-plus, long range, all-weather fighter.[14] See Appendix C for additional Phantom specifications and statistical data, including its limitations.

Official USMC photo of author dressed in full flight equipment ready to launch on a hop in the VMFA-232 Red Devil squadron at MCAS El Toro, California.

These two training classes were vital and included everything necessary for a life and death situation or emergency. Often the complicated and sophisticated high-performance jet broke or something just quit working. The Navy and Marine Corps didn't want any plane or crew lost due to lack of knowledge or judgment because things happen quickly in high performance, high-speed planes and things that happen tend to escalate. Throughout military and civilian aviation, more crashes are caused by pilot error than anything else. There was no failure here, just learn the plane inside out.

The training was the same for pilots and RIOs except for our cockpits. The pilot had over four times the amount of instruments and gauges, plus he had the control stick and rudders. RIOs did not have a stick, but had one thing the pilot didn't: a radar system—the AWG-10 Westinghouse pulse-Doppler radar. The AWG-10 system purportedly cost one million dollars by itself, while the plane was costing around three million at that time. The Marine Corps and Navy flew their Phantoms configured the same, but the Air Force flew D & E models with two pilots and a stick in the back. The more I learned about the plane, the more awesome it was. We never quit learning as long as we were in a flying status. I was comforted knowing the H-7 Martin-Baker ejection seats in our J model were zero, zero seats. These seats were a life-saving feature since they allowed the pilot or RIO to eject without any airspeed or altitude. We all knew shit happened and had to be prepared. A bit of Group SOP was touched upon as well as safety and

The author's photo of a VMFA-232 F-4J Phantom in flight over the Santa Rosa Mountains of Southern California.

emergency procedures. Our hard seats contained survival equipment. I was about to learn how hard it was.

Back at the squadron daily grind, we looked forward to our first flights. The Red Devil logo was everywhere, including on the fuselage of the planes. And the "Whiskey Tango" (WT) squadron designator was proudly displayed on the planes' tails. Our squadron headquarters was a hive of activity. I met with Commanding Officer Lieutenant Colonel Hutchins, and he assigned me the collateral duties of ground support equipment (GSE) and ground safety. I was put into the duty officer rotation, that being line duty officer on the flight-line and squadron duty officer (a twenty-four-hour duty).

During the interchange, I assumed I had been summed up by "skipper" Hutchins just as I had him. I determined I'd always be on my guard with him. I didn't ask any questions but told the skipper I was honored to be in the unit. Walter P. Hutchins earned the nickname of "Willy Pete" in Vietnam from his W. P. initials. Willy Peter was the military vernacular for a white phosphorous (smoke) target-marking flare. After being dismissed, I went to Ops (the Operations section) and discovered my first flight was scheduled for the following Tuesday and I was Squadron Duty Officer that weekend. Welcome aboard!

I went to the GSE, met my personnel, and started becoming familiar with the organization and workings of the section. The GSE conducted everything in support of moving and starting the Phantoms. I toured the flight-line and watched two of my personnel working in unison to start a pair of Phantoms. The next day I had my mandatory physiology assessment by flight surgeon, Lieutenant Commander (Doctor) Bouvier. Bouvier was a bit of a character but ended up being an asset to the unit and deployed to Vietnam with us. My anxiety about joining the unit was easing up. That Friday I attended my first AOM and met most of the 232 aircrew and ground officers. Saturday, much to Jan's consternation, I stood my first twenty-four-hour duty beginning at 0700 hours. Some others were scheduled on inconvenient days, like holidays, birthdays, and our anniversary.

Tuesday morning I ate very little breakfast. Jan wished me good luck on my first flight and I headed to the base. It was a gorgeous spring day. After spending some time in my GSE shed, I headed to my 0900 brief, taking a Dramamine tablet on the way. I could barely swallow it.

Some pilots took a dump to lighten up. Dumps before flights weren't my thing; I cleared my head, not my bowels. Though excited and nervous, I had high hopes for a really great flight. Nugget pilot, "Pappy" Patrick was the pilot of my virgin Phantom hop. (Though Pappy had lots of flight hours in the Phantom, VMFA-232 was his first squadron out of flight school and he had not seen combat; therefore he was a nugget like me.) Pappy's call sign was "Tarheel." He was from North Carolina, of course. I liked him instantly. Pappy progressed slowly, covering aircraft pre-flight, launch, flight conduct, recovery, and communications. At this point, each flight was customized to Marine aviation, El Toro MCAS, MAG-33 (Marine Aircraft Group) SOP, 232 SOP and our Phantoms.

This flight was the most basic I ever flew in the F-4. We were going VFR east over the mountains toward the desert, looking around a little, doing whatever, and coming back to El Toro where Pappy would point out landmarks, etc. Back at El Toro we'd do some touch and goes, field mirror landing practices (FMLPs), and land after reaching bingo fuel. It was my introduction to everything: the plane, the base, squadron maintenance and flight-line, the area around the base, local communications, and all procedures related to them. Pappy asked if I had any questions. I said none but mentioned my airsickness. Pappy said, "Bring a barf bag with you."

I replied, "I always do." After a weather briefing, we headed to flight equipment. My anxiety elevated so much as we walked, I didn't know if my Dramamine was working.

After suiting up, we went to maintenance to review our plane's yellow sheets. I met the maintenance officer, Major Villarreal. He asked if this was my first hop. I answered, "Yes sir," hoping it wasn't that obvious, and then asked, "Don't you like flying in these planes?"

Villarreal responded, "You don't see any wings on my chest. Knowing what I know about this plane, you wouldn't catch me in one."

I asked, "Why's that?"

Villarreal replied, "You can strap two rockets to a stone and make it fly but that doesn't make it safe," and walked off. I was about to experience that feeling and dismissed his comments. We grabbed our helmets, oxygen masks, and knee-pads and headed out onto the flight-line.

We located plane Number 8 and I just stood there looking at it. I was about to fly in the greatest plane built to date. It was the fastest, most versatile tactical fighter attack plane in the U.S. arsenal. It didn't matter if it was loaded with armament or not; it just looked awesome. As I tried to wrap my head around it, Pappy said, "Let's get started." He said the plane captains were there for assistance and proceeded to the first checkpoint in the pre-flight. We pre-flighted the plane from nose to tail together for my first time, knowing NATOPS dictated separately. After this flight, I always did it solo. Pappy told me to take my time through the whole process and then said, "Climb up."

I grabbed my gear and climbed into the rear cockpit. My plane captain helped strap me into the hard seat and attach my Koch fittings. (Pronounced "coke," these are the fittings that connected us to the parachute straps.) I attached the leg restraints around my lower legs and adjusted the height of my seat. The restraints retracted our feet in the event of ejection (another added safety feature of the seat). A few unfortunate aircrew lost toes on the bulkhead prior to this feature. I put on my helmet and the plane captain connected my oxygen mask to the fitting that went through the hard seat. The hard seat actually contained a small oxygen bottle of its own which gave us fifteen minutes of breathing to reach a livable atmosphere, whether from being under water or above 18,000 feet. I attached my oxygen mask to my helmet and sucked in some "air," pure oxygen from a diluter-demand system of delivery. Our oxygen came from a bottle of liquid oxygen (LOX) inside the fuselage that was one of the gauges we had just checked during pre-flight.

The plane captain removed the safety pin from my ejection seat and showed it to me, a no-fail requirement. Without the pin being removed, I could not eject. I gave him a "thumbs-up" acknowledgment and he departed the plane. I saw Pappy give a left-handed two finger run-up motion to the plane captain and I heard a click in my headset, indicating that power had been applied to the plane. Pappy was starting the left engine. There was no way I was backing out of this. As I gave a smile to my GSE lance corporal, the left engine began to windmill and come up to military power, idling at 70 percent.

I looked about the cockpit and started becoming familiar with the instrument locations as they came alive, with the ADI tumbling a bit before settling on straight and level. I knew not to crank up the radar system yet because emitting signals on the flight-line might make some young plane captain sterile. After locating the radio, I put in frequencies I needed for the flight. Some were pre-programmed, allowing push button control. I located the communication/navigation (COM/NAV) console and the TACAN receiver, our primary means of navigation. Pappy keyed his mic and asked me, "How do you read?" I pulled my oxygen mask over my mouth and replied, "Loud and clear" using the left foot control button on the floorboard. The right was for broadcasting outside the plane. Occasionally mistakes were made. I never made that one but made plenty of others and was about to make more. Several aircrew earned nicknames from their mistakes; I never earned one.

I was a tightly wound bundle of nerves as the right engine came up to military power and Pappy motioned for disconnect of the ground support equipment. Our Phantom was now running on its own power. I reached between my legs and put down the safety flag of my ejection seat's alternate handle. I would use it if I could not get to the primary one, the overhead curtain rings. All that remained before taxiing was verifying the gauges that indicated all systems were within acceptable parameters and put the plane through control surfaces checks, all stuff the pilot did. Those were done with hand signals because of jet engine noise. Flight-line and ground support equipment personnel wore "Mickey Mouse" ears for protection. Hearing loss among aviators and aviation related personnel was commonplace.

I took the opportunity to perform a radio check with squadron common. Ops read me loud and clear and I put my gloves on over sweaty palms. I heard a click and what sounded like air rushing when Pappy said, "Put your mask on so I can test the 'hot mic.'" I did and left it on the rest of the flight. We normally flew with hot microphones and oxygen masks all the time. Instant communication was necessary especially during tense times. My heart was pounding as I put my sun visor down and awaited Pappy. Pappy came up on hot mic and asked, "Are you ready to go, back there?"

I answered, "Yes, sir."

Pappy said, "Call me Pappy" and with that, he ran up the engines a bit and taxied our plane away from the flight-line as the plane captain threw him a salute.

Pre-flighting aircraft occasionally took longer if anything that might down the plane for flight came into question, such as hydraulic or fuel leaks. Phantoms were notorious for both. In fact, it was joked about. If a hydraulic leak would soak one rag the plane could launch. If it was a two "ragger" it was downed for repairs. Planes often went down for maintenance or routine and time sensitive checks. Planes were frequently declared not fit to fly and sorties were cancelled if another bird couldn't be substituted. A plane that broke during flight was often nerve-wracking. Sometimes it meant declaring an emergency or the worst-case scenario, aircrew ejection. Zero eight was a good one and we taxied toward the duty runway.

I took a very deep breath and let it out, slowly trying to relax. That jogged my consciousness to contact ground control for taxi instructions. I called, "El Toro ground control, this is Whiskey Tango zero eight, a single Foxtrot 4, requesting taxi instructions for an eastern departure, over."

Ground control came back, "Whiskey Tango zero eight proceed to runway zero seven, the winds are calm, the altimeter is two niner, niner one, and call for clearance to cross the three four duals."

I noted this new twist as I responded, "Whiskey Tango zero eight copies, two niner, niner one" and wrote the altimeter setting on my kneepad. I didn't acknowledge the three four duals, leaving it to Pappy to correct me or do it himself. I turned my radar system on, placed it in standby and ran the computerized internal check for system status. I left the navigation computer alone for this first flight.

The "three four duals" were a pair of 10,000-foot runways that ran compass headings 340 degrees (northwest) and 160 degrees (southeast). They had to be crossed in order to launch east off the 8,000-foot, zero seven runway. This runway had a minimum climb rate to clear the Santa Ana Mountains, no problem for the Phantom. Neither was the 8,000 feet since its nose usually came off the runway around 3500 feet. Crossing the three four duals was a major safety issue due to aircraft launching or landing, making clearance mandatory. We were told to hold short. After two Phantoms from the 334 squadron landed, we continued to runway zero seven. I left my canopy up because we still had a ways to taxi. I loved the fresh air before and after a flight and consistently put my canopy down at that last possible moment and up at the first opportunity. My excitement grew. I was about to receive a kick in the ass that many men would give their right nut for.

Then Jan popped into my mind, knowing that she never understood the significance of this moment or the elitism of Marine aviation that I was now experiencing firsthand. All the hard work, the studying, the training, the sacrifice, and even the number of barf bags filled and all the bullshit I had endured, came down to this moment, the ride of a lifetime.

My thoughts were interrupted by Pappy who said on hot mic, "Terry, you're doing fine, don't be nervous."

I responded, "Thanks" and instantly knew my nervousness was apparent. But his comment was apropos. Our plane arrived at the apron of runway zero seven and I waited for Pappy to confirm his compass heading, etc., before contacting the tower. When he put his canopy down, I did also and adjusted my seat once more. The amount of room in tactical jet cockpits, the amount of canopy clearance, and the fact that aircrew are securely fastened restricting movement could seriously affect claustrophobics. I never had claustrophobia nor was I ever afraid of heights.

I switched to the tower frequency and requested permission to take the runway for engine run up. It was granted and Pappy advanced the throttles and positioned our Phantom on the centerline. I began feeling warm, which was not good for nausea. I realized that the airplane air-conditioning system functioned just like cars: not efficient while standing still. I opened my a/c vent as wide as it would go and pointed it straight at my face, though little was exposed. I always flew as cool as I could get. As I fiddled with the a/c, I felt the left engine come up to 100 percent power briefly and then the right. I knew Pappy was checking everything out and I actually relaxed. Pappy backed off the throttles to military power and said to me, "All systems go, wings down [not folded], flaps at one half, ready for takeoff."

I confirmed the wings and flap positions visually, a NATOPS safety requirement, and said back to Pappy on hot mic, "Roger, flaps one half, ready for takeoff" and then keyed my external mic and called, "El Toro tower, Whiskey Tango zero eight's ready for takeoff."

The tower came back, "Roger zero eight, you are cleared for takeoff, winds are zero one zero degrees at 5 knots" and instantly Pappy came off the brakes and advanced both throttles to 100 percent power. The Phantom began slowly moving down the runway. Before I could think how slow the movement was, boom, Pappy went into full afterburner and the plane practically jumped forward, throwing me back against my seat and seriously accelerating as it continued down the runway. It was loud inside the cockpit but I knew it was even louder outside (thunderous and causing one to quiver from the vibration if physically close enough or from the sound alone if not). It was something everyone turned to see if they were anywhere near it. Most of those individuals could only imagine it was the greatest kick in the ass when experienced. It truly was and I just had. Nothing the rest of my life would compare to this experience; it was not describable and it was awesome every time, even after it became routine. In a few seconds, as the thousand-foot markers passed by, the nose came up and the plane was airborne. As soon as the plane was climbing off the deck, Pappy retracted the landing gear and the plane quickly accelerated through 400 knots and over the Santa Ana Mountains.

I called the tower and requested a frequency change as we flew out of the El Toro control zone. It was granted and our plane was free to go where we wanted, staying out of restricted areas, including the APC, of course. Southern California had many restricted areas plus many civilian airports and commercial aircraft corridors, so during VFR flight aircrew had to vigilantly scan the horizon (one of my jobs). I was overwhelmed with joy. The experience was euphoric. I was recalling the aviator poem, "Oh I have slipped the surly bounds of earth and danced the skies on laughter-silvered wings...,"[15] when Pappy interrupted my thought with, "What do you think?"

I could hardly respond, but said "Phenomenal." My nervousness was totally gone. It was an out of this world sensation, all new, all amazing. Pappy headed the plane towards the Salton Sea and leveled off under18,000 feet. I switched my radio to squadron common, not knowing where else to put it. As I soaked it all in, Pappy asked, "What do you want to do?"

I replied, "Whatever you want, impress me." I knew giving my pilot a green light meant opening it up for aerial maneuvers but I also knew that I would be considered a "wuss" if I didn't.

Pappy said, "Hang on to your seat" and raised the nose slightly and threw the stick over, putting the plane into victory rolls, three or four, I wasn't sure. Unfortunately, that was the one thing that made me the sickest, the quickest. Visibility was really good in the F-4 except for the RIO seeing straight forward. The plane rotated around the nose and the whole sight of earth and sky spun around until the plane came back to wings level. As the usual nausea started in my stomach, I told Pappy not to do any more rolls for a while. Then he advanced the throttle into burner and pulled the nose up as we did a loop. The speed response due to afterburner was superlative and my G-suit inflated as four G-force came on the plane. Pappy rolled the plane upside down and maintained it for several seconds while I looked up out of the top of my canopy straight down at the ground; then he did a couple of barrel rolls. It was all fantastic. After Pappy righted the plane I asked for a little straight and level flight. What exhilaration it was, being free as bird.

Pappy said, "I'll show you around" and flew us to the Salton Sea at 0.9 mach, around 500 miles per hour. After seeing Lake Elsinore, the Salton Sea, the Chocolate Mountains, the El Centro Naval Auxiliary Air Station, and the Mexico border, Pappy said, "Let's head back and do some touch and goes."

I responded, "Roger that" and painted all kinds of things with my radar as we headed for El Toro. The plane's limitations weren't evident to me. Pilots enjoyed this type of hop because they were free to do what they wanted: no mission, just playtime, which didn't come along very often. I was impressed with Pappy's skills and the plane. It was the greatest thing I had experienced in my life.

On the way back to the base, Pappy pointed out lots more of southern California and then told me to contact the tower. My nausea was almost non-existent. I contacted El Toro tower for landing instructions and requested permission to do touch and goes. Pappy performed six perfect four-G touches and bolters before calling for a final. On landing, Pappy put it down like the others and popped the chute, rolling out on centerline. We taxied onto the apron and held so one of our ground personnel could tie up our chute. I switched to ground control and requested permission to taxi to our flight-line. As we began taxiing, I opened my canopy and unclasped one side of my oxygen mask. Pappy went cold mic. I relaxed, breathing the fresh air and was grateful I hadn't thrown up. I was thinking how awesome the plane and flight were as we taxied toward our flight-line, when the refuel probe started out. Oops, I hadn't pulled the circuit breaker. Pappy put it back in and waited. I knew what to do but I couldn't stretch far enough forward, at the right angle, to find the button on the circuit panel on the bulkhead beside my right leg.

Before I located it, to my chagrin, the probe came out again and Pappy retracted it for the second time. Pappy stopped the plane just off the flight-line and asked me if I knew what to do. I answered yes and said I was having difficulty finding it but to give me a couple more minutes. Pulling the breaker allowed for hot refueling without extending the probe. The probe actually extended out from the right side of the fuselage to the right of the radar intercept officer who was instrumental in helping the pilot plug into the tanker during aerial refueling. Once I pulled the breaker, we headed onto the flight-line. A plane captain guided us into position to park. Once the tires were chocked, the plane was shut down. Plane captains climbed up to insert our seat safety pins and mine asked how the flight was. I responded, "Unbelievable." As Pappy and I headed to maintenance, I realized my butt was sore but still gave a thumbs-up and smile to my GSE personnel.

I was now part of a very elite group, "crème de la crème," and swelled with pride. I had done it, achieved a goal I once thought impossible. I thanked God and silently took it all in. While signing off the yellow sheets, Pappy asked me how the radar functioned and if I had any gripes. The radar was good, I had no gripes, and we headed to flight equipment to stow our gear. As we arrived in the ready room just beyond the entry door, Pappy turned to me and punched me hard in the arm after which, as if on cue, numerous other aviators punched me repeatedly on both upper arms. I was now a Red Devil in one of the Marine Corps's finest fighter attack squadrons. I was awestruck by this unforgettable crowning achievement. I somehow felt even more proud than I had felt a few minutes earlier on the flight-line. Being part of a group, this select group, was intangible, euphoric, and awesome.

I hoped to fly high, proud and confident from that point forward, attempting to preserve the unit's reputation, integrity, and operational prowess. I prayed not to be the one who screwed that up. Pappy went over the flight with minor criticism and asked about the circuit breaker button problem. I said I had a solution and it wouldn't happen again. Finding it was never a problem from then on; forgetting it was. Pappy said that he felt the hop went basically fine, that he always liked some landing practice and hoped I acclimated quickly and had enjoyed the flight. I said I had and debrief was over. I milled around the ready room for a while to meet more peers, a melting pot of individuals from all over the country. A quick check of the flight schedule revealed I had a low-level navigation hop with X.O. Zych late the next day. I went home puffed up but Jan seemed disappointed with my exuberance and there was no sex that night. Many more going from extremely high to low experiences were in my immediate future.

It was March 21, 1968. Unbeknownst to me, exactly one year hence, March 20, 1969, VMFA-232 was scheduled to leave El Toro heading for Chu Lai, Vietnam.

Chapter 11

The Devil's in the Details

ajor Zych was very informative about squadron events during our brief. He said the squadron was reaching our quota of personnel and planes. He said we were deploying to Yuma, Arizona, for two weeks of intense air to ground training (bombing, rocketing, and strafing) on March 31. I knew Jan would be pissed but had no idea what was in store for me. He briefed our low-level flight over the desert, we called a Roadrunner 4, and we headed for our plane (Number 5). Plane 5 ultimately had major significance for Zych and me. Part of our hop took us over Twenty-nine Palms and the Marine Corps Air Ground Combat Center (MCAGCC) on the edge of the southern Mojave Desert. Most of the Marine desert training, active duty and reserve, took place there. We finished our practice landings after sunset but it was not yet dark, a night flight time we called a "pinky."

I arrived home late and Jan lit into me. She accused me of having an affair and all kinds of bullshit. I fought back and said that flights were going to be scheduled for as early as 4:30 AM and as late as 11:00 PM and I was not in charge of scheduling. I informed her that the squadron would also do some flying on weekends and that the whole squadron was deploying to Yuma in another week for a two-week stint. In her anger, Jan blurted out that she would spend the two weeks with some of her California relatives, cursed me, and stormed off into the bedroom. While looking for food, I remembered her birthday was in two days. The next day on my way home I grudgingly bought her a card and gifts.

A few days later on my dad's birthday, I was scheduled for two flights on the same day with Captain Don Berger. Our morning hop was briefed for a 30-degree dive angle delivery of bombs and rockets. Nearly all the bombing flights out of El Toro went to the Chocolate Mountain Range in the desert of southern California near the Arizona state line. Since I was lead RIO and it was my first ordnance hop, I paid very close attention. Our divert base was Yuma, which I would soon become very familiar with. The weather was good and there were no NOTAMS (Notice to Airmen—pilot information like runway closures, etc). We pre-flighted our planes loaded with 2.75-inch rockets in packs of nineteen each and six thirty-pound practice bombs we affectionately called little blue bombs because of their size and color. We boomed out of El Toro and headed east to the Chocolate Mountain target area. The Chocolate Mountains were named that because their dark brown color contrasted starkly with the tan sand. I checked our flight in with the range controller and we were told to hold. Knowing what I was about to experience gripped me while we circled.

I was in a plane that was going to intentionally, steeply dive at the ground at speeds in excess of 500 miles per hour and pull in excess of 4 Gs climbing out of the dive to get back to altitude and do it over and over again. I knew I'd be using a barf bag. Live ordnance added a unique and potentially fatal variable to tactical aviation, carrying with it a critical element of physics and aerodynamics. Miscalculations could ruin one's day. Numerous bombing pattern scenarios called for the plane to actually be in the bomb fragment envelope at release but fly out of reach of the fragments as the plane accelerated away from the target and the fragments decelerated due to air friction. The little blue bombs didn't pose that threat. While we bored holes in the sky, Berger was talkative. We had a great conversation before being called in on target. He was just the third pilot in the squadron I'd flown with. Each pilot had his own idiosyncrasies, mannerisms, and capabilities.

Our conversation was interrupted when the Chocolate Mountain range cleared us onto the "Rakish Litter" target. I checked us in. We were given our run-in heading, the winds, and altimeter reading. Wind speed and direction is important because wind moves the bomb during its fall to earth. The altimeter setting was important because the aircraft's actual ground level (AGL) on target could be affected by a barometric pressure drastically different from our point of origin. It was the same as when landing and taking off from an airport, which was accomplished at the airport's elevation and not zero (sea level). Our planes took interval and we set up to make our runs on the target. "Taking interval" is when the wingman (Dash Two plane of the flight) separates from the lead plane (being Dash One) a sufficient distance so that each plane can safely conduct his run on the target. I acted calm but soon needed all my faculties just to keep up with what was going on. Staying ahead of the plane was tantamount. My job was communication, helping the pilot maintain altitude and airspeed, reading off altitude and airspeed verbally in the dive, and giving the pilot a "standby" moments before calling "mark, mark" at the release ("pickle") altitude, which was 8,000 feet this day. I also had my eyes outside the cockpit some in case someone flew into our restricted area and then I recorded my pilot's hit information, clock position, and feet from the target bull's eye.

Dive angle, airspeed, and sight picture were pilot variables also affecting ordnance delivery. A good bomber pilot develops a good sight picture during his runs. Not all pilots were good bombers and not all good bombers had good days. Nobody batted a thousand but every pilot in the Marine Corps developed the mastery of every facet of military aviation. Every pilot had his strengths and weaknesses and so did RIOs. In the final analysis, most Marine pilots who flew fighter attack planes were best at bombing because the whole reason for Marine air was supporting ground forces. All our practice was for combat operations, preparing for warfare, currently Vietnam, the real-life scenario.

I didn't have time to be nervous anymore. Berger called, "Dash One's in hot," put G-force on the plane and pulled the nose down 30 degrees, sending my stomach up into my throat.

I heard Rakish Litter call back, "Roger One, you're cleared hot." I was watching the console, watching the altimeter unwind and then realized I needed to be calling out altitude and airspeed over the hot mic. Eleven thousand feet completely passed and I called off 490 knots, then 10,000 feet, then 9,000 and said, "Standby," paused, and at 8,000 feet, called "Mark, mark." Berger pickled a bomb, pulled back on the stick putting G-force on the plane and brought the nose up, ending the dive. As the nose came through the horizon and began to climb, Berger called, "Dash One's off" and as the G-force eased up I caught my breath. The physiology of it wasn't that bad but it still brought on nausea. Occasionally the flight's lead pilot was able to use his personal call sign. Our commanding officer was Red One and he loved to use it. If the flight had more than two planes, additional ones would be dash three, dash four, and so on. A flight of four was considered a division while two aircraft were a section.

In a few seconds, while climbing back to 12,000 feet, the controller announced, "Dash One, your hit was three o'clock at sixty meters." I didn't know if that was good or bad but wrote it down and thought just six more runs to go as I heard over the radio, "Dash Two's in hot" and the controller acknowledge, "Roger Two, you're cleared hot." The targets we were hitting were well marked and were used day and night. The bull's eye was a circle, 30 feet in diameter. Pilot's scores were summarized into an average known by the acronym CEP, circular error probability. Zero was the best, meaning all hits were in the bull's eye. During actual bombing, CEP's would have two representations. The first one was the percent on target or effective coverage. Zero was 100 percent. The second was target destruction percentage in reverse, the amount not destroyed. A zero/zero CEP was 100 percent on target with 100 percent destruction. The larger the numbers, the less effective (worse) the pilot was. Not many of the pilots (especially the newer ones) obtained the coveted 0/0 CEP. The destructiveness of the military's arsenal of weapons compensated greatly for imperfect accuracy.

Our plane leveled off at 12,000 feet and entered a gentle left turn. I breathed deeply and reported to Berger, 480 knots. Twelve thousand feet was not an exact altitude to be maintained and therefore I never mentioned it to my pilot unless he was quite a ways off, high or low. From this point on, each dive, drop, pullout, and level-off occurred during the completion of the elliptical racetrack pattern we flew above and around the target. I grunted a bit as Berger pulled the nose down and headed into the next dive. I was on top of the airspeed and altitude and the drop went fine. After the plane pulled off the target, I recorded our next hit.

On the next run, I started sweating and relaxed as much as I could during the brief level left turns. That was also my opportunity to gaze outside the cockpit for horizon reference and scan the skies. While doing so, I observed Dash Two pulling down into their dive. After our next dive, I asked for cold mic and threw up while our plane climbed back up to 12,000 feet. I came back up in the gentle left turn and told Berger he could go back to hot mic. After the sixth and final bomb dive I vomited once more. After firing our rockets, Dash Two joined up and we departed the target area. I never missed calling altitude or airspeed and recorded all the bombing data. Firing rockets was fun. Nineteen came out of each pack in a shotgun effect and were devastating when they impacted and exploded on the ground.

I regained my composure on the way back to El Toro. Berger did not jump my ass, saying being in the back seat took some getting used to. Even though Berger showed some understanding it was still a problem. Because it was not discussed, I had no idea that several RIOs were also having some airsickness issues. After our planes landed and taxied onto the apron, ordnance personnel visually checked us over for misfires, etc. before we taxied back to our flight-line. This routine culminated every live ordnance hop. It was an important procedure, reducing mishaps, accidents, and possible fatalities, the obvious ones being dropping ordnance someplace other than on a designated target, doing damage to the plane, and not being able to drop or fire ordnance.

Debrief went fine and Berger looked ahead to our afternoon flight, asking me if I would be up to it. I said I was and that I'd see him at briefing, hoping I WOULD be up to it. My brief for the afternoon hop was in two hours. All of a sudden, I realized that the briefing was mine because I had to plan where to go. After peanut butter crackers and a Coke, I returned to the ready room and planned a round robin trip to Las Vegas. It went fine.

I was scheduled for an angle calibration with the skipper the next day. I hadn't wanted to fly with Lieutenant Colonel Hutchins already and went home not knowing what the flight entailed. I called my father that evening to extend birthday wishes and then tried to get some sleep. I tossed and turned all night. At briefing the next morning, I learned that angle calibration meant practicing dive angles and improving pilot sight picture. Hutchins was brushing up on his bombing expertise for the next week's sorties. I was not intimidated by him; I just dreaded being in his back seat so soon. He was a very experienced and capable F-4 pilot, a lieutenant colonel in the USMC and commanded a tactical fighter attack squadron. His command presence and aviation knowledge were awesome. He could eat up lieutenants unintentionally. I took two Dramamine tablets before launching. Our flight went to the Twenty-nine Palms MCAGCC where there was an airfield, ground support, and a slew of desert targets. I threw up a couple times but made it okay. The hop had little RIO involvement. Under the cool, calm boss façade was a human being and our conversation during the flight was amiable and devoid of motion sickness talk. The hop took away some of Hutchins's mystique.

Our Friday AOM outlined the deployment. Sunday, Jan drove to her aunt's place in Glendale. This was one example of couples managing separation due to military orders and scheduling. I relaxed and watched some basketball, developing a fondness for the Lakers. On Monday, I headed for the base, staged my luggage and attended an administrative briefing. I flew a low-level hop to

The author's photo of two Red Devil Phantom jets outbound from MCAS El Toro, California.

Yuma with nugget pilot Perrow. The hop was fun. We flew just feet off the desert floor, which for a brief time was below sea level, an unnerving sight on the altimeter. When we checked into the MCAS Yuma tower, they gave us the altimeter setting and visibility of 125 nautical miles, the distance of a particular mountain peak. Yuma was an excellent base for intense air to ground weapons delivery and it was not yet hot. I was ill prepared for "intense."

Most of the squadron sections were there and active when our planes arrived. After briefings from various section heads, the next day's flight schedule was handed out and we were dismissed. Some personnel went to the club. A few brave souls went to San Luis across the Mexican border. I cautioned my ground support equipment guys about the potential of bad things happening in San Luis and how it might affect their career. A bunch of us officers went to town for Mexican food. The group got boisterous and egos competed for the most outlandish aviation tale. Nuggets like me just listened but I'd have my own soon enough. The town bars and restaurants were obviously used to it because no one shut it down. The food was good, not as good as Tex-Mex, but I savored it and the socializing.

For me, 1968 April Fools' Day was no joke; it started with a bang. At 0800 hours, I had a 30-degree dive bombs and rockets hop with Ron Perrow as my pilot. Perrow and I were wingman (Dash Two) to lead pilot Major Gruhler. The briefing was standard stuff with a "no shit" bingo fuel (absolute minimum) of 6,000 pounds of gas. Bingo fuel was not an issue due to the close proximity of the Chocolate Mountain range to the base. We dropped mostly practice bombs the first week. The hard stuff was saved for the second week, those being 250, 500, and 1,000-pound fragmentary bombs, 2.75-inch rockets and five-inch Zuni rockets, napalm, and a 20mm Gatling-type machine gun. Both the 500-pound and 250-pound bombs could be configured with retardant fins. The purpose of the fins was to allow the pilot to fly a little slower and lower onto the target for accuracy of delivery. In combat, this would make our plane more vulnerable to ground fire. When napalm and 250- or 500-pound bombs were loaded together on the plane it was commonly referred to as "napes and snakes" and considered "soft" ordnance. "Snakes" came from the bomb's name, Snake-eye. It wasn't soft to the enemy.

After our planes checked out, we launched. Once at the Whiskey Impact area, Perrow took interval. I knew exactly what to expect and braced myself. Perrow adjusted a lot in the dives, quickly bringing on nausea. After a few dives, I started sweating profusely and after a couple more, threw up. In spite of feeling like hell, I performed flawlessly. I normally did better on morning hops but wasn't coping that well on this one due to dropping our twelve bombs singly. I threw up some more and longed for the flight to be over. After expending our rockets, our planes joined up and headed back to Yuma. We were on the ground in minutes with a flight time of barely over one hour. I was extremely nauseous and opened my canopy as soon as I could for some fresh air. After debrief, I headed for the Bachelor Officer's Quarters (BOQ) to get some horizontal time before my afternoon hop with Perrow, dropping 30 degree bombs and rockets again. I didn't know how I could cope. I lay down on my rack and prayed for peace and healing without eating any lunch.

I took two Dramamine tablets after I got up and headed to my briefing. Perrow was a good pilot but a so-so bomber. Executive Officer Zych briefed us and we headed to our planes. On the way to suit up, Perrow asked me how I felt. I responded, "I feel okay at the moment, we'll see how it goes," knowing full well it wouldn't be good. I had high hopes for the two Dramamine but feared they might adversely affect my health at some point. I just knew I needed relief, somehow. We launched and were on target in minutes. I was feeling dull as the Dramamine kicked in. For me, it was a lousy day and the deployment was just beginning. Apparently I was the fool this day but I wasn't laughing as the plane headed down at the target. Knowing that our squadron's operations would begin in Vietnam on April Fools' the next year added depression to my nausea. We were cleared in hot and I called off airspeed and altitude. Perrow's hits were better on this second hop but after several runs I was nauseous again. The good news, if one could to call it that, was that the flight didn't last that long. Towards the end of the flight, I was sweating profusely, my mouth was watering uncontrollably and my fingers and toes were tingling. I threw up but never missed a call.

There was nothing I could do. With each successive run, the feelings intensified as I began losing my focus. I feared reprisal or being ostracized but more importantly felt there was a safety concern. I did not want to jeopardize myself, my pilot, or the mission and wondered how the hell I was going to make it through the deployment. Thoughts of quitting crept in. When the flight was over, I beat it back to the "Q" (BOQ) and fell asleep for a couple hours. I made evening chow just before it closed and ate like a pig. On the way back to the Q, I checked the flight schedule. My heart sank. I was scheduled with the skipper in the morning for a 45-degree bomb and rocket sortie and in the afternoon for a flight of strafing with X.O. Zych. April Fools' my ass!! It wasn't a joke; it was self-imposed torture.

The next morning at 0730 hours, the skipper briefed me, his lead RIO, and wingman nugget pilot Gus Fitch who had Captain Kondo in his back seat. Kondo, a mustang officer, had been one of my NFO school instructors and seemed like a really nice guy, unlike many mustangs who were real assholes. Mustangs were enlisted Marines who got commissioned and many of them had chips on their shoulders. However, like many other mustangs, Kondo was (unfairly in my opinion) reverted back to a Chief Warrant Officer after our combat tour. The skipper covered the 45-degree angle of bombs and rockets delivery, communications, etc. and the four of us suited up and launched. Our "Red One" flight was immediately cleared onto the "Rakish Litter" target range. We set up on the target quickly and the skipper and I were cleared in hot. Hutchins lined up on the east side of the target and called, "One's in hot," turned hard port with lots of G-force and pulled the nose down, to me, an unbelievable amount to begin the dive.

I caught my breath as our plane straightened up to wings level in the dive. I felt as if we were going straight down. I had never seen so much horizon and ground forward from the back seat before. Much of what was normally shielded by the pilot's ejection seat in front of my console came into view. I thought I could see the edge of the target. I quickly drew my attention back inside the cockpit and to the altimeter. It was unwinding at a very fast rate and I called it off quickly and the airspeed too, now over 500 knots. Then it was "mark, mark" and the skipper dropped his first two bombs and quickly put over five G-force on the plane. I grunted as silently as I could and my vision went temporarily to black and white even with the G-suit. I experienced a grey out for the first time.

The steep dive angle, G-forces and top airspeeds in the dive were all new to me and very exciting. Though awesome, I was instantly affected by the shear dynamics of it and my nausea began at the end of the very first dive even with two Dramamine pills. I recorded the skipper's hit data of three o'clock at 30 meters and dreaded the next six runs. The skipper apparently was not a bad bomber but in the next dive he actually adjusted his sight picture by pushing the stick forward temporarily, putting some brief negative G-force on the plane. It lifted me off my seat. My stomach went into my throat bringing my nausea on faster. The skipper's adjustment was good because his hit was 12 o'clock at 10 meters, right in line and very close to the bull's eye. Vomiting was now inevitable.

My worst case scenario, throwing up in the skipper's back seat for the second time, was about to come true. I concentrated on the business at hand and fought the nausea with all my might. After pulling off the target on the fourth dive, I requested cold mic and started vomiting hard. It was all dry heaves because there was nothing in my stomach as I hadn't eaten any breakfast. I did it again two runs later and a little on the last run. The skipper's bomb hits were pretty good and then he put the rockets in the bull's eye. I congratulated him. I was barely able to make the communications for the flight as we headed back to the base. I was grateful for a lazy break but dreaded debrief. ("Break" is a term aviators use to describe a maneuver used during the landing sequence. Once the flight is cleared to land, all the the aircraft in the flight fly over the runway by the tower and then turn and separate to land singly. The break can be hard or lazy. A lazy break is when the pilot turns slowly and reduces speed. During a hard break the pilot snaps the plane left and pulls with G-force, slowing down sufficiently to lower the landing gear. The first time I experienced a hard break, when "snapped," my head hit the canopy.) The skipper had a few criticisms for Fitch and then turned to me and asked, "Anything to add?"

I said, "Nothing for the flight, Sir." I knew he wanted comments on my airsickness and I told him 45-degree dives were new to me and that I still needed some time to get used to the back seat. I left it at that; no optimism or pessimism, just asking for some time. We were dismissed.

I headed back to the confines of my BOQ room and crashed. My mind was a shambles and my body was too. I had another flight in three hours. I decided on rest rather than food, set my alarm clock and tried to doze. It would be hard and almost impossible but that was exactly what I needed. When I arrived at my afternoon briefing, I still wasn't over the nausea from my morning hop. I took another Dramamine and prepared for the worst. The X.O. briefed the hop for 10-degree strafing runs utilizing a centerline-mounted Mark 4 gun pod (a Hughes double barrel Gatling-type 20mm machine gun). In aviation vernacular 20 mm (millimeter) was referred to as twenty "mike, mike." The MK4 delivered 6000 rounds a minute. The X.O. cautioned wingman nugget pilot, Wayne Flor, not to exceed the three-second burst time limit due to possible barrel melt down and covered the fact that every tenth round was a tracer. Tracers helped the pilot aim the rounds on target and once on target, the pilot utilized the rudder to steer rounds across the target horizontally for effectiveness. The X.O. covered the low and slow advantages of the 10-degree dive and cautioned us not to go below the minimum altitude, which could make ricochet hits a possibility.

Once again, I was lead RIO and handled all the communications. After the brief concluded, our flight launched and headed for the Beagle Leash range. Once on target, Dash Two took interval and our planes were cleared hot. Zych headed in on the target and began firing. The neatest thing occurred as the gun pod fired. The plane not only seemed to slow a little from the recoil, but it also lifted the plane slightly. I loved the sensation and the awesomeness of this weapon. Sadly, it did not always work correctly and malfunctioned for wingman Flor, who ended up just flying circles around the target until Zych and I completed our runs. I barely got nauseous on this flight. I celebrated by going to early chow and devouring my food. My exuberance vanished as I read the flight schedule for the next day. I had a 45-degree dive bombs and rockets flight with the skipper again in the morning and then a bombs and rockets flight with Major Logan in the afternoon. I went to bed early, but slept poorly.

The next morning the skipper's brief was identical to the previous day's and for me the hop had the same outcome. I couldn't tell if I was making any progress and the skipper didn't broach the subject this time. I tried eating a little light lunch hoping for less nausea that afternoon. The afternoon 30-degree bombs and rockets flight with Major Logan was interesting. Logan had been an A-4 Skyhawk pilot who had transitioned to F-4 Phantoms. Skyhawk aircraft were subsonic attack planes and had been in the USMC inventory for some time and were primarily used as close air support (CAS). I liked Logan and wanted to do well on the hop, though still in recovery mode. I couldn't help wondering why I was being scheduled with senior officers so much. Our wingman was nugget pilot Beau Mace. The brief and launch went fine. I got sick after a few runs and vomited intermittently the rest of the flight, having difficulty with some of the communications for the first time.

Logan did a lot of correction during his runs but he was probably the best bomber in the squadron. Most of his hits were in the bull's eye and one time during a dive when I got to release altitude and called "Mark, mark," Logan replied, "Not there yet," and continued until he was satisfied before releasing his bombs. His hit was a bull's eye. Being sick didn't keep me from being impressed. During debrief, I apologized to Logan without making any excuses. I left for the solace of my BOQ room. I wasn't feeling well or hungry. I was dejected, discouraged, and melancholy. I wondered how it could get any worse. I hadn't talked to Jan in days and called her that night. She was in good spirits and having a good time with her relatives. There was so much loud merriment in the background I cut the call short because we couldn't carry on a meaningful conversation.

I was scheduled with nugget pilot Owen the next morning for 30-degree dive bombs and rockets and in the afternoon with X.O. Zych for the same thing. Owen and I were on Major Cagle's wing, whose call sign was "Tex." I got sick on both hops but threw up in the X.O.'s back seat that afternoon. Being sick on flights was bad but in the back seat of the executive and commanding officer was worse. I felt awful. At debrief the X.O. asked about my problem. I said I thought it would get better with time. It was April 4, my mom's birthday, but the buzz in the ready room was Martin Luther King's assassination. I called home that night and wished my mom happy birthday. I tried to hide being in the dumps but she read despondency in my voice. I confessed I was having airsickness problems and tried changing the subject to current events. I hated being negative on her birthday and wished that my situation and that of the world were better. Her next year's birthday would be worse. My next day was too. I was scheduled with Logan in the morning for bombs and rockets and the same ordnance with Captain Bob Snyder in the afternoon.

The next morning Logan briefed 45-degree bombs and rockets, my worst nightmare. Our wingman was pilot Fitch again and he had Captain Lepore in his back seat. I was surprised to see Lepore, my NFO instructor/mentor. He was now a newer member of the squadron than I was. Logan and I led the flight. I lasted several runs before getting sick and eventually throwing up. From then on in the flight, I didn't do that well. The dynamics of that flight were devastating to my system. I wholeheartedly welcomed the relatively calm flight back to the base. Logan did not mention my airsickness at debrief and I avoided Lepore. I somberly headed to the Q. I ate a few crackers and lay down. I felt skinnier.

Snyder led our 30-degree dive bombs and rockets flight that afternoon. Snyder had the nickname of "Tokyo Bob." Snyder briefed our flight with wingman pilot Rice, for bombs released singly. It meant a minimum of thirteen runs on the target, since we were dropping twelve practice bombs, and a longer flight, both disastrous for me. I took two Dramamine tablets, knowing full well it wouldn't do the trick. Our flight launched to the Rakish Litter range. Our pilots did their thing and we RIOs did what we could to help. Snyder was not a good bomber. His hits were all over the place and I recorded every one of them. It did not take me long to begin feeling nauseous due to my debilitated condition. I fought valiantly not to throw up for several runs but eventually had to. Due to the number of runs, I had the dry heaves several more times in the flight. I had difficulty with calling the airspeed and altitude and nearly missed one pickle altitude due to being in the bag. I called it slightly past, knowing it was within the margin of safety and wouldn't affect Snyder's hits anyway.

I longed for the flight to end. Nothing else mattered: Snyder, the Marine Corps, Colonel Hutchins, the next day's flights, or sunset. I had reached the "I'd just as soon die," moment. Back on the flight-line, I was slow getting out of the plane. When I stepped onto the deck, Snyder was in my face hollering, "You are the worst RIO I have ever flown with. You are worthless and should quit" and turned and headed to maintenance. Was he right? I gathered up my stuff and headed into the ready room for debrief. I handed Snyder his stats and sat chagrinned. Snyder debriefed and sent Rice and his RIO, Clark, on their way. Snyder inquired of me an explanation. I told him that I was still getting used to the F-4 and this type of flight and being scheduled for more than one a day was very hard on my tendency toward airsickness. In the full ready room, Snyder berated me and loudly asked why I had come this far. I reasoned, "Because I felt I could overcome it once I was in a squadron."

Snyder retorted, "You aren't worth a shit as a RIO and should get out of the squadron."

Major Schnippel overheard the conversation. He pulled me aside afterward and said, "I can make anyone in my back seat sick on any given day. Don't let this bother you." I loved him for that. I said thanks and went to look at the next day's flight schedule. It was Saturday and I was scheduled for only one flight, a morning hop with pilot Mace for 45-degree bombs and rockets. Finally I wasn't scheduled twice in one day or with a senior officer. Somehow, I saw it as a relief and sheepishly wandered back to the Q to collect my thoughts. I fought back tears. They came anyway. I contemplated quitting and might have if it hadn't been for Schnippel's comments. I didn't want to be a ground officer but knew the flight surgeons couldn't help me. It was my dilemma to solve. As I lay on my rack pondering, I crashed hard. I declined an invitation to go into town for dinner because I didn't feel sociable. I headed to the officer's mess and ate alone in a funk.

The next morning, Mace and I were on the X.O.'s wing for 45-degree bombs and rockets at Beagle Leash. Amazingly, I didn't get sick until near the end of the flight. I had the rest of the weekend off. I did laundry and Saturday night went into town for Mexican food with about fifteen fellow aviators. Being out on the town was pleasant and airsickness issues never came up. Most of the pilots ragged on the senior pilots' bombing abilities and most of the RIOs ragged on several pilots, senior and junior. I hit Snyder pretty hard and all the RIOs agreed. I asked why Snyder didn't come on these outings. One of the pilots said that he did't have time. "He has a girlfriend at every duty station."

I offered, "I thought he was married."

The answer came back, "He is." I drank Cokes but well into the evening most of my peers had a good buzz going, becoming boisterous and animated. Amidst it, some of the week's negative experiences diminished. Sunday was totally devoted to relaxing by the pool and playing billiards. Somehow, Executive Officer Zych and I paired up and dominated the pool table for quite a while. He was better at playing pool than piloting. He had transitioned from helicopters to jets. It explained why he was often behind the plane. My ping pong playing wasn't that bad either and it ended up being a good day.

The next day, with only one flight scheduled (30-degree bombs and rockets with Major Logan), I fared pretty well. Logan did excellent. To my knowledge, it was the squadron's first zero/zero CEP. On Tuesday, I was scheduled with Snyder for a morning bombs and rockets flight. The briefing and flight were strained due to our previous encounter. I performed about as well as I had with Logan but Snyder did not. Even so, Snyder was less than cordial after the flight and I left the building as soon as possible, checking the next day's flight schedule on my way out. I couldn't believe my eyes. I was scheduled for three hops, one with the skipper, one with Schnippel, and one with Logan, all senior officers. I had no idea how I would make it through the day, nor how I would take my Dramamine. It was going to be a total boondoggle or what many Marines would call a gaggle fuck. I had no propensity for the common military curse vernacular ("fucking A" being one of the more popular expressions of the day), but would have to make a Herculean effort to keep flight two or three from being a total wash. Now was an ideal time to quit if I was going to. I rose the next morning to offer up the guts I had left.

Hutchins briefed the 10-degree napalm and 30-degree bomb delivery and we suited up and headed to our planes. This was my first napalm hop and the skipper pointed out what to look for on the fuses at each end of the canisters, three loaded on the centerline in staggered positions under the belly of the plane. Our flight launched and headed for the Whiskey Impact range. The napalm was a one-run ripple and the fireball in my rearview mirrors as we pulled off target was phenomenal. I watched Dash Two drop theirs and marveled at the awesome destructive firepower of this weapon. The 30-degree bomb runs went fine. I got nauseous at the end but amazingly didn't throw up.

The briefing for my second hop was barely over an hour after I got back from the first one. I took another Dramamine, gambling on not overdosing. That flight of bombs and Zuni rockets went fairly well and I ended up vomiting just a couple times near the end. Oddly, I was happy with the outcome considering how bad it could have been and glad Schnippel left the airsickness issue alone. After recovery and debrief, I had just two hours before my next flight. I had not eaten in eighteen hours and was not hungry. I needed rest. I went back to the Q to lie down for an hour. I took a Dramamine before brief, though really scared about the effects. My flight with Logan did not go as well as the previous two but better than I expected. It was 30-degree Zuni rockets that had high explosive (HE) heads and that meant fewer runs on the target. That helped a little overall but I got nauseous early in the flight, fought off vomiting as long as I could, and then had nothing but dry heaves. Logan did well. I was a mess. I left the ready room trying to decide whether to eat or sleep. I slept.

My next morning's 0900 hour briefing was with X.O. Zych for 30-degree Zuni rockets with HE heads, my only flight that day. I thanked God the deployment was winding down. The flight went well for Zych and me. My last deployment hop was with Logan. Logan did very well again. As we came off the target on the last run, Logan remarked, "You did pretty good today, Lieutenant."

I said, "Thanks" and felt like there was light at the end of the tunnel. The next day I flew in the skipper's back seat on our return flight to El Toro. I knew exactly what this flight was all about and did my best to prepare for conversation. The skipper got into it right away. I agonized over the answers to his questions, trying to be positive. I indicated that despite the airsickness, I was glad for the ordnance deployment and flight time. I said I felt I was beginning to adapt and looked forward to more flights and new operational scenarios. I knew I was telling the skipper what he wanted to hear, hoping it would come true, and that it didn't sound too much like bullshit.

Hutchins finally changed the subject and the remainder of the flight, albeit brief, was pleasant. The whole squadron was dismissed for the weekend after a 1400 hour All Officer's Meeting (AOM). The next Monday's flight schedule was already printed and I was surprised I wasn't on it. Then I looked at the read and initial and found out why. I had the twenty-four-hour duty on Sunday. Shit, I thought, I can't even have a weekend with my wife. I decided not to tell her about the duty until Saturday. I went home and started laundry. Jan was actually glad to see me when she got home. We went out to eat and then back home to bed. I might have kept her up half the night if I hadn't been so utterly exhausted physically and mentally.

My Tuesday flight was canceled because our bird went down mechanically. Operations were cancelled altogether the next day due to issues related to our plane's recent heavy usage. By Thursday, however, it was business as usual and I was scheduled for two hops. The morning flight was with Captain Snyder, my nemesis. Our instrument round robin actually went well. The afternoon flight of bombs and rockets with Flor was a different story. Flor was a very junior pilot, consequently, a wingman. Our thirty-minute flight to the Chocolate Mountain range should have been an easy smooth flight. But Flor constantly adjusted the plane attitude and speed. I was nauseous by the time we got to the target and sick during the bombing. Being sick on the flight back to El Toro had never happened before and I asked Flor if he could fly a little smoother. He replied, "I thought I was." Other than Snyder, Flor would be the only other pilot I didn't like or like flying with.

I wished for one flight per day but had two the next. My first one was a morning hop with Snyder. Our plane was down and did not come up for a couple hours. I hated delays because it changed my Dramamine timing and I was somewhat leery about flying in a plane that was just cleared to fly. There had been some close calls and declared emergencies in our unit already. Once the flight launched, it went surprisingly well. Snyder was not friendly, but talkative. I found out that Snyder was the aviation safety officer of the squadron. For a fleeting moment I thought Snyder was a human being after all and not just the asshole part of one. I barely made it back in time for my flight with nugget pilot Sellers. I got nauseous on the bombs and rockets flight, but Sellers did pretty well.

Many of my flights were now repetitive but they weren't necessarily routine. I learned something new almost every day and each new experience brought just that, aviation experience and ability. I had many new types of flights to experience. The next morning I launched with Logan on an aerial refueling hop, scheduled as an IFR (in-flight refueling). Nugget pilot Stokes, who had RIO Foltz in his back seat, was Dash Two. We flew over to Twenty-nine Palms, made contact with and practiced plugging into a KC-130 tanker plane. We made several dry plugs and then on the final plug, took on fuel and headed back to El Toro. The KC-130s had a drogue basket at the end of a long hose trailing the plane from each wing as much as thirty feet, so two aircraft could tank simultaneously. The refueling took place at about 20,000 feet initially but once the F-4s started taking on fuel and getting heavy, the tanker would start descending to gain and maintain speed, a technique termed "tobogganing."

The turbo prop KC-130 Hercules was a great plane but not the best tanker because of its top speed, about 245 knots during the refueling process. Since the Phantom's refueling probe came out the right side of the fuselage near the RIO, the pilot couldn't take his eyes off the tanker to look at the drogue as it came close to the refuel probe. That made the role of the RIO critically important during the process. The RIO's responsibility was to get the pilot to plug the probe into the drogue basket using verbal commands. This was

Author's photo of a VMFA-232 Phantom about to refuel from a KC-130 tanker with the refuel drogue visible.

harder than it sounds. Air turbulence made it almost impossible, even with a good radar intercept officer in the back seat. It required great aircrew communications, coordination, and rapport. This day things were ideal. Logan and I were on the left wing. I was enjoying a good view of everything when the flight was cleared onto the tanker.

Logan extended the probe and asked if I was ready. After I replied, "Yes Sir," he advanced the throttles. I departed from Navy jargon (port and starboard) and used commands left, right, up and down. Logan and I made a good team and connected on our second attempt, then plugged in six more times with the final one wet (taking on fuel). The F-4 got really heavy once it was nearly full, another reason it earned the aircrew nickname "super hog." Occasionally, a pilot might have to use afterburner just to stay plugged in. That was the time to disengage. It all came down to physics and aerodynamics, that is, thrust-to-weight ratio and coefficient of lift. Logan and I had a good day. Proficiency at aerial refueling was extremely important for obvious reasons, extending flight times, distances, emergency low fuel situations, etc.

The next day, I had a ground controlled intercept (GCI) flight over the desert. It was my second flight with pilot Mace. To my surprise, we had a brand-new plane, which had just arrived from McDonnell-Douglas still painted a primer grey and devoid of our squadron markings. I was going to have fun on this flight. Mace and I were wingman to Major Mavretic, whose call sign was "Maverick." His lead RIO was Dobson. I did as well with my intercepts as I had at NFO School but without air sickness issues. I knew this practice was leading up to air combat maneuvering (ACM), which included supersonic intercepts and multi-plane engagement scenarios. It was now May and a lot more flight scheduling was coming. For the squadron brass, especially the skipper, it was all about flight hours, flying experience, and squadron statistics. The skipper had to have the squadron battle ready by early 1969. It was almost summertime and I was doing better with flights and feeling better in the plane.

Chapter 12

The Devil Made Me Do It

hough bombs and rocket hops were now fewer, I got scheduled for one with Tokyo Bob. We were Dash Two on the skipper's wing. I was really up for this hop and hell bent on restitution. On the very first run I was all over Snyder for being either high or low on altitude and on run-in, either fast or slow on airspeed. I was right on with communication commentary in the dives and totally in sync with the pickle altitude. I did not cut him any slack and kept it up during every run, without getting sick. When we got out of the plane back on the flight-line, Snyder came over to me and said, "I was wrong about you," and walked away to debrief. Vindication—I had nailed his ass. Giving Snyder's poor stats in front of the skipper was over the top. My afternoon flight with Rice wasn't as good.

My next day's VFR instrument flight with Tom Billison was a "gimme" hop and I brought my camera. I planned to do a round robin into the desert, fly over the Grand Canyon and then return home. The flight was easy and as it progressed, Billison asked me if I wanted to fly through the Grand Canyon instead of over it. I responded, "Sure," knowing it was a huge no, no, and figuring he wasn't serious. We could do whatever we wanted during the flight as long as we obeyed flight rules and restricted areas, but the canyon, of course, was restricted. As our plane neared the canyon, Billison lowered the plane's altitude and airspeed. He entered the canyon just west of the main entrance and lodge, hoping to hide the plane's numbers and any other identifiers. I was curious and shocked at his next statement, "There's a cable stretched across here somewhere." It would have ruined our day if we had hit it but I dismissed the thought and started taking pictures.

We flew below the canyon rim, weaving above the Colorado River until we got to the end. Billison hit minimum afterburner and pulled the nose straight up until we reached ten thousand feet and leveled off upside down. I shot a picture of the ground out the top of my canopy, capturing the Hoover Dam. It was a totally awesome and exhilarating experience, one I wouldn't have had if I'd quit, one that few people ever experience. I couldn't wait to get my film developed and there were no repercussions for what we did. I never confessed it to anyone except Jan, who didn't share my enthusiasm.

I was scheduled in the skipper's back seat for my first ACM. It was unfortunate because it was my second flight of the day, the recipe for disaster. I didn't want two flights in one day but any issues with scheduling were my problem, not theirs. I paid very close attention to the briefing. The old

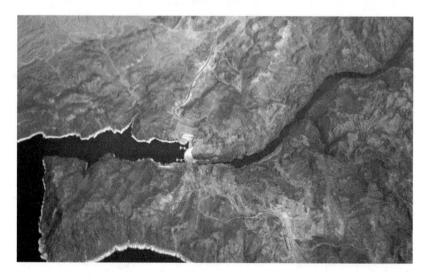

A photo of the Hoover Dam from 10,000 feet taken by the author through the top of his canopy while the plane was inverted, just after flying through the Grand Canyon.

terminology for this type of flight was "dog fighting." Two planes were set up to fly at each other head to head and once there was visual acquisition, each pilot attempted to maneuver his plane onto the six o'clock position of the other for a kill shot, which would be accomplished with a Sidewinder missile. Historically, two good pilots had difficulty obtaining an advantage. The problem was the F-4 didn't maneuver that well behind certain planes (MiG 15s and 17s could out-turn it) even though the Phantom wasn't "thrust limited," meaning it had unlimited power. Eventually, all the ACM training would be married to intercept scenarios where technology and aerial ability merged into modern air warfare.

During the brief the skipper delved into aerodynamics and coefficient of lift, thrust-to-weight ratios and got bogged down with mathematics until finally getting back to the conduct of the flight. Aerodynamics in the flight meant physical and physiological dynamics in the air. During the brief I quickly realized it was going to be worse than 45-degree bombing runs. The RIO had little responsibility except trying to find and/or keep track of the bogey plane, monitor instruments, and scan for any idiot who strayed into our restricted airspace. Our planes launched and I got our flight cleared into the restricted area. Once we headed toward each other, the fight was on. When the skipper acquired a visual of our "adversary," he slammed the stick to the left. Not being prepared, my head hit the canopy. I had no idea that a plane that heavy could maneuver the way it did. After a small period of time the skipper reversed the plane to the starboard with over five G-force in the opposite direction and I knew I was going to be really sick on the flight. The Phantom consumed lots of fuel conducting air combat maneuvers. It wouldn't be consumed quickly enough for me. Our two planes entered a scissors pattern with neither at an advantage so the skipper called it off to set up again. I was getting nauseous.

The vertical element was not used this day but during the skipper's second run he lost a visual of our adversary and asked me if I had it. He had our plane in a tight left turn with lots of G-force. While strongly resisting the urge to vomit, I attempted to see the "bogey" at our seven o'clock position. I could hardly get my head around and with my G-suit tightly pressing my gut, I pulled my right hand up along my body and up under my chin, using it to help turn my head to look. I did not see him but threw up shortly thereafter. The hard turns and G-forces were almost violent and using afterburner added to the effect. I was glad when we reached bingo fuel and returned to El Toro. On the way back the skipper asked how I was feeling. "I'm better," I replied and added, "Colonel, this was my first ACM. I will get better with this type flight just as I have all the others." Hutchins was silent. I went home and was going to crash for a little nap without eating but Jan wouldn't have any part of it. I was still nauseated and cratering from the Dramamine. Instead of napping, I exploded. She had no concept of what I'd been through, being thrown all over the sky. I told her that her attitude sucked, stopping short of calling her an unsympathetic bitch. I went into the bedroom and even with the adrenaline flowing, quickly went to sleep. Jan woke me up after two hours, apologized, and we ate the excellent dinner she fixed.

My next flight seemed innocuous enough: a retirement flyover for a general's retirement ceremony at the Marine's Camp Pendleton in San Diego. I was in Logan's back seat, again. We were in a flight of four Phantoms. X.O. Zych led the flight and briefed us. We launched, contacted the tower at Pendleton, and were told to hold at 3000 feet over the ocean until notified it was our turn to fly over the parade deck during the festivities. While holding, the three other birds flew a loose chevron formation while Logan and I flew outside the group before assuming the slot (trail) position. I took photos of those birds, one with the southern California coast in the background. The flyover for the retiring general was a conglomeration of helicopters, jets, and prop planes. While boring holes in the sky, Logan remarked, "If we survive this, we can survive anything!" I thought this was an inane flight and didn't question Logan's surprising remark since I barely had seventy-five hours in the Phantom. Flyovers were difficult to coordinate due to the numbers of aircraft and their relative speeds. Though impressive viewed from the ground, they were dangerous gaggles in the air.

Before I got too bored, the tower called us in over the bleachers. Logan carefully maneuvered into the slot position and our flight assumed a tight diamond formation. We descended to 1,000 feet AGL and headed east. The slot position is tricky because of the exhaust from plane number one and the aircraft's proximity to all three of the other planes. As we flew over

The author's photo of 232 Phantoms off the west coast of Southern California waiting their turn to fly in a diamond formation over the parade deck during a retirement flyover at Camp Pendleton. His plane almost crashed less than fifteen minutes after he took the photo.

the parade deck at 500 miles per hour, Zych signaled burner and all four F-4s lit minimum afterburner, accelerating into an ascending lazy left turn. Before I could complete my thought of being the highlight of the show and how grandiose we must look from the ground, my exuberance quickly vanished when my plane pitched violently over 30 degrees nose-down. It was so sudden that the negative G-force threw me up against the canopy, even though I was tightly strapped onto my hard seat. That collision cracked the visor of my helmet. My camera hit the canopy, denting it. My nav bag on the floorboard beside my left foot came up into the air in front of my face, with all its contents inside. I was instantaneously scared shitless. I had no idea what happened but knew it was bad and potentially cataclysmic.

My mind was racing like sixty but I did not panic; I went into survival mode. I recorded everything that happened visually at lightning speed. Just as quickly as the plane had pitched nose down, it pitched nose up over 30 degrees, slamming me back into my seat under extreme positive G-force and my camera slammed into my gut. At that moment, I reached down for the alternate ejection seat handle between my legs and pulled it out of the detent. I held it there without completing the action. I did that instinctively because the positive G-force was so great that I could not raise my hands over my head for the curtain. At that moment I heard Logan blurt into the mic, "disengaging." That was the last transmission I heard and with that, the plane pitched nose down again. Once again I hit the canopy and so did my camera, putting another dent in it. I was terrified and knew the plane was losing altitude. I knew Logan was trying to gain control of the plane and maneuver away from the formation, but my worry was hitting the ground. The cause of our diving was a mystery and I was no longer able to communicate with anyone.

I knew it best not to eject when in a negative G situation because the seat might hit me in the ass with such force that it could break my back, a consequence some other aviators had suffered. I also knew it was better to stay with the plane if it could recover and land safely because ejecting did not guarantee survival. I was at an impasse. During that second negative G-force maneuver, my nav bag came up in front of my face with all the maps and high-altitude charts suspended in the air. The next nose-up attitude slammed me back into the seat at which time I had the presence of mind to see if the master caution or eject light were on, solidifying my choice to go. Neither was lit. I had no idea what was happening in the front seat but I was sure Logan was doing his best to save the plane and us.

As the situation rapidly progressed, during that positive G-force moment, I felt possibly the plane was under control. That moment quickly passed when I was thrown up against the canopy during another negative G nose-down attitude. My camera hit again suffering another dent. Again, I kept the alternate handle out of the detent but less than the inches required to eject. The airspace in front of my face was filled with maps, dirt, and debris as evil thoughts of circuit breakers popping and systems failing flashed through my mind. Before I panicked at that thought, the plane pitched nose up again, and again I slammed back into my seat. It was like the scariest, most violent roller coaster ride ever and I knew it couldn't continue. I felt we were dangerously nearing the ground. So, according to my training, with lost communications and the plane out of control at less than 10,000 feet, I should eject, or at least I had every right to. But I didn't. I rode it out through one more oscillation and the plane smoothed into a left-turning shallow dive. I peeked out of the cockpit at the ground. The trees looked really close but we were still well above them!

I didn't know it at the time but the other three birds of our flight had separated some and my friend Doug Harlow was watching my plane from a higher, safe distance wondering what the hell happened and how I was, since we looked really close to the trees. I never did look at the altimeter. I didn't need to. Logan had gotten control of the plane and was beginning to climb. I slowly eased the alternate ejection seat handle back into its detent assuming the immediate danger was over. As I surveyed the instruments on my front console, my eye caught Logan peering back at me. I gave him a "thumbs up" and then I saw the lights on my radio disappear and knew Logan took control of them.

In the meantime, pandemonium broke loose on the ground. The three-star general did, indeed, get his show. Three West Coast news stations filming the event had gotten great footage of the whole incident, which they plastered all over the six and ten o'clock news later that day. Once my plane disappeared over the hill northeast of the parade deck, it was assumed that it crashed. Fellow RIO Fred Griffin was standing the squadron duty that day and told me later that the phones lit up, overwhelming him with calls. Because I had lost communications, it was thought I punched out, which, of course, I had come very close to doing. Meanwhile, back in the plane, I was trying to clean up the mess in the back seat and pushed in a few circuit breakers that had popped out. Logan requested that Dash Two of our flight come over to us for a "look see." I communicated with hand signals to Harlow in that bird as it got alongside us. Harlow tapped on his helmet on the side where his ear was and gave me five fingers. I tapped the side of my helmet and gave him a "thumbs down," indicating no radio, "Nordo" for short. Harlow's pilot gave Logan a "thumbs up" for the visual, indicating that they could not see any external damage. Logan started dumping fuel.

I knew we were headed straight back to the base to get on the deck as soon as possible. At this point, I was left with my thoughts. I wondered how close we had come to having a mid-air collision with the other planes in the flight and knew that some or all of us could have been killed. It was a thought I didn't like. "Flight pay is hazardous duty pay" came to mind. Logan declared an emergency and made a straight-in approach at El Toro. Dash Two escorted us nearly all the way back to the ground. I was glad to hear the air rush of the landing gear as it extended and then the thud, as it locked into place on final approach. Logan took an arrested landing, reducing the chances of any other malfunctions. Once the plane's hook engaged the wire at the end of the runway, the plane decelerated from 145 knots to zero. That's when my mic cords, male and female ends, came forward into view. Obviously they had disconnected during one of the negative G-force oscillations. I plugged them together and heard a click in my headset. I keyed my mic to let Logan know I was back up on com.

As we taxied off the runway, Logan asked me how I was and I told him "Okay, just shaken up a bit." I then pulled the refuel probe circuit breaker and silently thanked God and Logan for delivering me home. Back at the flight-line, before exitting the cockpit, I cleaned house. I scooped up the maps and things and found Logan's flashlight on my floorboard and his shroud-cutting knife lodged in the console between the front seat and back seat. Those were testaments to the abnormal attitude and forces on the plane. I also discovered that my camera not only had four dents, but had also taken a photo during the melee. I watched Logan as he climbed down the steps on the side of the plane. At the bottom, when he turned toward me, he looked as white as a sheet. As Logan and I gingerly walked to mainte-nance, Logan asked me how many oscillations I counted. I replied, "Four." Logan said, "Me too," and that is all we spoke of the incident until a briefing, at the skipper's request, during the next AOM. Logan's words about survival had been prophetic.

As best maintenance could figure, inexplicably, the pitch augmentation, the computerized gyro stabilization for the up and downward movement of the nose on the plane, failed once we entered burner over the parade deck and caused the plane to pitch nose down. The plane was over stressed with nine and a half positive G's and six and a half negatives Gs. Plane number five became a hangar queen and never flew again. Logan was so stiff the next day,

The photo is of the author with his principal pilot, Major Gene Brown, assisting with a maintenance test. The author is on the plane, with pilot Brown (right) and a Staff NCO (left), as they all inspect the left engine intake. Official USMC photo.

A photo of pilot Brown (left) and the author in the back seat getting assistance strapping into their Phantom jet by two enlisted plane captains prior to a maintenance test. Official USMC Photo.

In this photo, pilot Brown and author Thorsen give thumbs up indicating they are ready to taxi off the flight line and take off on the maintenance test. Official USMC Photo

This photo depicts pilot Brown, center, and author, right, reviewing the results of the test with the maintenance Staff NCO, who is seated. Official USMC Photo.

he could not get out of bed and did not fly for several days. I was offered a no-fly day the next day. I declined, hoping it would earn me "brownie" points and nervously flew a generic flight unaware of other significant airborne emergencies in my future. The evening of the incident, I was dismissed early to go home. I could not get the incident out of my mind as I drove. I told Jan about it but played down the potentially dangerous outcome. As the two of us watched the evening news, to my surprise, the footage of our planes was broadcast and Jan caught her breath.

I then knew just how bad it looked from the ground, how close a brush with death it was, and why it was thought that Logan and I had crashed. I watched it again at ten but Jan wouldn't. The footage confirmed the four oscillations and one of the stations gave the squadron a copy of the footage for retention and safety purposes. During that week's AOM, Logan reviewed the hop's emergency and how he managed to get the plane back to the base. He told everyone in the room how the control stick came completely out of his hand at the start. This harrowing and death-defying experience was uniquely ours. Logan always had my respect and gratitude. The skipper praised us for saving our asses to fly another day. I was praised separately for keeping a cool head and not ejecting. The squadron brass now had an inkling of what I was made of.

Chapter 13

Green with Pride

My first intercept flight with the skipper was scheduled the next week. I hoped it wasn't another "check me out" flight. The flight was in the restricted area out over the ocean beyond the Air Defense Identification Zone (ADIZ) in international waters. I contacted the Doubloon controller for our subsonic intercepts. The Doubloon Restricted Area was a designated airspace located over the Pacific Ocean that was used by military aircraft for maneuvers, including intercepts. On my first run I locked on the bogey, took a Judy, and directed Lieutenant Colonel Hutchins in for a "Fox one" and then immediately began maneuvering him in for a "Fox two." As our plane approached 30 degrees off the bogey's tail at one nautical mile, I swelled with pride as I told Hutchins, "In range, you've got the dot."

Hutchins called "Fox two" and the intercept was terminated. I breathed easier. Inside I was bursting with pride as Hutchins complimented me, "Nice run Lieutenant."

I replied, "Thanks," all the while thinking it was a great run and a thing of beauty! I was in my element, I knew it, and it showed. I was never nervous around the skipper again.

On our wingman's turn to run his intercept, I relaxed. All my runs were good, our flight was done, the range time was up, and we were at bingo fuel. I led us back to El Toro in a state of euphoria, crossing the ADIZ en route. Crossing the ADIZ was a big deal. Fighter jets would be scrambled if any unidentified or unauthorized plane came across it and thus violated U.S. airspace. During debrief, Hutchins seemed pleased with the flight's results and our RIO performances. Hutchins reminded us that the Fox two scenario was a little unrealistic because enemy pilots weren't going to maintain an unaltered heading, altitude, and airspeed while an aggressor positioned himself in range off his tail to shoot him down. ACM begins if the Fox one missile doesn't blow the "enemy" out of the sky. The drawback of the Fox one scenario was (at that time) Raytheon's Sparrow missile reliability.

I was also pleased with the flight and hung around the ready room for a while. I hoped this was a good omen for the week. I was scheduled for a refueling flight the next day with Executive Officer Zych and came in early to spend some time in my ground support equipment shed. With that, ground safety, standing duty, training, and meetings, there was very little spare time. On my way to my brief, while walking toward the squadron headquarters and ready room, I heard and felt a loud explosion. I rushed toward the flight-line. My ground support personnel were running around all over the place. There was no fire, just panic.

During engine run-up of one of our birds, the flywheel of one of our machines used to start the Phantom's engines fragmented and pieces of the hot metal burst through the unit's housing. One piece of the flywheel hit the plane's fuselage where it covered the left engine intake. The centrifugal, inertial force of this propelled piece made about a fifteen-inch track up the side of the fuselage and lodged there. It could have just as easily gone completely into the fuselage or impacted the rear cockpit area and/or the RIO or possibly the Number 7 fuel cell right behind him. Luckily, the largest fragment hit the concrete flight-line beneath the unit, making a good size gouge, and came to rest under the plane parked next to the one they were starting. Fortunately my two lance corporals had the machine parked alongside the aircraft correctly and they were both safely positioned while starting the plane.

The only other significant piece came out of the unit's left side, leaving a hole in the red painted line indicating the flywheel's rotation axis. That piece came out with so much force it flew over the squadron headquarters building, over 200 feet away, and landed in the grass next to our headquarters sign. No one was hurt and no fire resulted. My personnel performed well. Next came the clean-up and paperwork. The incident had to be reported and one plane repaired. The skipper was ambivalent about it, although clearly upset it happened and a plane was damaged. All I could think of was it could've been so much worse. The skipper had me make some changes to my incident report, exerting as much control as possible. It wasn't lying; it was doctoring. I felt there wasn't enough emphasis on ground safety in the squadron.

Zych and I had a good in-flight refueling hop that afternoon. We had a total of nine plugs into the tanker. After the flight, I gathered my stuff from my locker and headed home. When I got to my car in the squadron parking lot, I discovered I couldn't get into it. I had parked in the end space where it adjoined our sister squadron's parking lot with the spaces striped ninety degrees to ours. A pickup truck with a trailer hitch had backed into a space adjacent to mine and backed the trailer hitch into my driver door where it still was, with the ball of the hitch pressing a dent in the door. I was pissed and knew that it was someone from VMFA-334 so I proceeded there. It turned out to be the squadron's Executive Officer, Lieutenant Colonel Jenkins. Jenkins got livid and tried to bite my head off, inappropriately exercising his authority. Since I was parked well within a designated space, I wouldn't have any part of it and demanded that he fix my car at his expense or I would notify the base MPs. Then Jenkins capitulated and once I got an estimate, he paid me.

Less than two weeks later, Jenkins was dead. He had an airborne emergency during a night flight and crashed into the Santa Rosa Mountains, east of the base. All that was found of him was thought to be a piece of his ear. His RIO safely ejected but impacted the mountainside and died of his injuries before help could reach him. Everyone was solemn for days, but operations continued.

I had several good hops without nausea, returning home late one night from a ground control intercept flight. Jan again started accusing me of having an affair; I was not. I hadn't the time even if I had the inclination, nor did I have time for her crap. She was lessening much of the positive I had going. I went to bed mad and did not sleep well. Fatigue and stress were not desirables while flying in supersonic jets; they were recipes for disaster.

The author poses in front of plane #5 on the flight line of VMFA-232 at MCAS El Toro, California. The photo was taken for the author by pilot Ken Owen.

Fatigue affected my mental acuity and made me less resistant to air sickness. Stress affected my focus. My energies needed to be on making sure I became a good Marine officer in the squadron and RIO in the back seat. I felt I was doing both.

On Monday, I had another new wrinkle, a one-plane flight to assist ground troops at Twenty-nine Palms. My pilot was Lieutenant Colonel Bond, from 334. We proceeded to Twenty-nine Palms and contacted a ground unit. The unit commander requested that our plane fly at low levels at a relatively fast speed so they could track our plane with their Redeye missiles. The Redeye was a man-launched missile capable of shooting down a low-flying plane. Bond flew our plane in a figure-eight pattern back and forth over the unit so all the personnel could practice acquisition and tracking. At bingo fuel, Bond came up on the radio and told the ground commander we would make one more run. The commander asked if we could do something special for the troops since they were about to deploy to Vietnam. Bond agreed, saying nothing to me. Bond flew directly over the unit at a very low altitude. As we passed over the unit, he hit afterburner and pulled the aircraft straight up to 10,000 feet and rolled out on top. The unit commander came up on the radio and excitedly said, "Fantastic, thanks."

Bond replied, "You're welcome, good luck. I'll be there in September," as we headed back to El Toro.

The next day, I had a ground control intercept flight with a SATS launch, another first for me. A short airfield for tactical support launch was a land-based catapult shot just like those on an aircraft carrier. I did not mind having a cat shot land-based, but never wanted to hit the boat (carrier) nor be stationed aboard one. All Marine pilots qualified aboard a carrier, practicing launches and recoveries both day and night, because Marine units were regularly stationed aboard them. A regular takeoff in the F-4 was a kick in the ass but cat shots were even more spectacular. The conduct of the launch was much the same as that aboard a carrier. My pilot taxied our plane into position and it was attached to the shuttle of the steam catapult. My pilot extended the plane's nose gear to increase the angle of attack. The catapult launcher gave the engine run-up signal and my pilot advanced the throttles to 100 percent power, assessing the gauges. The launcher then held up his hand, palm towards the pilot with all five fingers extended, at which time the pilot advanced his throttles into afterburner and immediately gave the launcher a salute. The launcher drew his hand down to the ground and the catapult sprang into action sending our plane forward, accelerating it to 175 knots and airborne in mere seconds. I was slammed back into my seat and our plane jumped into the air so quickly I could hardly believe it. It was an incredible, absolutely fantastic experience. Our intercepts were fine and I enjoyed the flight, including the arrested landing at the end.

The next day, Executive Officer Zych and his wingman took cat shots at the beginning of their flight. During Zych's launch, he failed to take his feet off the brakes as his plane catapulted and consequently sheared both the main landing gear tires. It was another example of how small the margin of error is and how one's whole day could be ruined in an instant. It was also an example of Zych's being deficient in the jet environment. Snyder got me on the horn and asked if I had a camera. I asked why and he elaborated. While Zych was busy dumping fuel, preparing for an arrested landing, I quickly drove home and got my movie camera. Snyder and I photographed him as he made a picture perfect landing, catching the wire. The deck was fouled because Zych could not taxi off the runway. Two new tires were installed and the plane was towed back to the flight-line. Zych was embarrassed about his mistake and took a lot of kidding. But our day's events were overshadowed later that night by the assassination of Robert F. Kennedy. I had now been less than twenty-five miles from both the Kennedy brother assassinations. It was a depressing coincidence, but as I was learning, time and life went on. A short visit by Jan's family, operational flights, and Jerry Leist's Marine wedding with crossed swords made June 1968 pass faster than one of our jets in afterburner. Jan's funk, after her family left, dissipated more slowly.

My first hop in July was another air combat maneuvering flight in the skipper's back seat. I did better because I was rested but still had a little trouble keeping a visual of the bogey plane. I acquired the bogey in my mirrors two separate times and was able to tell the skipper the plane's location while only barfing once. The skipper gave an okay debrief but he clearly was agitated. My second hop in the same day was with "Pappy" Patrick for some landing practice and didn't even last an hour. Upon examining our Phantom after the flight, we found guts, blood, and feathers between the ramp of the right engine intake and the fuselage. Apparently we had a bird strike on one of our approaches and weren't aware of it. Bird strikes were not a common thing in our unit and this one missed our right engine intake by mere inches. We were lucky the bird wasn't sucked into the engine. Foreign object debris (FOD), in the form of flocks of birds, has brought down airliners. A fodded engine on landing could have been catastrophic. Base personnel walked our entire runways every morning for debris that could be sucked up into our engines. My only two hops with Pappy at this juncture were notable: virgin Phantom flight and a bird strike.

All aircrew stayed busy training or performing our collateral duties when not flying. My next new wrinkle was a night refueling flight with pilot Sellers. Night refueling added another degree of difficulty to the already challenging endeavor. The flight actually went fairly well and the team of Sellers and Thorsen successfully plugged into the tanker seven times. When we returned to El Toro, during the landing sequence, Sellers turned our plane from the downwind to begin his final approach to the duty runway too early and our plane was too high and fast at the approach end. Sellers quickly realized it, broke off the approach and called the tower to tell them he was taking it around. On the downwind of the second approach he was about to do it again when I chimed in on hot mic, "Extend your downwind." Sellers straightened it up and continued until I said, "Okay" and then he started his turn. The landing went fine from there.

The next night brought a night close air support sortie with the center-line mounted 20mm Gatling gun on the Rakish Litter target range, another first for me. I was in the lead plane with Executive Officer Zych again. Our wingman was Ron Perrow who had Tom Knudsen in his back seat. Both pilots did well. I loved the sound and feel of that weapon. On the post-flight inspection of his aircraft, Knudsen found a hole in the right wing of their plane. The hit was obviously a ricocheted bullet from being too low in one of their runs. Perrow and Knudsen were very lucky they didn't kill themselves. During debrief, Zych admonished his wingman, then covered other points of the hop.

My next night flight was a night intercept over the ocean with Schnippel. Our wingman pilot was Owen with RIO Watson in his back seat. During the flight, Schnippel had the air conditioning pretty chilly. For the first time ever in the F-4, I asked for the temperature to be raised a little. Schnippel responded, "I didn't think it could ever be too cold for you?!"

I responded, "This is a first." After a couple runs, my radar screen went dark. Our plane had lost a generator. The remainder of the flight was canceled and we returned to El Toro without incident. I was relishing my role as a radar intercept officer and being savvy with emergencies.

Chapter 14

Baby, Light My Fire

Late one morning, while busy in my ground support shed, I got a ground safety call from maintenance. One of the airframe lance corporals was working near a plane's tail section when that plane's tail hook dropped onto his left foot. The lance corporal was wearing his steel-toed boots, in accordance with regulations, but his toes still got crushed. I knew the skipper had already been notified but without consulting him, in accordance with regulations, I called the group safety officer to make him aware of the incident. The group safety officer came to the hangar, bringing the wing safety officer with him. They conducted an investigation on the spot and made a report to me, in accordance with regulation. Later in the day, I visited the young man in the base hospital. It was unknown at that time whether he would keep the toes or not. The lance corporal was in decent spirits due to pain medication. I went home after the visit and received a call from the squadron Admin officer saying the skipper wanted to see me in his office at 0800 hours the next morning. I knew the skipper was pissed and a good night's sleep was out the window. Sadly, the lance corporal lost the toes and received a medical discharge. Was he the lucky one? Things would have been totally different if the hook had hit his head.

At 0800 hours the next day, the skipper went into a tirade yelling and cursing at me for my insolence. I put up a small defense citing the regulations and directives but Hutchins was adamant that I should have consulted him before I reported anything to any higher body. He claimed I should personally consult him for his prior approval of any action or reports. All I could do was muster, "Yes, Sir," and left when instructed. It was an obvious safety violation. If the hook had been secured with the small cable made for that purpose, it could not have happened. I didn't appreciate chastisement for being and doing right. That which drove me to succeed and help conquer my air sickness, now affected me negatively. I couldn't claim victory of a battle much less the war. Being uncompromising was sometimes a pain in somebody's ass but there would be times it saved mine. I tried to keep a low profile for a while. My highlight of the day was playing some hoops that afternoon.

All aircrews were being scheduled for more night ordnance hops. I had one the next day. When I got home late, Jan and I had a terrible fight and I went to bed wishing I'd never married her. The next morning Jan said she was going to enroll in a modeling school. Though angry while driving to the base in a thick blanket of smog, I pondered her decision and my life in general. I was having success in the squadron operationally while my personal life was taking a nose dive.

Launching aircraft under instrument flight rules (IFR) due to low visibility was not a problem but if the smog did not lift, recovering them at El Toro would be. However, operations went on as scheduled. I had my first flight with the squadron's Air Force exchange pilot, Captain Lowry (who was rumored to have crashed a plane). Lowry and I had a low-level nav and intercept hop over the desert with Gruhler and Castonguay. After launching, while ascending through the smog, I marveled at how absolutely, totally white it was and experienced my first case of vertigo. As I trained my eyes on the instrument panel to alleviate my dizziness, the whiteout brightened. Just as our plane emerged from the "clag" (as we referred to it), our plane went silent and all instruments null.

I instantly assumed we had a generator failure. Lowry had the "RAT" (Ram Air Turbine) out in no time and the basic instruments plus our radio came back to life as the turbine produced auxiliary electrical power. Lowry keyed his mic and asked me if I could read. I replied, "Yes, Sir." He then explained that we had a double generator failure and were on RAT power. Without panic, I asked what our course of action would be and Lowry said we would divert to Yuma, pretty much where we were headed. I told Lowry this was my first double generator failure and asked if he needed me to look up any emergency procedures. He said no as we headed to Yuma. While en route, we filled in Ops O Schnippel. Our wingman flew formation with us and then headed back to El Toro. We landed without issue and taxied our bird to a Marine training squadron's hangar where repairs could be made.

Since there were full Phantom maintenance facilities at Yuma, I had hopes of getting home that evening. Jan and I and several other squadron couples had been invited to Tex Cagle's house for a social evening. My hopes were quickly dashed, however. Lowry and I were ordered to stay with the plane until it was repaired. A maintenance crew and parts were being flown in by helicopter that afternoon. I called home and told Jan the news and that I doubted I would be back for the evening's events. I told her that the best-case scenario was I would be home late but, if not, I might be in Yuma for some time. I asked her to pack me a small bag of clothes with some money and take it to the base squadron headquarters and give it to Ops O Schnippel. I told Jan that he would get it to me on a plane headed to Yuma on a cross-country hop. I ended the conversation with "Thanks, I love you, and I have no way of knowing how long the plane's repairs will take." Lowry and I checked into the BOQ.

That evening my package from Jan arrived. She had sent me a pair of pants (no belt), a shirt, one pair of socks and underwear, and ten dollars cash, but no shoes. The reason for sending me stuff was that all my personal items (wallet, jewelry, uniform, etc.) were in my locker back at the squadron. Fortunately, the BOQ supplied toiletries. I, with a large number of my squadron mates passing through Yuma on their cross-country hops, headed into Yuma town for Mexican food, as usual. I had spent most of my money less than four hours after I received it. I was embarrassed wearing my ugly reddish tan flight boots with navy slacks. The plane was not repaired that night and was declared "hard down." I called Jan and told her before turning in for the night. She was not pleased. I wasn't either. The next morning Lowry and I got in touch with Schnippel. We tried to convince Schnippel to let us catch any plane we could back to El Toro. Schnippel said no, stay with the plane, thinking it would be fixed that day and we would be able to fly home. It did not get fixed that day.

I was pissed. I had no money or clean clothes, including underwear. It was Saturday but for Lowry and me there was nothing to do, nowhere to go, and no way to do laundry. I went back to the Q and washed a pair of underwear by hand and hung them up to dry overnight. I lay down on my rack and took a nap. I got up hungry. Lowry loaned me some money and we went to the officer's mess then checked on the plane. It was still down. When we returned, I called Jan collect. She was livid and extremely angry at the squadron and the United States Marine Corps. I was too, but that didn't help me and I ended the conversation. I found a smut novel in my nightstand and after reading a little of it was both horny and depressed. I showered and went to bed.

The plane was not fixed on Sunday either and I was now outraged. Lowry and I called the squadron headquarters again asking if we had permission to get a flight back to the base. Once again, the answer was stay with the plane. I washed another pair of underwear before I went to bed that night. The plane was still not fixed on Monday and I had had enough. On Tuesday, without authorization, I caught a flight on a Navy S2F (nicknamed by Navy personnel as a "stoof with a roof") and flew back to El Toro and had Jan pick me up at the base. I went straight home and never checked into the squadron. I went back to work at the squadron the next morning, Wednesday, and checked in with Schnippel who made no comment to me. The plane was finally fixed later that week and another aircrew flew it back to El Toro. I was so mad I didn't give a rat fuck if that plane ever got back.

I was flying again right away. No issue was ever made about me returning without authorization. I was prepared if there was. My payback was being scheduled for a cross-country hop throughout the next weekend. I planned a flight to NAS Dallas for refueling and while refueling, I contacted my parents. Jan went to stay with her aunt in Glendale again. During the cross-country flight, many thoughts rolled through my mind. I thought of Jan and how her non-coping affected my stress level and how much her negativity was impacting our relationship. I wondered why our being away from home didn't draw us closer together but was tearing us apart instead and her getting into modeling didn't help. I decided we needed to enjoy California. To me, the Big Sur, Yosemite, Sequoia, San Diego, and San Francisco were calling.

My next couple of flights had airborne plane issues and we quickly returned to the base. Mechanically down planes were commonplace. Radar units were also breaking frequently but when working they kicked ass. During my next GCI, I took a 100-nautical-mile Judy on my first run. As my intercept developed, I gave my senior pilot, Joe Ezell, a command to the starboard for separation, paused, then port hard to close in on the bogey. I was concentrating hard on my scope and working the intercept solution as I commanded Ezell to go port harder and climb. With the plane in a nose up attitude and hard left turn, everything was looking really good and I was about to tell Ezell he had the dot for a kill shot when Ezell told me to look at our eleven o'clock position. Though unusual, I took my eyes off the scope and peered out of my canopy to see a jet airliner just before Ezell turned our plane upside down and pulled down and away so we wouldn't climb up into the APC airspace. My response to Ezell was, "Oops, no wonder I had such a good lock-on."

Ezell chuckled and we requested another set up. I then remarked, "But it was a good run, wasn't it?"

Ezell responded, "Yes it was." I hoped I hadn't alarmed any passengers then quickly thought it could've been their excitement for the day.

I was glad Ezell caught it in time. Our controller didn't mention it and that was the end of it. For me, it was a lesson learned, but it WAS a good intercept. When Ezell and I got back to El Toro, the weather was deteriorating so Ezell requested a ground controlled approach (GCA). As we were cleared down to 2,000 feet, the Marine traffic controller said he had an unidentified aircraft closing on our position. Ezell replied, "Keep us updated." Our plane was now totally in cloud cover and totally vulnerable due to poor visibility. The controller came back with, "Whiskey Tango one four descend to and maintain one thousand feet," then followed with, "the bogey is still closing on your position." Ezell requested a read on the amount of separation and asked if we should take evasive action. The controller's voice was shaky as he said, "Your blips are about to merge on my screen." That was enough for

Ezell who replied, "We are powering and climbing to five thousand feet" and immediately added afterburner and climbed. I held my breath.

It most likely was some general aviation nut with very little experience and not much working knowledge about air traffic in his locale. It's not a good idea to be joy riding in the big boy's airspace. A small plane might not bring down the Phantom but would surely ruin his or her day. Our jet climbed quickly as the uncomfortable seconds passed. While wondering why our controller didn't have more definitive information on the plane, he announced, "Whiskey Tango one four, you are clear."

Ezell responded with, "Roger that, set us up for our final approach and landing."

The controller came back with, "Yes Sir, turn left to 2-7-0 degrees and descend to three thousand feet." We landed without incident. It was a reminder that nothing was a sure thing. I wondered how close to a mid-air we had been.

On the cross-country flight that I prepared for the weekend, pilot Ezell and I flew to Eglin Air Force Base in Florida via Davis-Monthan AFB, in Tucson, Arizona, and NAS Dallas, of course. Davis-Monthan was interesting because of the "bone yard." Hundreds of vintage aircraft "mothballed" and stored out in the open there presented quite a sight. I called my parents while at Dallas. They didn't know military aviation interfaced with the FAA and ATC airspace. Back then many people were not aware that we didn't put our high-performance jets into civilian airports because the airports didn't have the ground support equipment or the JP5 jet fuel we required. On the return trip, I put us into Holloman AFB in New Mexico on our last leg home on Sunday. That's when things got very interesting. Holloman supported Phantoms but was a highly restricted area. There was a narrow east-west corridor for approach and departures. When I contacted the base tower for approach, there was very little radio traffic. As the base came into view, it was a huge sprawling landscape of concrete and hangars. Curiously, there were no aircraft to be seen on the flight decks. The base had the eerie aspect of a ghost town.

After landing, ground control instructed us to taxi onto the apron and wait for a "follow me" truck. In a few minutes, an Air Force blue pickup truck appeared with a lighted "follow me" sign on the back. Ground control instructed us to follow the truck. The truck led our jet to a flight-line outside of one of the many closed hangars. The truck driver put chocks on our wheels. Ground control radioed us to prep our plane for refueling, shut it down, and get in the truck. I responded, "Roger that" and we did. Ezell and I got in the crew cab truck and were driven to the base tower where there was an empty snack bar that had vending machines. We had soft drinks and chips and relaxed a little. After what seemed a very short time, our truck-driving airman appeared in the snack bar and informed us that our plane was ready to go. Ezell and I got back in the follow me truck and were driven to our plane. Magically, there were two plane captains and ground support equipment to start the plane. Our plane was run-up, checked out, and ground control gave taxi instructions for a western departure. We took off and were cleared out of the control zone without ever seeing another plane. As we leveled off at cruise altitude heading back to El Toro, I said to Ezell, "Was that place classified secret or what?"

Ezell replied, "I'd say so."

A frontal system of ominous-looking clouds with tops over 50,000 feet was spread out before us. I didn't remember anything of this magnitude in our weather briefing but we were heading right into it just as the sun was setting. I knew it was going to be a bumpy ride. I switched my radar to infrared and scanned for "holes." I told Ezell, "I'm painting the skies and will direct you through the less dense areas." It started to get really dark and somewhat turbulent. It was raining hard and lightning was all around us. I put Ezell through a series of turns to circumnavigate the "thunder bumpers" and after many nerve-wracking minutes and being thrown all over the sky, we came out into smooth air close to home. I got a "well done" from Ezell and we both breathed easier. Another week without a weekend had come to a close. I was getting tired of it but the Marine Corps owned me. I arrived home to another cold reception.

Chapter 15

California Dreamin'

The next morning at the squadron, I put in for a couple days off. Jan suggested we spend some time with her relatives. I told her no way (or maybe I said, HELL no). We went to Big Bear and Palm Springs and had a good time, free from stress, daily duty, and flying. Back at the squadron I was informed that the Group had scheduled a ground safety inspection for the following Tuesday. Amazingly by the end of business on Monday, everything that I had been attempting to get maintenance to do on a daily basis to be safe was proudly on display. It was a thing of beauty. Later that day, I had a hop with Major Cagle. He was a colorful fellow with a relaxed air about him and was a competent pilot with a good sense of humor. After engine run up, our wingman's plane went down for maintenance and Cagle and I had a free hop to do whatever we wanted.

Cagle decided we would fly over the mountains a bit and then come back and do some practice landings. When Cagle had our Phantom back near the base he asked me to contact the tower and request that we be able to fly over the control zone at 5,000 feet. I thought it an odd request but did it and it was granted. I had never had a bird's eye view of the base and wished I had brought my camera. After performing three touch and goes, he asked me to contact the GCA for some radar approaches. I contacted ground control approach and after a frequency change, Cagle was in the driver's seat, he thought. A supervisor came up on the radio and asked if Cagle minded a student controller (supervised, of course). Cagle responded, "Sure, why not? I'm not that good at this myself." I laughed out loud. Then the student started lining us up way off the runway. It was fun but after three approaches, Cagle told the student, "Bring me down for a final." I liked Cagle from then on.

In August, the squadron deployed to NAS Fallon, Nevada, for two weeks of intense air to ground ordnance training. In spite of Jan's negativity, I was looking forward to it. "Hey Jude" was the popular Beatles' song for the moment and Jose Feliciano's "Light My Fire" became the squadron's selected song to get our engines started and airborne. My air sickness was now a non-issue, even with two flights in one day. I cautioned my enlisted personnel about casinos and brothels during their weekend off. I financed my weekend in Reno with gambling winnings and on Monday we were back throwing ourselves at the ground and putting bombs and rockets on the targets. On one of my hops the second week, pilot Mace, and I were returning from the range as a cold front was coming through. The sky was ominous, like one of our famous Texas squall lines. The winds were at 45 knots, and gusting, in direct crosswind to the runway. When Mace lined up with the runway (more correctly off the runway), I thought he was nuts. He "crabbed" so much into the wind that I could see the entire runway from the rear seat and started to pucker a little. When our plane was over the runway edge, Mace straightened up and smoothed it out into a perfect landing. It was a thing of beauty and I told him so. Mace said, "Thanks" and then added, "a little hairy wasn't it?"

I replied, "It was from back here, but I never doubted you for a minute."

It was now early fall in southern California. Our sister squadron, 334, was already in their first month of operations in Vietnam and the presidential campaign was in full swing. I had already decided to vote for Nixon, not because I liked or trusted him (or any other politician for that matter), but because I hoped he might end the Vietnam War and thereby eliminate the need for our squadron to deploy. At the time, public sentiment was becoming very strong against the war as were students on university campuses. Whatever my beliefs were, Jan's were stronger and she was very vocal about them and not always in the right circles. I finally got a weekend off and Jan and

I drove up to Big Sur. We visited the Hearst Castle and San Luis Obispo and enjoyed a beautiful sunset at Morro Bay. It was a much-needed diversion. Every time I "got away," I made an objective assessment of my status quo from a different perspective, from the outside looking in. This often resulted in decision-making revelations. I had time to just appreciate creation. There was a great deal of solace in this and especially at this moment in time. It put things in perspective, realizing God was in control. I marveled at the grandeur and beauty of the Big Sur scenery and accepted my finite existence and position in the universe.

On Monday it was back to the grind, honing our aviation skills. The squadron was becoming a cohesive, experienced battle-ready unit. Fitch and Knudsen got a really different kind of hop. They were tasked with flying a refurbished F-4B from Miramar, California, to Da Nang, Vietnam. Fifteen minutes out they experienced smoke in the cockpit from an electrical fire. They were lucky to make it back to the base without crashing. I was obviously not the only one experiencing airborne emergencies. After a heavy dose of flying in October, Jan and I took a long weekend to visit Lake Tahoe, Yosemite, and San Francisco. The fall colors in Yosemite Valley were gorgeous and I decided right then it was the most beautiful National Park in the park system and aligned with Ansel Adams and John Muir's love of it. Seeing deer grazing on the grass in the valley with the morning sun shining on them wasn't just majestic and spiritual; it was cathartic.

Tuesday after the trip Nixon won the election and the war did not end. Back at the squadron, I learned that there was a one-week mini deployment to Yuma the whole week of Thanksgiving for air to ground ordnance practice and I was scheduled to go. It had to be punishment. So far for the year, I had had the twenty-four-hour duty on Jan's birthday, was on a cross-country on our anniversary, and would be deployed on Thanksgiving, all in addition to my other scheduled duties. I wondered what else they were going to do to me. I had no idea how the other officers were faring but knew the Corps had us by the yang. Jan was pissed and went to stay with relatives again.

At Yuma, this smaller group bonded well and performed well. I made the best of my time there and socialized with my peers. I also flew with two pilots who were getting ready to join 334 in Vietnam, Tyson and Noggle. Tyson, whose nickname was "Doc," was a character and I liked flying with him. Noggle was a bad pilot, and a worse bomber, even though he had an aeronautical engineering degree from MIT. He made me nervous. I was always leery of any pilot the first time I flew with him. On Thursday, we had the traditional Thanksgiving meal at the Officer's Club and afterwards I called my parents and Jan. The conversation with my parents was better. I flew back to El Toro in the back seat of Lieutenant Colonel Braddon, another pilot who was going to join 334. After the deployment, Jan and I planned our Christmas trip home to Texas.

Flying got lax after Thanksgiving. There were some night hops and intercept work in preparation for the missile shoot in January. I flew an intercept hop with the skipper and one at night with Mace. I completed an ACM without throwing up for the first time. I had another intercept hop with Ezell. During our first run, my radar broke and all we could do the rest of the flight was bore holes in the sky as bogey. Radar unit malfunctions and break downs were now becoming very commonplace. I was unaware of it at the time but our radar units wouldn't be used much in Vietnam. Ezell, a fellow Texan, and I talked a lot during the flight. Ezell was a nice guy and a good pilot. He got married in college like I did and had two children. He was not from the area of Texas that I was but we still had the Texas connection and instant rapport. My last flight before Christmas vacation was with Major Noggle. I really was uncomfortable flying with him and not just because he wasn't a member of 232. Noggle, for all his smarts, didn't seem to have a feel for the plane. After the flight, I was ready to stand down and get out of "Dodge."

Christmas 1968 was a somber affair for the Thorsen family. There was lousy news almost every day about the Vietnam War, including weekly casualty rates. My mom seemed the most depressed overall and I could not say much in the way of encouragement except that it was safer in the air than on the ground, safety being a relative term. We stayed at Jan's parents' home and Jan wanted to spend lots of time with them. I pointed out that once I deployed, she would be with them full time. Without being argumentative, I told her in no uncertain terms I would not shortchange my folks on this trip. It was not a happy holiday, happy time, or a fun trip. A dark cloud hung over it. I took my brother aside and told him in confidence, "If I am missing in action,

I am dead. Do you understand what I am saying?" With a solemn face, he nodded his head.

Aircrews had heard rumors of unspeakable torture and death for downed pilots and aviators. We received official briefings and classified information confirming this prior to our departure. We would also receive jungle survival training. I attempted to present an air of confidence about my upcoming tour and even tried to back it up with statistics but mainly I tried to enjoy the moment for what it was, though strained. I knew I would only briefly see my folks in March when I brought Jan back to Texas. I conveyed as much detail about the deployment as I could. I told them that I would write often and obtain cassette recorders so we could exchange audiotapes. I also asked my dad if he wanted to play a game of chess through the mail. He did, of course. Though my parents were very proud of me, underneath it all, they were worried sick, especially my mom. Mom worried about everything, all the time. Knowing this, I attempted to reassure her now and later in correspondence. Christmas gift unwrapping was secondary to everything else. Jan and I conversed very little during our drive back to California.

Things were pretty slow around the squadron between Christmas and New Year's but not without excitement. I found out that I had the twenty-four-hour duty on New Year's Eve. My being dumped on was an understatement. Not being a drinker didn't mean I would be less celebratory. The odds of being randomly selected were next to zero. Jan was pissed too. She didn't like much of anything at the present time and I couldn't blame her. On December 30, Forney and I had a desert intercept hop with refueling. I took my movie camera. The intercepts went fine and we refueled and headed back to El Toro to do landing practices. We did so many that I lost count even though it was my job to keep track. After the flight my butt was really sore. The flight had lasted over three hours.

On New Year's Eve day, I launched on an intercept hop over the ocean in Executive Officer Zych's back seat. My pilot from the previous day, Forney, was on our wing with Matzen in his back seat. Once airborne and joined up, I checked us into Doubloon restricted area. We were flying straight and level over the ocean into the restricted area when all of a sudden my plane experienced a small boom followed by a short period of uncontrolled flight. As Zych got control of our plane, it went suddenly silent and began to descend. All of this happened in mere seconds and my first thought was that we were going to eject if we didn't explode first. I recognized a double generator failure immediately and expected Zych to extend the Ram Air Turbine so we would have auxiliary power and could communicate. That did not happen and the plane silently continued to descend. The silence became deafening as all my senses were now heightened to fever pitch. I was beginning to get scared. Other than pray, there was nothing I could do except support my pilot or eject.

Since I wasn't hearing anything from Zych, I wondered if something had happened to him. I looked at my console to see if the eject light was lit. It was not. Then I worried that Zych may not have the sense or the ability to push the button. My consolation was that if Zych ejected, I went 1.75 seconds before him. The silence was interrupted by something I had seen only one other time. I saw Zych's panic-stricken face with his oxygen mask off through the left console and then heard him scream, "Terry, can you hear me?"

I tore my oxygen mask off and yelled, "Yes Sir, put the RAT out." I put my mask back on and soon heard a click and then a whirring noise. I asked Zych, "How do you read?"

Zych came back on hot mic and said, "Loud and clear" and then continued to tell me the bad news. Our plane not only had the double generator failure I recognized but also a left engine flameout. Without panic, I cleared my head and focused. I'd been through many emergencies, but this was new and just beginning.

I looked up flameout/re-light procedures in my kneepad manual while wingman Forney came reasonably close to look us over. I informed Dash Two of our situation and Zych chimed in with additional info about operational systems. Forney said that our plane appeared normal on the exterior; in other words, it didn't look like anything fell off or was on fire, and that he witnessed a big black puff of smoke come out of the left engine exhaust. I asked Matzen to get us out of the restricted area and heading back to El Toro and onto squadron common frequency. I assumed we would make an emergency straight-in approach to the base. We were still losing altitude at this point and I wasn't sure I was going to see 1969. I then turned my attention to Zych and said, "Let's go for a re-light." Zych replied, "Roger that." Zych seemed overwhelmed with it all and not in control.

I started reading the procedure off my kneepad and talked Zych through the re-light sequence. The procedure was to come around the horn and shut the engine down, allowing it to windmill. Then advance the throttle and depress the ignition for as long as thirty seconds. If it did not light, repeat the procedure after three minutes. If it did not light then, we couldn't retry for thirty minutes. I wasn't crazy about that scenario and hoped for a light on the first attempt. Zych was silent and I immediately realized that the engine hadn't started. The next three minutes seemed an eternity. I repeated the directions, while Zych voiced them back to me. Zych hesitated during repeating the instructions and I felt he had left something out the first time. On the second re-light attempt, I reminded him he had thirty seconds before discontinuing ignition. I barely completed that sentence before the engine came to life and up to military power. I exhaled upon hearing this beautiful sound.

We had lost over three thousand feet during the procedure. Zych, for the moment, was silent, and I assumed he was monitoring gauges. He leveled off our plane and announced to Forney that he had a re-light and the engine appeared to be running normally. I knew we were still in a state of emergency but also knew we did not need to declare it or immediately land. We cleared the restricted area and headed towards El Toro, heavy with fuel. On squadron common frequency we made Ops aware of the problem. Major Schnippel heard part of the conversation and my friend Doug Harlow, who was standing the Ops duty, told me later that Schnippel asked who was in the back seat, then said, "No, let me guess, Terry?"

"Yes Sir," Harlow replied. At this point Zych wanted to dump fuel. For whatever reason, even though our manual said the F-4 could dump fuel on RAT power, ours wouldn't. Burning off fuel was a slow and nerve-wracking process. I hoped nothing else broke during the interim. Murphy's Law says it won't be good if it did. The generators would not come back online and they hadn't successfully done it in one of my planes yet.

Zych had me review our landing procedure. I reminded him that with a double generator failure, a functional utility hydraulic system was an unknown, and that the landing procedure is treated as though the plane actually had a utility hydraulic failure. That meant blow down the gear and flaps pneumatically. Zych also decided we would make an arrested landing. The thinking was without the utility hydraulic system, we might lose nose gear steering on roll out. Apparently Zych now had his thinking cap on. As the time went by slowly, I contemplated my future. The coming year, 1969, loomed large. Though 1968 was history-making enough for me, 1969 would surpass it easily. At bingo fuel, I contacted the tower and requested an emergency straight-in approach for a routine arrested landing. There was nothing routine about it. The tower came back with confirmation and cleared all other traffic out of the control zone. I had my procedures ready. I had little confidence in Zych at this point and realized I needed to walk him through everything.

Zych slowed the plane to 250 knots and descended to 1500 feet. I was very anxious and somewhat scared of a critical failure on final. I reviewed the procedure with Zych. It sounded easy enough. Carrying it out was another story. I knew everything had to be projected further back in order to compensate for the slower sequencing mechanics and Zych's reaction times. I reported the initial to the tower. Zych began his approach and I related the procedure, gear first, and then blow the flaps down. I monitored our airspeed indicator to make sure Zych was on the money. Blowing the gear down was a one shot, irreversible procedure. They would not come back up and if they didn't go down and lock, landing was going to be hairy to say the least. The sequence was: lower the gear handle, pull the circuit breaker and then pull the gear handle aft to activate the pneumatics. The handle must be held aft until the gear lowered. If the handle was released before this occurs, the action was incomplete and the gear would not lower completely down or lock in place, possibly collapsing on landing.

Zych lowered the handle and pulled the circuit breaker. I held my breath. Zych pulled the handle aft and the gear began to lower into position. The familiar sound of the wind noise of the gear in the air slip was music to my ears but I did not hear them lock in place and exclaimed to Zych, "Don't let go of the handle." The nose gear locked in place first. After a while the right main locked into place and then it seemed as though nothing else was happening. Zych exclaimed, "The left gear is barber poled." (The pilot's landing gear indicators resemble a barber's pole.) I reiterated my plea, "Don't let go." I knew that the pneumatic pressure was now low but still working. I was now worried that the gear would not be down by the time we were cleared to land but more importantly not lock in place at all. It was better to make a belly landing than to make a landing with only one main gear down. Since the procedure was irreversible, we would have to land with whatever the results were, good scenario or bad. The left main remained half way down and our wingman reported it to us. Zych replied, "Roger that, we have the indication." There was nothing else to do but wait.

My heart was pounding. At some point, holding the handle aft would become futile and we would have to take it around and approach with plan B. Plan B sucked. I had the flap procedure ready if all went well. Finally, the left main locked in place. I loudly exhaled. We were now getting really close to the base and I didn't want to make another approach. Zych wanted the flaps down. I reminded him that he would only get half flaps and quickly reviewed the procedure. Before I finished, the tower cleared us to land. I told Zych to lower the handle and pull aft. Two issues could potentially result, besides them not lowering at all. They could lower asymmetrically, creating control problems, or there could be an aileron droop, which would require them to be disabled. I thought Zych had enough going on without this possibility and also thought a no-flaps landing seemed a better scenario with an arrested landing, but I was not the pilot. The flaps lowered fairly quickly and (more importantly) correctly. Zych lined up on the runway and made a nice, soft, landing. After our plane passed the catch wires, Zych lowered the tail hook and it dragged along the surface of the runway creating sparks as the plane began slowing from 150 knots.

The plane rolled out on the centerline without any nose gear steering issues. Before the plane came to a stop (after almost two miles), Zych raised the hook. An inch of the metal must have worn off because of that faux pas. I never mentioned it but maintenance couldn't miss it. Our wingman landed after we cleared the runway and the field resumed normal operations. Disaster had been averted. Zych taxied the plane back to the flightline. On exiting the plane, I took one look at Zych and realized, for the first time, one of my pilots was wetter than me after a flight. I did not comment, thankful I had defied death again, and then the two of us walked to maintenance so Zych could complete the lengthy yellow sheet gripes. As we walked, I silently thanked God I was going to see the next year, fully aware it was going to be life altering. I called Jan and never mentioned the emergency to her. I told her I was busy and would call her at midnight to wish her Happy New Year.

No cause for the generator failures or flameout was determined but the plane remained in maintenance for quite a while. The flight began a new reputation for me: emergencies. Pilots didn't know whether to avoid flying with me because of them or fly with me because of my emergency experience. I remained diligent and stayed current on emergency procedures. At our first AOM of '69, Hutchins asked Zych to review our in-flight emergency. Zych described the emergency and all the procedures he and I followed, excluding minor mistakes. To my surprise, he gave me partial credit, including keeping calm. He carefully omitted his shortcomings, panic, and the tail hook. In short, he did pretty much what I expected and told everyone how he brought the plane home. Most of the RIOs knew the truth about Zych after flying with him a few times and for some reason I had flown with him a lot. The tail hook did not get by maintenance personnel. RIOs don't lower tail hooks. The flight wasn't mentioned again. Aviation was comparable to police work: mostly routine with interruptions of stark terror.

By 1500 hours, the squadron was a ghost town. My twenty-four-hour duty progressed through the evening and into the night. At about 2200 hours, I received a call from the group duty officer, Captain Garrison, who informed me that one of our planes was leaking fuel. I told the captain I'd take care of it and went out on the flight-line to check. Sure enough, plane Number 7 was leaking fuel out of the left wing dump port. I placed a five-gallon plastic bucket under the wing to catch the drippings and went to my staff non-commissioned officer on duty. I told him to get maintenance duty personnel to take care of it immediately. That should have resolved the issue. But no, within an hour Garrison called back and said the plane was still leaking and demanded that I take care of it forthwith. A superior officer with a hair up his butt was just what I need to end one year and start the next.

Knowing it was wrong, I got a little sarcastic and replied "Captain, you are aware it's New Year's Eve, aren't you?" And before he could tee off on it, I continued with, "our staffing is low but I will get someone on it right away."

The captain let it pass and reiterated, "Get it done, Lieutenant."

I replied, "Yes, Sir" and hung up. I called my NCO and pressed, "I've got the Group Captain on my ass about that plane. Get it done and inform me when someone is here to do it." In less than thirty minutes the NCO said, "Lieutenant, one of the flight-line corporals is out there right now, Sir." I walked out to the flight-line in time to see a corporal walking toward the leaking plane with a lit cigarette in his mouth. Before I could demand he snuff it, he tossed it into the five-gallon bucket under the wing. I thanked God the captain never saw it and that there was no explosion. The fuel snuffed it. The corporal knew this and was making a point; JP5 fuel was a low grade of kerosene that didn't light easily. He started up a Tud, the nickname for a weighty, high-performance tractor, latched onto the nose wheel of the Phantom and turned it 180 degrees so it was facing downhill. The leak stopped. I thanked the corporal, cautioning him to never let me catch him smoking on the flight-line again. We exchanged New Year's salutations and the corporal peeled out in the Tud. I was amazed by this powerful machine with 3000 psi hydraulics like our planes. It had to be a huge waste of taxpayer money just like the Group Captain. I did not write up the corporal.

I called Jan at midnight. We exchanged pleasantries and New Year's wishes and promised each other kisses. Our conversation was somber and devoid of expectations and goals for the next year. In truth, the outlook was bleak. We knew the war was not ending but were unaware "Tricky Dick" had his date with reality approaching. After our conversation, I was left with my thoughts. An extraordinary year lay ahead, one which would affect me physically, emotionally, spiritually, matrimonially, politically, experientially and yes, even astronomically. I assumed it would impact me more than any other in my life and I wondered if I was prepared. My first flight of the New Year gave me an indication.

On January 2, Major Schnippel and I had a GCI over the desert. Our two Phantoms boomed out of El Toro heading east. We were about halfway there when Schnippel said "Oh, oh."

I immediately replied, "Oh, oh, what?" Schnippel said he was reading RPM fluctuations on the starboard engine and the exhaust gas temperature was running high. I asked, "Are we going home?"

Schnippel replied, "Yep" and I communicated the issue to our wingman and that we were heading back to El Toro. Our wingman asked if we were declaring an emergency. I was waiting for Schnippel to respond, since it was his call. Schnippel came up on the radio and said, "Not yet." Twenty-nine Palms was the closest airport except for the small civilian airport at the south end of the Salton Sea, which we would use if things got really dicey. I referenced the engine issue in my emergency manual and I reminded Schnippel to monitor the oil pressure of the engine and watch for spikes in the exhaust gas temperature. Any vibrations in the engine dictated it be shut down.

We were in a "land as soon as practical" situation and I joked to Schnippel, "I don't want to hear about a fire warning light."

Schnippel responded, "Roger that." I knew Schnippel had his hands full and I remained calm and attentive but asked about dumping fuel. He replied, "Everything seems to be holding okay for the moment." I wondered if it was a faulty gauge. All pilots and aircrew relied heavily on gauges and they were the last thing suspected but were occasionally faulty. A pilot who remains calm with a fire warning light has a really cool head. But, failure to act quickly and correctly could result in dying in a fireball falling to earth. Schnippel kept me updated. With less than thirty minutes flight time back to El Toro, we began dumping fuel. The temperature continued to fluctuate, often over acceptable limits but Schnippel did not shut the engine down. We made our approach and landed without incident. Schnippel shut the engine down on roll out. Was Schnippel glad I was in his back seat? He never said but my reputation remained intact.

Because of the irregularities, the engine was replaced. Aircraft that have an engine or engines replaced require a test hop, including a Mach 2 run. Captain Keenan and I were scheduled for a test flight the next week. I was excited about flying twice the speed of sound for the very first time in my life. Shortly after takeoff, all hell broke loose. Circuit breakers popped out and smoke filled the cockpit. Keenan started dumping fuel and immediately declared an emergency. Keenan dumped cabin air pressure to clear it out.

Our cockpits partially cleared and quickly heated up. The air conditioning system was not working in addition to a lot of other stuff on the plane. I asked Keenan if there was anything I could do. Keenan said, "Hang onto to your ass, I'm putting this thing back on the ground." All I could do was pray, and I did. My ass was going wherever his did. Keenan made a picture perfect landing and shut the engine down on roll out. I complimented Keenan and the flight was logged for barely two tenths of an hour. I decided I didn't want any test hops anytime soon and my Mach 2 run could wait. On the way to flight equipment, I recalled that this was the same plane Schnippel and I were in with engine trouble. Once again, I had cheated death.

The squadron started preparing for our live fire missile shoot. Aircrews were scheduled for intercept sorties practicing for the event that was taking place the following week at the Point Mugu NAS, north of Los Angeles. Every squadron aviator had to fire a Sparrow and a Sidewinder missile before going into combat. Except for cross-country flights, instrument flights, and test hops, all flights were exclusively tactical in preparation for combat. West Coast missile shoots took place in a restricted area offshore near Oxnard, California, an intricate mission, planned to the most minute detail. Safety demanded it. There could be no accidents, no mistakes, or mishaps. Missile shoots were also expensive. Each Sparrow missile was like dropping a Cadillac car off the wing. Every facet of our training came into play but it did not go like clockwork.

Aircrews took turns rotating up to Point Mugu and were briefed before launching. The day of my shoot I was scheduled with Logan. We were Number two on target. Our plane and missiles checked out and our radar was up and fully operational. Dash One had a successful launch and Logan and I were vectored from our holding pattern into the target area toward the drone. The controller vectored us into position and began calling bogey info. I acquired the target, verified all my settings, and took a Judy. As I vectored Logan in for a Fox One shot, everything was picture perfect. As we closed on the target, we were cleared to fire and I told Logan to standby. I was glued to the radarscope and my heart was racing. When the circle on my radar scope constricted around the target (optimum scenario), I told Logan "You've got the dot." Immediately, Logan pressed the firing button on his control stick and whoosh, the Sparrow missile came off the rail, heading toward the target. As it guided, it inexplicably quit tracking and my scope cursor started panning back and forth across the screen as if nothing was going on. I checked all my settings and found no fault with my procedure. I remained stupefied as we proceeded to the next target for our Sidewinder shot.

I didn't have time to dwell on my "Fox one" but recalled hearsay that this Raytheon missile had reliability issues (not knowing then that it was still using vacuum-tube technology). Everyone in the unit had heard about the two Navy Phantoms who came off their carrier in the Gulf of Tonkin and engaged two MiGs. When they fired their missiles, the missiles flew straight into the ocean. They were lucky to make it back to their ship with their asses and planes. The Raytheon Company later claimed that the aircrew had "cold soaked" the missiles; in other words, they weren't ready to fire. I was now in the business and knew bullshit when I heard it. I'd never heard of "cold soaking." Once Logan and I were over the Fox two target area, I had little to do. Logan and I were directed toward a flare floating on a parachute dropped by another aircraft. Logan was cleared to fire once he was in range and had a good "growl" in his headset. The Sidewinder was an excellent and very reliable missile. It could home in on a match at night at one nautical mile. Cautions were don't let it home on the sun or a friendly exhaust and do not fly through the explosion debris. Once fired, the missile would hit the heat source it was pointed at, pulling as many as twenty-eight G's if necessary. Logan scored a direct hit on the flare and we returned to Point Mugu.

At debrief, I indicated that I had done everything correctly and that it all looked good at release. The range controller in charge had no explanation and could find no fault with the radar operation, me, or Logan; even so, I felt as though I had done something wrong. The missile just inexplicably lost its lock and track. Logan and I were credited with a "kill" anyway because range personnel felt the proximity fuse detonation could have brought the plane down. What a crock of shit, I thought. I knew they were padding their stats. I didn't cherish the thought of going into combat with Sparrow missiles. Years later, Raytheon perfected the Sparrow and it became a superior missile.

After the missile shoot, all flights in January were to round out each aircrew's training in preparation for the ORI, Operational Readiness Inspection.

It was our last requirement for deployment. New details and dates of deployment operations were coming out almost daily. Our scheduled departure date was March 19. We were flying our F-4s across the Pacific Ocean (Trans-Pacific, or abbreviated, TransPac), and into Vietnam. It was all classified secret. We were going by way of Hawaii, Wake Island, Guam, and the Philippines. After looking at the map, I wondered what other way there was.

Our operational readiness test, scheduled mid-February, would be a three-day affair conducted by the 4th Marine Aircraft Wing (MAW) out of New Orleans. The inspectors would critically review, observe, and evaluate every facet of the squadron. Each section was subject to inspection. The official title of the exercise was MCCRES, Marine Corps Combat Readiness Exercise(s). I related the plans and dates that I could to Jan that evening. I tried to candy coat my imminent deployment and combat service. We both ended up crying and Jan called her parents to relate the news. We decided to move her back the first week in March. I would stay a few days in Texas and fly back to California and live in the BOQ until the squadron departed. I wanted our days together, roughly six weeks, to contain as much normalcy and intimacy as possible. There wasn't much of either.

The last week of January was busy and eventful. I had both an intercept hop and night bombs and rockets with senior pilot, Major Gene Brown. I liked flying with Brown. Our accuracy on the night hop was good. There was no chance of intimacy this night. I got home about 2300 hours from my night hop and had a 0530 briefing the next morning. Jan was silent for a change. The early hop was a section ACM, a new wrinkle. It was a four-plane scenario pitting two aggressors against two bogeys. It was interesting, exciting, and a little dangerous, conducted with a whole new set of rules. Trying to find or keep track of two bogeys was difficult but the hop went fine. Our aircraft were all over the sky each time we engaged. I was pleased I only got a little nauseous.

My night ordnance flight with Brown the next day didn't proceed as briefed. Immediately after getting airborne, we experienced a "wheels warning light" when Brown retracted the landing gear. We aborted our mission, dumped fuel, and landed with the ordnance, contrary to procedures. On February 1, Hutchins announced that pilots and RIOs would marry up, meaning pilots and

RIOs were paired and would principally fly together from that point on and into combat. I was paired with Brown. We made a good team and I was happy to go into combat with him. I never knew how the pairing was accomplished nor was I queried or allowed input of my choice for a pilot. Many years later I learned that Brown chose me.

The Operational Readiness Inspection was the following week. It went pretty well except very early into the inspection, during an arrested landing, pilot Mace had a cable break. The plane was slung off the right side of the runway and into the mud where it mired and sat the remainder of the inspection. It was a grim reminder of just how quickly things could go wrong. Even so, the squadron was declared ready. The mired plane was extracted with a crane and repaired with no problems.

On my next flight, Brown and I, after aerial refueling, returned to the base to engage in some ground controlled approaches. On one of our approaches we were behind a helicopter. Every time the helicopter pilot made a transmission, his voice reverberated. He also progressed so slowly toward the runway that Brown and I had to bolter out of our approach to keep from flying up his butt. Being a seasoned RIO, I felt the helicopters should stay out of our jet approach, not our base, just the GCA. Our next sortie was a supersonic intercept, another new wrinkle for me. Though a learning experience, it was boring. The turning radii were horrendously large due to the thin air and the bogey being visible because of the contrail bands ("connies"), so the whole scenario was unrealistic. I loved flying that high because the air was smooth as silk. Pilot Keenan and I had a "napes and snakes" sortie the next day, including refueling. Our napalm hits were awesome.

I now had a little over 200 flight hours in the F-4 and felt completely prepared for combat. I just wasn't anxious to go. Though confidence was a very important component of combat readiness, over confidence was a killer. I knew operations in a hostile environment would be the same and different at the same time and maybe unpredictable or even fluid. Training was the only preparation the Marine Corps and our Commanding Officer could provide. Nothing can completely prepare a man or woman for the realities of combat. Preconceived notions never approach the actual experience.

I conveyed none of this to Jan as we drove to Texas in early March. The time with my family flew by. The three days were overshadowed with the impending departure. At the church Jan and I were married in, on the Sunday before my flight back to LAX Airport, my pastor invited me to speak to the congregation. I asked for their prayers and then quoted the Scripture, John 15, verse 13, "Greater love has no one than this; that he lay down his life for his friends." Though Jesus's words, they seemed appropriate. I spent the afternoon with my parents. Everyone was somber, my mom totally depressed. I tried to be optimistic about it all and played up the aviation aspect one last time. I wanted to tell my father more but withheld specifics. His birthday was March 27 and my mom's was April 4. I promised them gifts from foreign lands. I promised them that I would write and call and informed them our operations began on April 1.

The next morning, my parents and Jan and her parents went to the airport to see me off. There were lots of tears as the time to board the plane arrived. I never forgot the sadness in my mother's eyes. I knew she felt she was losing her son. I hugged Jan, kissed her, and did one of the toughest things I ever did, waved goodbye (not knowing if I would return alive), turned, walked down the ramp and got on the plane. I spoke to no one, asked for nothing and tried to keep from crying, unsuccessfully. Back at El Toro, I checked into the BOQ. That night I ate at the Officer's Mess. While eating without being hungry, I couldn't believe my eyes. I saw my recruiter, Major Nelson, at the table next to me. When I finished, I spoke to him. Nelson was heading to a squadron in Da Nang. We exchanged pleasantries. I withheld my negative feelings about certain aspects of the Marine Corps. Nelson expressed well wishes to me and his pride in my accomplishments thus far in my career. I wished him luck and headed to the Q to try to get some sleep.

Restful sleep would be rare for quite some time. For several days there was little flying but lots of administration and deployment organization. We had to have our affairs in order. Regardless of what went on squadron wise, life itself would go on, pleasant or not. The only loose ends would be those that an individual failed to take care of. I encouraged and cautioned my Marines to adhere to policy and be prepared. I wrote my parents thanking them for helping me be the success I was and apologizing for having to deploy.

A VMFA-232 squadron stock photo of the full complement of squadron officers and aircrew, with their respective last names superimposed, prior to deployment to Vietnam. Many are now deceased.

On March 18, one day before departure, Brown and I had our last stateside hop: aerial refueling with very windy conditions. The tanker was on station over the desert. Due to the high winds, the refueling drogues of the tanker were oscillating by as much as ten feet above and below center. As Brown throttled our jet forward and lined up on the port drogue, I gave voice commands in a seemingly impossible scenario. We closed in toward the wildly swinging drogue and unbelievably caught the bottom side of the basket on its way up, connecting on our first try. After Brown disengaged, our elation quickly faded. After trying over and over again without success, we reached bingo fuel and headed back to El Toro. Our wingman and his RIO never plugged in a single time. It was not a confidence booster for any of us, considering we were heading over the Pacific the next day to Hawaii. We all knew it was successfully tank or ditch in the ocean.

Chapter 16

Bombing Charlie to Hell

At 0700 hours on March 19, the entire 232 squadron, in a state of melancholy, staged personal effects outside the maintenance hangar for shipment to Chu Lai base. Aircrews headed into the ready room. The atmosphere was somber with lots of long faces. The hour of departure had arrived, we thought. The first flight led by the skipper, which I was a part of, assembled for briefing before heading to our planes. Brown and I were dash three of the eight-plane formation. Before launching for Marine Corps Base and Air Station, Kanehoe Bay (on the north side of Oahu, Hawaii), all eyes were on the weather report. Sustained headwinds of 55 knots threatened to cancel the flight. After an hour of waiting and debating, the flight was rescheduled for the next morning. All the liaison and services en route had to be rescheduled. My emotional angst started all over during the next twenty-four hours. Fuel computations allowed for sustained head winds up to 50 knots. Any higher was cutting it close. Our aviation motto: never push a bad situation unless survival dictates it. I went back to the Q and wrote letters home. My parents' letter requested they send Jan flowers on her birthday and I apologized for the inconvenience and anxiety I was causing everyone.

The next morning with winds of 45 knots, the first wave of 232 planes boomed out of El Toro at 0900 hours. It was a magnificent sight and sound. After our formation crossed the ADIZ, we were on our own. I thought it was Pappy who broke radio silence with, "Thirty minutes out and I'm horny already."

Hutchins's RIO, Captain Kondo, instantly replied, "Radio discipline."

I quipped to Brown, "What are they gonna do, make him a Lieutenant and send him to Vietnam?" Brown chuckled. I was acutely aware of the possible punishments, most being worse than the twenty-four-hour duty on New Year's Eve.

Some of our checkpoints along the way were Navy ships. About halfway to Oahu, Kondo made contact with the KC-130 tankers and flew us towards them until we made visual contact. The pressure was on: tank or swim. Oddly, the skipper was the only one who had a little trouble getting connected, but the entire wave refueled successfully. Brown and I connected on our first attempt and he breathed a sigh of relief. We weren't aware our wave of planes was photographed by someone in the lead tanker. Years later, a black and white copy of that photo was published in *The Continental Marine* (a 4th MAW publication), for a seventy-fifth anniversary Marine Aviation write-up. It showed the Red Devil Phantoms with Brown and me taking on fuel on the port wing of Tanker #2. While I was in the Marine Reserves at War College in Quantico, I saw that same photo in color on page 155 in a book at a mall bookstore.[16] The book title was *Vietnam: The War in the Air*, which I bought of course. I took great pride seeing it in the book.

Just after the last checkpoint before Hawaii, with about 100 nautical miles to go, Mace's plane malfunctioned and lost power to 80 percent. It was a critical problem and their plane making it to Kaneohe was an unknown due to increased fuel consumption. Our flight had to leave Mace and RIO Varni to deal with their dilemma on their own. When our seven-plane flight got to Kanehoe, we requested a VFR landing. It was granted and after five and two-tenths hours I was glad to get my aching ass on the ground. That soreness quickly vanished when the local command handed me a Mai Tai in a pineapple. I loved them from then on. Mace and Varni arrived about thirty minutes later on fumes. The ramps on their plane's engine intakes had inexplicably programmed (a process that reduces the amount of air coming into the engine intake) and had to be repaired before

This photo shows VMFA-232 Phantoms refueling over the Pacific Ocean
en route to Hawaii during their TransPac to Vietnam. The USMC photo is
a reproduction from a book titled Vietnam: *The War in the Air*. The same
photo was published in the *Continental Marine Magazine*, a 4th Marine Air
Wing publication. The photo was used in an article commemorating the
75th anniversary of Marine Corps aviation.

our flight departed. Military aviation hiccups always kept things interesting.
Wave two arrived the next day.

We had three full days in paradise before proceeding and we made the
most of them. They passed at lightning speed, seeing Blowhole, sunbathing
on Waikiki, eating on the strip, and snorkeling in Hanauma Bay. I decided
then to meet Jan in Hawaii for my one-week R&R, when I was eligible
(if still alive). I wrote home about the beauty of the island and took photos
like crazy. I called Jan. She was less than cheerful, but said she missed me
and was glad I was enjoying Hawaii. Our time in Hawaii was not all play,
however. We had a briefing by the the local command, part tactical and part
political. We were briefed on the indigenous people of South Vietnam and

their various religions, politics, customs, and plight. It was not pretty; in fact it was mildly depressing. Trying to be encouraging, a chaplain gave a lecture on religious beliefs. My religious beliefs brought me great solace but I knew that was no assurance of survival. Anxiety concerning what lay ahead could only be diminished, not overcome. Such thoughts and our impending departure overshadowed the beauty of Hawaii.

I called Jan on the twenty-third and wished her happy birthday. The next day we were airborne at 0800 hours heading for Wake Island, our last leg requiring aerial refueling. The sky was a beautiful blue just like the ocean. I thought we were flying into Hell by way of Heaven. After the Johnston Island (atoll) checkpoint, there was nothing but ocean. But that part of the ocean was significant. While en route to Wake, our flight crossed the International Date Line. This imaginary line was significant for two reasons. Once past the line we had traveled so far west we were east and in passing the line, longitude 180 degrees, we gained a day. There were numerous cheers and kudos over the radio until someone blurted out, "I feel younger!" The pleasantries ended and I reflected on the milestone. I congratulated myself on having come far and accepted my future and fate.

Wake Island atoll was just 2.85 square miles in size in the middle of the Pacific Ocean. Civilian and military personnel called this atoll home. Anyone stationed on Wake must have pissed somebody off. Amenities didn't abound on the island. I collected seashells during the day and watched a movie that night; no one dared go swimming due to sharks.

The next morning the flight launched out of Wake and as the Dash Four plane, Forney and Matzen, got airborne, Forney called out over the radio, "I've got a canopy unlock light." It was very quickly followed with, "There she goes" as his voice was covered with the sound of rushing air. Brown told the skipper that we would lag behind a little to check on them and started a gentle left turn. The skipper nixed Brown's maneuver and told him to join up, that Forney could handle it. He did. Forney dumped fuel and made an emergency landing after the remainder of the flight was airborne. The plane was downed for repairs, waiting for a replacement canopy from Hawaii.

The rest of us headed west toward Anderson AFB on the United States Territory of Guam, part of the Northern Mariana Islands. Guam, like Saipan and many other islands in the chain, had experienced fierce fighting during World War II and had a lot of history. The Guam populace was extremely proud to be the U.S. Territory where the sun rose first every day. I saw two of those sunrises while there. After landing, I made a beeline to the Base Exchange to buy my mom and dad's birthday presents. While shopping, I peered across the aisle and was astounded to see one of my high school acquaintances standing less than six feet away. I called out his name in shock. He was as surprised as I was. He was in the Navy and shopping while on shore leave. I mailed my parents' gifts and headed for the Officer's Mess. I saw and photographed as much of the capital, Agana, as I could. It whetted my appetite to see more of the world. Guam was a tropical paradise in its own right and I wished I could've seen it without the combat requirement.

The following day, our birds, including Forney and Matzen, headed for Cubi Point at Subic Bay in the Philippines. It was an enormous naval station and airbase. We had two days at this beautiful setting. But it had an ugly side too, which I would ultimately see firsthand. It was the stuff of legends, the infamous Olongapo "Red Light District." Everybody went into town except for me and a handful of others. I went to the O Club for dinner and then gambled at the slot machines. The next day, the squadron had organizational meetings and another lecture on the Vietnamese people. Aircrews were issued blood chits, propaganda sheets, and Vietnamese money, things to be used in case we were shot down and were able to coerce locals into helping us. I had more confidence in my snubnose .38 revolver.

With the squadron starting operations in four days, there was still much that needed to be accomplished, including jungle survival. Many personnel were less than attentive due to their previous night's activities. Our squadron launched on our last leg the next morning and headed west for Chu Lai, about fifty nautical miles south of Da Nang. It was the afternoon of March 29. Our advanced party personnel were in place to greet our planes. We had arrived at our home away from home for the next thirteen months.

As Brown and I climbed down from our plane, we stepped on hot, humid, and hostile foreign soil. Our plane was quickly backed into a concrete reinforced steel revetment as we proceeded to the maintenance hangar, getting a tour of the flight-line en route. At Administration we received our living quarters and other assignments and were dismissed to get settled in. The radio station in Admin caught my attention. The female voice of Hanoi Hannah was berating American military activities in Vietnam. She started a new diatribe on air operations and then unbelievably said, "Welcome aboard Red Devils. You will be rocketed tonight." I realized two things instantly. Our classified secret arrival was not a secret and I was in the combat zone in earnest. Hanoi Hannah was a regular fixture for the rest of my time "in Country."

Major briefings, orientation, and a complete tour were arranged for the next day. I located my SEA (Southeast Asia) hut, stowed my gear, and scoped out the surroundings of my accommodations. SEA huts were rectangular barracks on stilts. They were about twenty feet wide by about thirty feet long and provided space for up to sixteen cots. They had corrugated steel roofs. The walls were half plywood on the lower portion and screening on the upper portion. The screening was covered with plywood panels that could be raised and lowered. Due to the promise of rockets, we all worked diligently fortifying our bunkers with additional sandbags. Fellow RIO Devere looked at our little settlement of "hooches" and remarked, "Look, we're in Watts." The nickname stuck. Later, I went into my hut, assembled the mosquito netting over my rack, and laid my flak jacket near the head of the rack and my helmet on the "bedpost." While doing this, something moving on the floor caught my attention. A reddish iguana lizard with about a one-foot-long body and an even longer tail was checking me out. I thought, "you can be my hooch mate but I'll kill you if you get in bed with me."

I was thrilled to discover the chow at the officer's mess wasn't that bad. Back in my hooch, I tidied up as much as I could and tried to relax, without success. I wrote letters home, read a little and played my guitar. Being in a combat zone presented a new form of anxiety. Not too long after sunset I lay down hoping to get some sleep. Rockets began to explode as the air raid siren sounded. I donned my helmet and flak jacket and rushed into the bunker. Quickly, all of us who had fortified the bunker earlier hunkered down. Devere had a flashlight. We sat there with solemn faces dimly illuminated, waiting out the attack. Rocket attacks became a fairly regular thing, but so was their inaccuracy. This one, like lots of subsequent others, did not last long. Between the attack and waiting for the all-clear, everyone in the bunker

A photo of the author in front of his Southeast Asia (SEA) hut berthing quarters in Chu Lai, Vietnam. The SEA hut housing community was nicknamed "Watts." The photo was taken by one of the author's peers.

had time to think, reflect, and some of us waxed philosophical. Then jokes, quotes, and numerous statements were bantered around. I started with, "What makes grown men act like this?" Soon we were laughing at ourselves. No one from 232 was injured. More injuries like bumped heads and stubbed toes occurred from rushing into the bunkers than from rockets. At the all-clear, we settled back into our racks.

I stared at the ceiling, while every imaginable thing, representing every emotion, crossed my mind. I prayed for sleep and safety but was never aware of having slept as dawn came. The sunrise itself was a paradoxical event. As I stared through the screening of my hooch looking east, I observed beautifully colored clouds and thanked God for His celestial creation and His majesty. Many, many glorious sunrises would begin the days of bombing, strafing, and rocketing. At our early briefing, reality set in. The previous night's rockets had fallen mostly on the other side of the base with no serious injuries. Even so, I was immensely angered, thinking "Welcome to the war zone." I was eager to retaliate against the perpetrators. Several weeks later, a rocket hit the Army hospital on our base and an ER nurse was killed when a piece of shrapnel tore through her jugular vein.

After the brief, we doggedly went about the day's business with heightened focus. Hanoi Hannah constantly forecasted doom but nothing she said was accepted as fact. We toured the area, locating the post office, the chapel, the exchange, all of 232's departments, and other squadron locations, including our parent command, MAG-13 Headquarters (HQ). (For MAG-13 history see Appendix E.) I was surprised to see a tennis court on the base. I visited my ground support personnel and told them not to listen to Hanoi Hannah's garbage but focus on the business at hand. Chu Lai was large but paled in comparison to the 1st Marine Aircraft Wing at Da Nang. Chu Lai Air Base was built by the Seabees and was also a combat base occupied by the U.S. Army and Army of the Republic of Vietnam (ARVN) forces. It was operated by the Marine Corps from '65 to '70 and was located on the coast near Tam Ky City, the largest city in Quang Nam Province.[17]

March 31 at 1300 hours, the entire squadron attended a welcome aboard meeting hosted by MAG-13. Commanding Officer Colonel Rash, whose name fit his personality and position, addressed our group. He outlined the mission and the scope of operations, group liaison, logistics and support, and just about everything pertinent to living and functioning at Chu Lai. He invited all the officers to the Officer's Club for dinner and drinks that night. Alcoholic drinks didn't sway me but I was sure ready to sit, relax, and chill out. We were surrounded by sand and affectionately referred to our location as "Yuma by the sea"; but Chu Lai's official nickname was posted as "Fighter Town." I loved it. The base chaplain offered encouragement, personal counseling, and an invitation to church services. Our administration, safety, intelligence, maintenance, supply, and operations held briefs amidst a hive of activity. I was surprised to learn I already had mail and a package.

The rest of the squadron was dismissed when aircrews moved into the ready room for air Ops briefings. Various air and ground controllers addressed us, getting us up to speed for our missions. All information was classified secret and we would soon all be issued a classified secret Crypto wheel. It contained the secret codes for all Pacific operations, including Vietnam. South Vietnam was divided from north to south into four sections: I-Corps, II-Corps, III-Corps, and IV-Corps. Except for limited Air Force and Army unit operations, I-Corps from the de-militarized zone (DMZ) of North Vietnam, south to II-Corps (which was about fifty miles south of Chu Lai), was the fighting and defending domain of the USMC. The DMZ was a ten-mile width of land between North and South Vietnam, designated no man's land, and extended along the 17th parallel. It was an identical set up to the 38th parallel between North and South Korea. Like Korea, the enemy pretty much ignored the sanctions, especially at night.

To the north, China was hostile. Civil wars raged in Laos and Cambodia but much of our focus was on eastern Laos and Cambodia and the Ho Chi Minh Trail. Our squadron became part of this concerted operation that at the time had a title I wasn't aware of called "Operation Commando Hunt." The Commando Hunt operation started in November 1968 and continued into April 1972, concentrating on the Ho Chi Minh Trail. Also unbeknownst to me, during my tour in Country the war was in transition from guerilla warfare supported by the North Vietnamese regulars to conventional warfare supported by Viet Cong guerillas but increasingly fought by the Peoples' Army of Vietnam (PAVN) regulars. The source of the enemy didn't matter to us. We supported our friendly forces whoever they were fighting. Concurrently with this transition was a movement of anti-aircraft artillery, from up north where aircraft had discontinued bombing (by presidential directive), south to beef up fire power against our air operations on the Ho Chi Minh Trail and its tributaries where enemy troops and supplies flowed into I-Corps.

The nearest ally was Thailand, well west of us. There were two Air Force divert bases there, Ubon and Udorn. Chu Lai was located on the coast of the Gulf of Tonkin. We wouldn't be involved in any operations south of I-Corps, like the Mekong Delta, including Ho Chi Minh City, then known as Saigon. I never got to see Saigon. Squadron personnel were seldom allowed off base (in the "Ville") for safety and security reasons.

The majority of U.S. offensive forces in I-Corps were Marines. Curiously, Chu Lai base was defended by the AMERICAL Division of the Army. I often spotted them in the Base Exchange. They always looked disheveled, dirty, and tired. I felt sorry for all ground troops in Vietnam, though I respected and

The author's photo of an F-4 Phantom jet taking off with full afterburner, at dusk, from Chu Lai Airfield in Vietnam. Chu Lai air base was nicknamed "Fighter Town."

appreciated them greatly. I also came to revere helicopter pilots and all personnel who flew in aircraft low and slow in the combat zone.

After the briefing, on the way to the post office to pick up my mail, aircraft were frequently heard taking off and landing. When I retrieved a package, the clerk asked, "You gonna open it?" I opened the package and was totally shocked to find a batch of homemade cookies my mom had sent me. I shared them with those around me and they were gone before I got back to my hooch. My mother sent me a new batch every week I was in Country. I cherished them and had the envy of my peers. She had my love and respect and I had hers and my father's.

The flight schedule for the next day, April 1, had been posted. Most of the sorties that day were live ordnance hops considered to be relatively safe, called TPQs (ground directed bombing). Each scheduled aircrew duo launched in a fully loaded plane and checked in with the controller VICE SQUAD who vectored them (via radar control) to a designated area where they dropped their bombs from a high altitude on command. These flights were probably not that destructive. Each new pilot flew with a seasoned RIO and green RIOs flew with seasoned pilots when possible. After the bombs were dropped, the aircrew took time to fly, also at a safe altitude, over much of I-Corps for familiarization before completing the fam hop. Landmarks like the Rockpile, the DMZ, Khe Sanh, A Shau Valley, and major towns like Hue, Phu Bai, Quang Tri, and Da Nang were noted. Da Nang was our squadron's primary divert base if Chu Lai was closed and there were numerous times it would be.

We knew most of our flights would be close air support but learned we would fly night escorts in addition to bombing flights across the border into Laos and Cambodia. These were classified secret and called "Steel Tiger" missions. They were conducted to help reduce anti-aircraft artillery (AAA, or "triple A"), located just outside the border of South Vietnam. Group Ops warned us about de-militarized zone border violations, and there was a growl frequently heard from a Surface to Air Missile (SAM) site just on the north side of the DMZ. According to S-2 intelligence, it was not an active site, which didn't relieve my anxiety about a possible launch every time I heard the growl in my headset as its Fansong radar painted my plane. BARCAP flights

Three VMFA-334 Phantoms executing a TPQ (ground radar directed) bombing mission in Vietnam. The photo is a reproduction of a 334 squadron stock photo.

(BARrier, Continuous Air Patrol) in the Gulf of Tonkin off the coast of North Vietnam, were mostly at night. These flights were to protect our "snoop and poop" aircraft (reconnaissance planes) from enemy aircraft aggression while they gathered information. We were cautioned about an offshore restricted zone north of Da Nang. It was an area where aerial refueling tankers flew a racetrack pattern, keeping a flight of two aircraft ready to be on target within minutes and was called an airborne hot pad. The magnitude and scope of 24/7 operations could not be overstated.

The time at the club that night was the beginning of a daily routine for many of our officers and aircrew, without restriction. The alcohol flowed and soon the club was loud and rowdy. I was against inebriation and never wanted to be less than 100 percent. I had other ways of escaping the reality of war. I was glad to find out Brown wasn't a big drinker either. The aviation community, including the Marine Corps, had its share of alcoholics. I ran into my friend, Jerry Leist, from 334 and we talked for a long time. Leist had been in

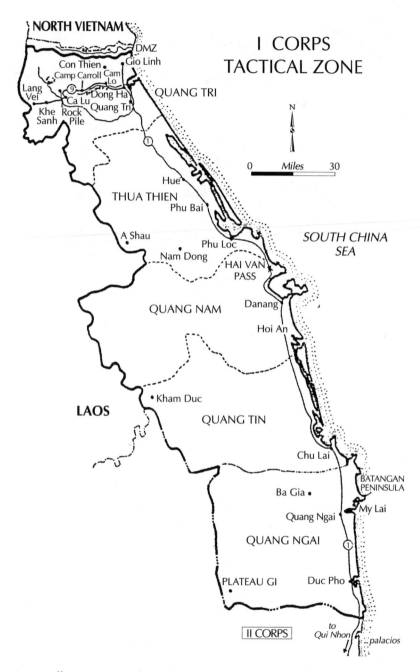

A map illustrating South Vietnam I-Corps demarcations and key combat
mission locations.

Country six months and had flown over 175 missions already. After our chat, I left to turn in early. I was tired but could not sleep. I tried writing letters but my heart wasn't in it. Finally I wrote my mom and wholeheartedly thanked her for the cookies and requested she "keep 'em comin." I wrote a little about the base and accommodations and finished with my love for my parents. There were no rockets that night. There wasn't much sleep either.

The sun began rising as I walked to my 0710 briefing. Brown and I were on the skipper's wing for our fam hop. Our Phantoms were loaded with twelve 500-pound cast-iron bombs to be dropped at a high altitude on a pre-determined area, a hot bed devoid of friendlies. We also carried four Sparrow missiles on the belly of the fuselage and a rocket pack containing two five-inch Zuni rockets each on either side of the fuselage just under the wing. The secondary part of our fam hop happened automatically, getting a feeling for how much air traffic there was over Vietnam. Being aware of this traffic became a very important role for RIOs and helped prevent mid-air collisions. All ordnance drops in which the "friendlies" (U.S. and NATO forces) were engaged with the enemy were conducted solely with an airborne controller. Killing friendly personnel was inexcusable but it had happened and great efforts were taken to prevent it. When it happened it was always someone's mistake and it was always catastrophic. I prayed all my kills were enemy.

I was glad to be Dash Two on the first hop. The brief and launch went fine and our flight, Love Bug 4-5-7, contacted Vice Squad. They handed us off to a tertiary controller who directed us out on the 270-degree radial of the Chu Lai TACAN. Brown flew formation on the skipper's wing and both pilots, on the controller's command, dropped the bombs on what we presumed was an A Shau Valley enemy stronghold. Our flight headed north, flying well within the South Vietnamese border at over 15,000 feet to avoid anti-aircraft artillery. We flew up to the DMZ and headed east to the Gulf of Tonkin and then south towards Da Nang, flying over Quang Tri and Hue. Hue City was significant not just because it was a sacred city but it became very well-known due the '68 American losses during the first Tet offensive. Our squadron began operations in a post-Tet era and U.S. military strength, preparedness, and air superiority had enemy operations in an offensive transition. During this hop,

I marveled at the number of craters caused by American bombing sorties and the amount of jungle vegetation that was prevalent.

Da Nang was a beautiful port city. I thought it might have been a great place to visit if it weren't in a war zone. Da Nang was one of the hottest spots in I-Corps. The mountains that partially surrounded it made it easy for enemy activity and difficult to defend. It was also a strategically important location. It was a huge complex of military personnel, equipment, supplies, and munitions. It was a port of major proportions, transporting everything associated with the war effort, thus a major target. The Hoi An River basin southwest of Da Nang was notorious for harboring the enemy and trafficking of contraband up and down the river. It was also a hotbed for skirmishes requiring close air support and many planes had been downed there. The pockmarked landscape in that area demonstrated the mobility and proliferation of the enemy and our pursuit of him. Viewing the damage brought to mind the expense of this war: $40,000 per kill for the Corps compared to the Army's less efficient $42,000. At bingo fuel, our flight returned to Chu Lai. As we landed, I remembered it was April Fools' Day. Sadly, the joke was on me.

After debrief, I hung around the ready room for a while to study the charts and maps of the area and, as usual, lost a game of Ace-Deuce to Allen. With nothing to do the rest of the day, I went to check on my ground support personnel and then wandered about the base. I purchased a few snacks at the Exchange and headed to my hooch to nap with the lizards. Sleeping soundly was difficult. I was a light sleeper and with operations 24/7, there was always some kind of noise; plus it was warm and humid. At the club that night, I tried to watch the nightly movie. It was difficult to hear for all the rowdiness. The 16mm movies arrived on three reels. They were never recent and were projected by an enlisted Marine who had to determine the correct sequence. Frequently the sequence was wrong and most nights he was subjected to shouts of "wrong reel" whether it was or not. I felt sorry for him. Watching the movie usually turned into an exercise in futility. Though it was somewhat of a diversion, it was mostly a sidebar to the real activity—imbibing alcohol. The young Marine got a break during infrequent floor shows. Most of the floor shows were Koreans who poorly imitated American rock and roll bands. Occasionally there were

American groups and even comedians. I appreciated their willingness to entertain in a combat zone.

While I walked to the ready room at 0630 hours the next morning, the beautiful sunrise did not brighten my day. After Brown and I critically examined the charts and maps, Brown conducted the brief. Our ordnance had been changed to Q bombs, 500-pound cast-iron bombs with delayed fuses. After launch, our two Phantoms dropped these bombs near the Ho Chi Minh Trail where they detonated twelve hours later, we hoped killing unsuspecting enemy around sunset. Our last "gimme" hop was that night, a TPQ. On each of these sorties we led junior pilots on their first combat familiarity flight. Things looked different at night. Though I was nervous about being lead RIO on just my second and third combat flights, the flights went like clockwork. I was vigilant outside the cockpit watching for both enemy and friendly aircraft and monitored my APR-25 scope for "triple A." On return from each of these flights, Brown led each "green" pilot into the break. There would be lots more breaks. We had performed as we had been trained. The "gimme" stuff was over.

After debrief, I completed the flight with a visit to Intel (intelligence section), for an S-2 brief and then Ops to review protocol, messaging, maps, and scheduling. I would have related any bomb damage assessment (BDA) if it had been given by the controller. There was none this day. I got in bed just in time for a rocket attack during which, fortunately, nothing fell near me. Near me or not, it was scary when the sirens went off and rockets fell. I finally got to sleep about 0300 hours. There was no mistaking I was in a war zone.

The next day I flew my first Close Air Support (CAS) sortie. Brown and I launched our flight of two Phantoms and contacted Vice Squad who passed us on to an airborne controller. Controller Cowboy and Indian asked us to hold at altitude. As we circled our target, we could see all hell was breaking loose on the ground and communications were voluminous and intense. Instantly I realized this was not going to be a routine flight but an emergency CAS mission. The whole area was hostile, crawling with an enemy that had one of our recon teams trapped on top of a hill in the A Shau Valley, a place not far from the soon-to-be-famous "Hamburger Hill." I could see the Marines were completely surrounded. Their chance of survival appeared hopeless. Muzzle flashes with both uphill and downhill trajectories were visible even from our altitude of 14,000 feet. Though the team was putting up a great fight, they were vastly outnumbered and about to be overrun by enemy forces, most likely North Vietnam Army (NVA) combatants. It was organized chaos and the sight was surreal.

The team's situation was critical and I quickly prayed they wouldn't die. Their only hope was a helicopter I observed hovering in an adjacent valley ready to pick them up if the pilot could get into position. A heavily armed Huey Cobra helicopter and our controller's OV-10 Bronco observer plane began making live fire low altitude dives, in concert, to kill the enemy or suppress their fire with devastating effect. In the midst of this barrage, the recon team popped a purple smoke to accurately pinpoint their location and the helicopter in the valley quickly maneuvered over them. The enemy forces directed their fire at the chopper as the Marine team rapidly climbed aboard. I was certain they were taking hits.

Amidst that hail of bullets, the chopper swiftly departed through the valley below. I couldn't believe they were staying airborne. My fixation with this scene was interrupted by controller Cowboy and Indian who had marked our target with a white phosphorous flare and cleared us in hot. The spectacle was over; it was time for us to go to work. As we set up on target our controller said, "Hit my mark at six o'clock at thirty meters. No, make that fifty meters, they're running downhill like scared rabbits!"

I radioed back, "Roger, One's in hot" and with that Brown and I and our wingman blew the hell out of the side of the hill with bombs and rockets. As we cleared the area, our two Phantom jets joined up and started flying back to the relative safety of Chu Lai. "Those guys nearly got their asses shot off," I said to Brown.

He replied, "We don't know that they didn't." At debrief, we were informed that the recon team, miraculously, was extracted without casualties, that our flight had received enemy fire and we were credited with twenty-two KBMA (enemy Killed by Marine Air). I was elated for the team but in the heat of the moment, never thought about enemy fire. Hanoi Hannah never mentioned this one over the air but the flight caused me apprehension.

I was not excited about my next day's assignment. I was scheduled to stand the "hot pad" with our sister squadron, 334, from 1200 hours until 1800 hours. Hot pad flights were usually emergency operations and required a ten-minute or quicker launch. Out of nervousness, I skipped lunch, took a Dramamine and headed to 334, departing from my normal routine. I would take a second one after four hours if necessary. Hot pad launches were nearly always close air support missions. Since the hot pad was a block of six hours, it could launch more than once. Hot pad sorties were often requested by friendly forces critically engaged by enemy fire and in dire straits. Those launches had other departures from the norm. A short briefing was taken by the lead RIO over the phone while the other three aviators got in their loaded planes. The RIO receiving the brief climbed into his Phantom with the engines running without pre-flighting his plane. He briefed the flight as the planes taxied out towards the duty runway to which they were given priority.

It seemed appropriate considering the life-saving results and BDAs. Since this was my first flight with 334, I was nervous about flying with a pilot unfamiliar to me (regardless of their six months of combat experience). I was not the first RIO to fly with them; my friend Terry Foltz was. Our squadron RIOs flying with 334 became a regular thing. My pilot was John Trachta and we were Dash Two. The flight was briefed for 30-degree "soft" ordnance of napes and snakes. While waiting, I got to know some of their aircrew other than at the club. Less than two hours into the stint, we got a call to support U.S. troops engaged with the enemy in the Hoi An River basin, southwest of Da Nang. It was not an "emergency" request but our flight still launched quickly and we were soon over the target area. The Hoi An was a hotbed of enemy activity and a two-run restriction was implemented by Group SOP as a result of many aircraft (and crew) losses in this area. Our flight put the ordnance on target and returned to the base with less than forty minutes of total flight time.

At debrief, I learned that the flight had received enemy fire (probably small arms). The type of fire didn't matter; any kind could potentially bring down a plane. Small arms fire was the least likely but if it did, it was referred to as a "Golden BB" shot. Once again, enemy fire hadn't entered my mind. Focusing on it brought this reality to mind—the enemy wanted me dead and every launch gave them an opportunity. I completed the six- hour hot pad without another launch, got to see my friend Jerry Leist, and spoke to Major Noggle with whom I had flown in the States. I had lots of hot pad stints ahead in both 232 and 334. I was never bitter about launching on one knowing I (my flight) had helped U.S. forces in need.

I already had four flights under my belt, earning six points towards my first air medal (twenty points per medal). Air medal count accumulated by flight, scoring one point for each combat sortie and two points if the flight received enemy fire, went out of country (across the border), or was at night. Using these criteria, compilations accumulated quickly along with our squadron statistics. I didn't give a rat's ass about the medals, only survival. I was scheduled the next day with Brown for an early CAS but disappointed to see I was scheduled that night with Snyder on a "Steel Tiger" hop. While digesting this, I realized I was starving and headed for the chow hall.

Brown and I launched early the next morning with napes and snakes in northern I-Corps. It was Good Friday. En route I marveled at the sky, which was azure blue and picturesquely dotted with billowy white clouds. After contacting our airborne controller, we were set up to bomb in a valley that was not easily accessed and required us to fly around a mountain prior to settling in on our run-in heading. We were cleared "hot" and told to hit the controllers' mark in the valley. I was uncomfortable for two reasons. One was the mountainous terrain we were dealing with and the second was the proximity of the mountain we were flying around to get on target. I was not used to seeing trees this close up while bombing. Oddly, the other side of the mountain was beautiful due to a cascading waterfall halfway up it. Finding beauty in the ugliness of a war-torn country was a strange irony. This beauty only helped mask the potential for all kinds of enemy fire possibilities and I resisted being captivated by its charm or view it for any length of time.

I was ready for this mission to be over before we were headed in hot. We dropped our napalm and Brown set up for our ripple all-bomb run. After calling "mark, mark," I quickly peered out of my canopy at the dense tree growth and was sure I saw muzzle flashes. Our flight quickly boomed up to the safety of 15,000 feet and as we departed the target area, the controller gave us our BDA. Sure enough, we had received enemy fire. We were soon over the ocean and back to Chu Lai. The pattern was busy. We were number five for landing. The delay gave me a chance to visually observe the size, scope, and layout of the base. Somehow a sense of pride entered my mind and I hoped our operations were making a difference in the war. After debrief, I headed to lunch. I had the rest of the afternoon off until my 1900 hour Steel Tiger brief. All I knew about Steel Tiger missions was that they were classified secret ordnance drops across the border in Laos and Cambodia targeting "triple A" sites. I returned to my hooch and started a long letter to my parents. In part, it read:

Dear Mom and Dad,

I can't remember what I wrote last so, I'll pick up from the time we landed here and since. Thank you all for the Easter cards and goodies. They (& mail) have been arriving intact and are welcomed whole-heartedly. It is a real morale booster to receive fresh home cooked pastries. I usually pass around a few when I first receive them, then hoard the rest in my hooch. Glad dad liked his watch …

This could be a beautiful country if it weren't wracked by war. Much of the countryside is scorched from bombing. We have air superiority here … Our enlisted work twelve hour shifts but all aircrews are on 24 hour call and scheduling, meaning we fly day or night, sometimes both. Our remaining schedule is lax as long as we take care of our collateral duties. Surprisingly, I have a new one, protestant lay leader. I will also be a customs postal inspector for a week. Officers must inspect any enlisted package but all us officers have to do is sign that we are not mailing any contraband. I have flown five missions to date …

Dad, let's get our chess game started. You're white and we both have king's pawns to the 4th; now your move … As yet, my creative mind is not in gear …

Reference Ike's passing, was he that great? I think perhaps he was just a man of our time, in the right place, at the right time, making some right decisions. His accomplishments speak for themselves, as do his mistakes and passivity ... I was not impressed, especially with his frontal assault on Germany's most fortified position (speaking of Normandy, of course). About a leader needed for our time—he will come. I believe it was Emerson who wrote of our American Revolution, "When our father says we must, youth replies, I can."

About our quarters, we, five of us, live in a 20 × 30' shack. We do have electricity. The quarters are really lousy and blowing sand coats everything. The base here is really big ... with all the squadrons, it is as busy as a major city airport ...

I am doing fine in all respects now. All I have to do is fight loneliness. I don't need anything ...

I certainly miss home and you wonderful people. Wish I could have been there for your birthdays. I was in thought.

Love, Terry"

After supper, I walked to the ready room for my brief. Major Gruhler, whose call sign was "Growler," was lead pilot with Paul L'esperance in his back seat. Snyder and I were on his wing. Our mission was to destroy AAA sites near the border of Cambodia. Many of these sites were devastatingly accurate because they were radar guided. Gruhler's briefing went like this: "Sunset was at 1858 hours, so it will be dark when we launch. Our Love Bug 4-5-5 flight has a time on target (TOT) of 2030 hours. We will fly lights out (Christmas tree out) contacting Vice Squad who will vector us west toward the border and pass us off to our airborne controller. For formation purposes, only the upper and wingtip acquisition lights will be on. This mission is classified Secret, NOFORN." (NOFORN means not for foreign dissemination.) "In two runs, we'll drop Rockeye first then CBU bombs from a pickle altitude of 10,000 feet in 45 degree dives." (I instantly thought, I'm about to fly a classified secret mission using secret weapons! How cool is this?)

Gruhler continued, "Afterburner will not be used during pullout due to the potential of visual acquisition. Our dives will begin from 15,000 feet, with the run-in heading assigned by the controller. Friendlies are not a factor. After our two runs, we will join up and return to Chu Lai for a VFR approach unless foul weather mandates otherwise. Any questions?"

There were none. I was not familiar with Rockeye or CBU ordnance (designated D14 and D15). Rockeyes turned out to be large cast-iron containers which, upon leaving the aircraft, opened up like an alligator's mouth, setting loose a large quantity of approximately twelve-inch rocket-looking devices (dart-like) that had armor-piercing explosive heads. The Rockeye expanded to a circle about one nautical mile in diameter and absolutely tore the hell out of the earth's surface and anything on it. Cluster Bomb Units (CBUs) were large ball-bearing looking devices with raised razor edges around their surface. Their delivery device was similar to the Rockeye and when the CBUs hit they would ricochet off of everything, tearing holes in all they came in contact with, preferably the triple A emplacements and enemy personnel. My only thought was, awesome!

We walked to our planes, launched, and headed west. Vice Squad passed us off to our airborne controller, which was probably an Air Force bird from one of the Thailand bases. It was pitch black at the border and eerie. The controller acquired our flight and briefed us as follows: "Love Bug 4-5-5 flight, your target is marked by the three 'logs' [lighted flares on the ground]. Your run-in heading is New York to L. A." (East to West—approximately 270 degrees magnetic). "Hit my mark at twelve o'clock at 500 meters, with Christmas tree out, do you copy?" The logs were just inside the Vietnamese border and the hits would be inside Cambodia across the border.

Gruhler responded, "We copy, Dash Two take interval."

I voiced in response, "Roger, interval." Snyder was silent, but was busy setting up for the runs and putting space between Gruhler and us. Radio transmissions were held to a minimum and as far as I was concerned so was my interaction with Snyder.

The controller came back, "4-5-5 flight, you're cleared hot."

Gruhler responded, "One's in hot." As our plane took interval, on the downwind portion of the pattern, I peered out of my canopy but saw nothing on the ground except the three logs. Then Gruhler's ordnance exploded, impressive even from our altitude. Snyder pulled the plane down into the dive and called in hot. At that exact moment, the ground lit up with muzzle flashes from the triple A sites we were trying to bomb. My sphincter puckered tighter than it ever had in my life. It was a "holy shit" moment beyond measure, absolutely terrifying. Though staring into the "belly of the beast" and perhaps death, I thought, "I guess we got their attention." I started reading off airspeed and altitude to Snyder. The muzzle flashes were now the target and we were heading straight at them. When I called "Mark, mark," it seemed to take forever to cease diving and start climbing without afterburner. Time sort of stood still due to the magnitude of the moment and while we were at the bottom of this inertial process, airbursts started going off behind our plane at our altitude. They dominated the view in my rear-view mirrors (all three of them) and they were working their way towards our plane.

Somehow my sphincter puckered more, as I expected to be blown out of the sky at any moment. Scared shitless but without panic, I invoked God's help. I saw airbursts predominantly in my left mirror and instantly screamed on hot mic to Snyder, "Break, starboard." Without hesitation, Snyder snapped the plane full right as hard as possible and held it until we were heading north. The airbursts continued to track in a westerly line, passing behind our plane. The muzzle flashes were greatly diminished as Gruhler made his second run. Our second run was delayed a little due to our irregular pattern. My heart was practically beating out of my chest as we dove toward the deck the second time. Fortuitously, the airbursts were almost nonexistent. Back up at 15,000 feet, we joined up with Gruhler and headed east to Chu Lai. I exhaled in relief. There was no damage to our plane. My frame of mind was a different story. I could not write home about this flight.

Gruhler had little to say at debrief; Snyder was totally silent. I was still in shock. As the four of us left the ready room, Snyder said to me, "Good call up there."

I replied, "Thanks, it was really tense wasn't it?"

Snyder responded, "Sure was." I guessed he was glad I hadn't quit. Solemnly walking to the club, I contemplated the remainder of my Vietnam service bleakly. I wondered how I was going to live through it and had difficulty putting this flight behind me. Naturally, I've never forgotten it. But, my next mission was coming; I was scheduled for the hot pad the next morning, Saturday, 0600 to noon. I did not stay long at the club and didn't talk about my first Steel Tiger flight. Back at my hooch, I had trouble going to sleep even though I felt I was developing the capacity to accept just about anything. The images I saw this night, now indelibly etched in my mind, splashed across my consciousness as I lay on my rack. I vowed again to be superlative in my approach to everything in the combat zone. I was concerned about the enemy's accuracy and glad the flight had had a successful outcome. In that regard, it was a Good Friday. War was indeed all these things: fear, anxiety, tragedy, sadness, elation, depression, humor, euphoria, and disappointment, and all amplified. Fatigue finally caught up with me and I slept.

For a welcome reprieve, Brown and I did not launch during our scheduled hot pad. I relaxed the rest of the day. The next morning, before my hot pad duty with 334 from 1200 to 1800 hours, I attended Easter church services at the base chapel. I had been to numerous military services by now. They were sterile in comparison to Protestant services back home but this service was good, perhaps due to my frame of mind. The choir special was inspirational and I was able to worship and pray. With all I had seen in the past few days, my prayer was simple, for God to preserve and protect me and my fellow Marines over the next thirteen months. And then I included all the Armed Forces, especially those on the ground. I had given up praying for the politicians and the president. I rationalized that my tour of duty was admirable and patriotic. But before I could even finish this prayer there was a commotion outside, followed by a siren sounding like the base emergency response vehicle. Sure enough, one of our Phantoms had crash landed. The crew reportedly had safely ejected. At the close of the service, I rushed over to check it out on my way to 334.

No one was allowed near the plane, which was upside down about fifty feet from one of the above-ground fuel bladders full of JP5. It was an unnerving sight with its six 1,000-pound bombs, still attached to the underside of the wings, sticking up in the air. Unless the plane exploded or caught fire, the fuel bladder was not the problem. However, the bombs were. Everything seemed to be stable and safe. But if one of the bombs went off it would detonate the other five and probably take half of the Chu Lai base with it. Emergency ordnance disposal personnel were already hard at work recovering the bombs. I didn't yet know what happened, but I knew bringing bombs back to the base violated SOP. They were supposed to be dumped in the ocean at a spot twenty nautical miles out to sea on the 0-9-0 degree radial of the Chu Lai TACAN.

I headed to the 334 ready room. RIOs from VMFA-232 assisting with 334 flights often caused us to be scheduled for more than one flight a day. I took a *National Geographic* magazine to read if it was slow. My pilot was Hajduk. We were Dash Two configured with napes and snakes, but the snakes were 500-pound cast-iron bombs with three-foot fuses. Upon impact, the bomb would explode three feet above ground, dispersing its fragments in an even more deadly manner. Their designation was D2Y/W (Delta Two Yankee Whiskeys) and nicknamed, "Yankee Daisy Cutters." We launched on a CAS mission in the A Shau Valley. Our flight got on and off target without incident. Back at Chu Lai, landing with our inverted Phantom off the right side of the runway was a grim reminder that not all the dangers of combat aviation were enemy oriented. Pilot error claimed its own share of casualties. I found out days later that the bomb damage assessment for this close air support mission included twelve KBMA. I had no remorse about killing the enemy and was not surprised when told the flight received enemy fire. I liked Hajduk and considered him a good stick. After the hot pad stint, I ate Easter dinner at the Officer's Mess and went to the club. My RIO friend "Buffy" (Doug Harlow) was there. To my surprise, he had been in the back seat of the plane that crashed. Our Air Force exchange pilot, Cliff Lowry, was the pilot of the flight.

Harlow voiced his version of what had happened on the flight. He and Lowry had returned from a flight without dropping their bombs. Lowry touched down a bit short on landing and the main landing gear tires were blown on the exposed runway edge that was being repaired. Harlow said the airplane climbed to get airborne but the right wing began dipping (stalling) due to their low airspeed. He indicated that at that time he intended to ride it out but Cliff ejected them. So, while entertaining the thought of staying with the plane, boom, the next thing Harlow knew was he was descending from just a few hundred feet altitude and landed hard on his ass in the middle of the runway. While in his brief descent he watched as Lowry's chute barely opened and then saw Lowry impact the grass off the right side of the runway. Harlow thought he was dead. He gathered his parachute and rushed over to him, finding him alive and stuck in mud. Harlow helped him out and that's when his ass really started hurting from his injured tailbone.

Emergency personnel took them both to the hospital where Harlow refused surgery and also, later, refused the Purple Heart he was entitled to. The plane had continued rolling right a short ways and impacted the ground upside down, skidding to a stop just short of the fuel bladder where I saw it. Fortunately, the engines shut down by themselves and there was no fire or explosion. Had Harlow "rode it out," he would have spent an unknown amount of time inverted in the plane until they could get him out (a harrowing eternity under the circumstances), if he survived being upside down that long. That is why the Phantom was equipped with the "command eject" feature. If the pilot goes, the RIO already went, 1.75 seconds before him. The 1.75 seconds is the reason Lowry almost died. He was milliseconds from it and, obviously, the Martin-Baker H7 seat saved his life. Neither of them ever explained why they didn't dump the bombs in the ocean. Lowry was

A photo of fellow RIO Doug Harlow's plane that inverted and crash-landed next to the runway at Chu Lai, Vietnam. The photo was taken by the author after the plane was righted and moved next to the maintenance hangar and scavenged for parts.

reprimanded for it but began flying again right away and Harlow returned to flight status two days later, sore ass and all.

Emergency ordnance disposal personnel loaded the removed bombs on another plane and they were dropped on the enemy later that day. After several days, the plane was righted, towed, and stored next to the 232 maintenance hangar where I photographed it. I was glad not to be involved with the paperwork. I'm sure it chapped Hutchins's ass. The plane was scavenged for parts and carted off to the bone yard, east of the base near the ocean. The runway was quickly repaired. At the completion of our first week in combat, the squadron was racking up missions and memories. Easter Sunday turned out to be quite eventful and my life philosophy and political views were undergoing a dramatic metamorphosis. The stark realization was that when shit happens, it can potentially be fatal, but life and flight operations go on.

Sadly, on one of Christianity's most auspicious occasions, things to me couldn't have been more dismal. I checked the flight schedule before retiring and as I walked back to my hooch, tried desperately to find something positive about the day. Then I hit on the obvious, Christ had risen and was alive here, even if I thought Vietnam was God forsaken. I was totally unaware that Easter services at my church back in the States had special prayers for me. While in my rack and beginning to doze off, I happily realized that my airsickness was, so far, not an issue. Air raid sirens awakened me at 0100 hours. I rolled out of my rack and into my flak jacket and helmet and hit the floor, without heading into the bunker. It was a good night also because there were no injuries.

Chapter 17

Dash One's in Hot

Monday my ass was dragging and I needed a good shot of adrenaline to get going. I got it on an early morning low-level close air support with Brown. Joe Ezell was on our wing with Watson in his back seat. The S2 brief indicated that Marines had been engaged with the enemy all night at a location in the A Shau Valley. Brown briefed the flight at 0610 hours with a TOT of 0715, launching with soft ordnance, for 10-degree runs of napalm and twelve retardant fin 500-pound bombs (D2a). I mused, "Looks like the gooks are going to have a hot breakfast today." As our two Phantoms arrived on target, controller Cowboy and Indian told us to prepare to drop using a 3-6-0 degree (due north) run-in heading. Cowboy and Indian put down a mark in the dense trees and requested us to hit his mark at six o'clock at twenty-five meters and cleared us in hot. Brown didn't waste any time and had the plane heading in on the target as I called, "Dash One's in hot." I read off altitude and airspeed and at "mark, mark," Brown pickled off the three canisters of napalm from the plane's belly, each coating and scorching about a football field-sized area of jungle floor and flora and, of course, anything else above ground (including people).

Dash Two did the same, and then Brown and I were in to drop our bombs. Our flight and others that morning were deadly accurate. The total body count was unknown to our flight but we were credited with seventeen KBMA and learned that air support had put the enemy in retreat. We also took fire. Cowboy and Indian turned out to be the front and rear seat in a Marine OV-10 Bronco. The Bronco had great visibility and was a prop plane with a large, high wing so it could turn on a dime and fly low and slow. It was perfect for the mission it had, but vulnerable to small arms fire. Cowboy and Indian were from Texas and Oklahoma, respectively. I loved working with them.

After the flight, I went back to my hooch and took a nap. All aircrews were coping with fatigue because of early briefs, late flights, standing the duty, hot pads, and flying BARCAPS in the middle of the night. Scheduling was a nightmare but our results so far were great.

After my nap, in the quiet of my hooch, I wrote letters to Jan and my family. I candy coated everything especially for my mom and Jan. So much had happened during the past week, I couldn't recall all the details anyway. I eventually wrote my dad about the classified Steel Tiger missions after I saw them written up in an article in *Newsweek* magazine, where they actually used Steel Tiger in quotes. I was determined to not lapse on correspondence to my mom and Jan because my mom, for sure, worried immensely. I had no idea how Jan was coping with me in combat. To help with our communicating, I purchased two cassette recorders at the exchange and mailed one to Jan so we could send audiotapes back and forth. That turned out to be a two-edged sword. It was good to hear each other's voice but sad at the same time, particularly when it revealed voice inflections that could not be masked. Jan never sent but a few. She gave the recorder to my folks. My mom had trouble making it work and the whole thing fizzled after several weeks.

While reading my Bible, I remembered my Protestant Lay Leader assignment and vowed to project and maintain a good image and be available for any enlisted Marine who wanted spiritual guidance. It turned out to be an innocuous position, probably just filling an X in a box. I knew God was with me and kept a Serviceman's Bible in my flight-suit vest pocket next to my heart and pistol. Survival was not guaranteed, just salvation. The lizards offered little companionship so I headed off to dinner and the O Club.

The next day was an administrative day with classified briefings by MAG-13, an intelligence briefing, and tactical analysis. All new RIOs were issued Crypto wheels containing all the secret codes for the Pacific Fleet and theater. Training in cryptology was birthed after the *Pueblo* incident, which occurred in January 1968 off the coast of Korea. We were required to use the wheels every day while in Country until further notice or unless compromised and/or another one was issued. Group operations officers reviewed the MAG-13 SOP with emphasis on the two-run maximum on soft ordnance, close air support sorties. New RIOs were trained on the Crypto wheel and shown how the classified codewords changed every day and were to be used for challenges, radio responses, border violations, etc. The wheels had to be checked out and back in for every flight and were kept under lock and key when not in use. I did not fly this day and checked on my "troops" at the GSE. This day came close to being a good one. I piddled around in the exchange and took a few photos of Chu Lai base.

When Brown and I had a morning CAS canceled, I thought I'd end up with two days in a row without flying. No such luck. I was scheduled for a night ground directed bombing flight. I loved dropping Yankee Daisy Cutters, Q bombs, CBUs, and Rockeyes, and just about all of them for that

The author's photo of several squadron hangars near the flight line of Chu Lai airfield, Vietnam.

matter. The next day I had the hot pad with 334, noon to six. When I arrived at 1145 hours, Harlow was nearing the end of his six-hour stint. We got into a discussion of just about everything from missions, to politics, our status in life and getting back to the USA. Harlow asked if I had heard the rumor that both F-4J squadrons were going to be pulled out of Vietnam and be sent to Japan. I said yes and asked who the source was. Harlow said right now it was scuttlebutt but it was supposedly from headquarters Marine Corps, and then he headed off for lunch. I launched on two close air supports and drew enemy fire on both. I did not write home about getting shot at a lot. Apparenty getting shot at was my new norm since I was no longer experiencing emergencies. It was mid-April and I'd earned twenty points for my first air medal without even knowing it. The question was: would I live to receive it?

I had the hot pad with 334 again the next day and was miffed that 232 RIOs were being tasked so often. I was paired with Major Noggle. We had one CAS mission that went fine until we returned to the base. At the three nautical-mile initial during our approach for landing, Noggle flipped the heat/defog handle to defog. Because it was very humid as usual and Noggle had the air conditioning on nice and low, the insides of our canopies were instantly coated with condensation. It was so severe we were IFR in the cockpits. He had created an internal mini-monsoon. I couldn't see shit and assumed Noggle was wiping off the front of his canopy for some visibility since the plane was rocking around. There was no way we could land like this. About that time the tower called, "Love Bug 4-5-1, you are cleared on final." I, knowing Noggle had his hands full and couldn't see, immediately called the tower with, "4-5-1, we'll take it around," before he had a chance to say or do anything. The tower responded, "Roger 4-5-1." Noggle now had the heat on full and our canopies were beginning to clear out as we flew over the duty runway and by the tower at 1000 feet. If the tower knew why we were going around, they'd be laughing their asses off; I wasn't and at the moment wasn't saying anything either.

Noggle turned left to head out over the ocean and into the downwind with our flaps and gear still down. I was feeling pretty proud of myself and packing my nav bag when I started feeling a sinking sensation, like my butt sinking deep into a soft, poorly supported couch. It was eerie and unnatural, one I had never felt before in the landing pattern or while sitting on the

Phantom's hard seat. That's when I quickly looked at my airspeed indicator and couldn't believe I was reading 125 knots! I panicked thinking we were seriously close to stall speed since the F-4 landed optimally at 145 knots and 19 degrees angle of attack. Knowing both our asses were about to fall out of the sky and into the ocean, I screamed at Noggle, "Power!" With that, Noggle went into afterburner, attracting everyone's attention on the base, and pushed the nose forward and got control of the plane and his landing sequence. We landed without incident but I decided, any more close calls with Noggle and I would refuse to fly with him. Noggle glossed over the incident during debrief. Getting killed by the enemy is one thing, but I for damn sure wasn't letting him do it.

Being scheduled for a late flight the next day, I slept in. It was my best night's sleep since arriving in Vietnam. After I got up, I went to Ops and Admin to check for changes in the flight schedule and to check the read and initial board. My name was on the Read and Initial. I was tasked with inspecting enlisted outgoing mail. I was also assigned Line Duty Officer noon to six. Failing to show up for assignments got individuals on shit lists. I'd been there enough times already. Being the Line Duty Officer was easy, just standing a lot. There were no issues to attend to this day and at 1800 hrs, I went to dinner and got ready for my ground-directed bombing flight that night. After the flight, I went to my hooch just in time for the sirens to go off. My roommates and I all dove into the bunker. These rockets were a lot closer but overshot us towards the beach and there were no casualties.

The next day I went to the Post Office and was trained on inspection and censorship. I devoted four hours to it that day and was done for the week. It was important for security, of course, but most of us officers thought it was total bullshit. Before leaving, I checked my mail. I had a package from my parents. I opened it and was totally delighted to find another batch of homemade cookies. While getting envious looks from postal personnel, I trooped back to my hooch to eat some. The mail was not predictable but it was regular and the only negative was when one of the cookie packages was crushed. Even the crumbs were good. I looked forward to mom's packages and loved her for them.

On April 15, RIOs Harlow, Devere, and Morgan were standing the 334 hot pad but Brown and I were scheduled for something new, a 232 air to air hot pad from 0500 to 1230 hours. Our planes were clean with no racks to store and deliver armament other than missiles, both Sparrows and Side-winders, designated D16s and D17s. Frame and Bacon were on our wing. In the middle of our duty, word came that a Navy EC 121 Super Constel-lation spy plane had been shot down ninety miles off the Korean coast. (The Super Constellation was a passenger plane in the States at that time.) News of the event spread like wildfire. None of us could believe there was no reprisal. Clearly, it was an act of war just like the capture of the *Pueblo*. We all wondered, "What the hell was wrong with our government? They were conducting a useless war in the shithole country of Vietnam and not attacking North Korea who clearly provoked it by killing thirty-one U.S. servicemen in an unarmed plane in international waters." Years later, I would be incensed to learn of President Lyndon Johnson's braggadocio about the Vietnam air war saying, "They can't bomb an outhouse without my say so." It was a bitter truth and it was a tactical error resulting in the loss of American lives.

I would further form a very biased view of war and conclude that politi-cians and military brass, especially tacticians, made strange bedfellows. Brown and I did not launch during our hot pad stint but we had another ground-directed bombing sortie that night. I was getting a lot of night flights and soon would experience Barrier Continuous Air Patrol (BARCAPs). These were flown mostly in the wee hours of the morning for one- and two-hour periods in the Gulf of Tonkin off the coast of North Vietnam. BARCAP aircraft protected our spy planes as they gathered information offshore from North Vietnam. The exact location of the spy plane was not supposed to be known. The BARCAP cover aircraft, usually F-4s, flew elliptical racetrack patterns at altitude to deter enemy planes (usually MiGs) from attacking the reconnaissance plane. All these flights were controlled by a Navy ship in the Gulf. The flight was totally boring unless enemy planes launched.

During the day, it was unnerving to see MiGs taking off and landing at Vinh, their airfield along the coast of the Gulf of Tonkin about halfway between the DMZ and Hanoi. Brown and I launched the next night for a 2200 to 2400 time on target, our first of many orbitings over the Gulf of Tonkin. The 0200 to 0400-hour stint was the worst; 10:00 to midnight wasn't so bad. Brown and I had the hot pad the next morning from 0600 to

1200 hours so I resigned myself to very little sleep this night. I had no idea. The flight went fine, there were no bogeys, and we returned to the base without incident. I headed straight for my rack. I hadn't been lying down five minutes when I heard a loud thud, followed in just a second or two by a long whoosh sound and after several seconds a loud boom. In a little bit the same thud, whoosh, and boom repeated itself. I had no idea what the new sounds were. They seemed to originate in the east and after the whoosh overhead, terminate in the west. It kept up for what seemed like hours. I finally fell asleep only to be rudely awakened by my alarm. When I observed myself shaving, I looked like hell.

Once I got to my brief I realized I was not the only one. I also found out that the thud, whoosh, and boom was the USS *New Jersey* battleship firing 16-inch RAP rounds across Chu Lai at suspected enemy rocket launching positions. RAP rounds were "rocket assist propelled" Naval gun munitions with an unbelievable twenty-two nautical mile range. They were accurate and effective and they fired them every night for a full week. I never got used to this noise but the rocket attacks temporarily abated. During our six-hour hot pad, Brown and I launched once on a close air support, dropping napes and snakes. The flight drew enemy fire but was otherwise fine. Back at the base, I checked with Ops for schedule changes. Sure enough, I had been scheduled for a late evening hop with a new pilot who was joining 334. Flying consistently with one pilot was no longer holding up. The sortie was a ground-directed bombing at dusk near the Laotian border. The hop went without incident. I liked the pilot, knowing first impressions could be deceiving.

The next day Brown and I had a morning close air support hop with hard ordnance, 1000-pound bombs. The hop was good and while I watched Dash Two head in on target, I marveled at the huge concussion wave the thousand pounders made when they exploded. I decided from that point on to carry my camera with me on certain hops and took still photos from the back seat. I also took movies with a super eight movie camera I purchased at the Exchange. Other RIOs took portable cassette tape recorders with them, plugging the earpiece in the mic receptacle and reversing it in their helmet headset to record missions. I did this a couple times, including a close air support sortie along the Hoi An River which received enemy fire. Back in the Chu Lai landing pattern we were just cleared on final when an Army "med-evac" (medical evacuation) helicopter came up on the Chu Lai tower frequency transmitting, "Chu Lai tower, Army med-evac 2-1-0 requests an emergency approach straight across the pattern to the hospital helipad. A few seconds might save this soldier's life." I didn't wait for the tower to respond or for Brown to say a word. I immediately came up on the radio and said, "Love Bug 4-5-3, we'll take it around." The tower came back, "Roger 453, Army 210 you are cleared straight in." Brown added power and climbed to five thousand feet as Army 210 came back, "210 copies, thank you." I instantly prayed for this man, who probably was not even twenty years old. "Damn war" I thought, as we took it around and turned downwind for landing. Once again, I felt fortunate not to be on the ground. I knew their hell was worse than mine.

Before my afternoon close air support with Brown, I wandered back to my hooch and wrote a letter home. I labored over words and things to write about. It partly read:

I got three letters from the Thorsen family today. I deeply appreciate it …. I can't think of anything I need except home baked goods and letters. There's good food here … We have a very good mess and the Exchange (retail store) has extra goodies (candy, chips, etc.). I have money to purchase anything I want ….

Pardon me waxing philosophical but it is time your kids started paying you back (in life) and I intend to do so through the remainder of your years. I don't mean this as an inference in an elderly sense. You should be deriving cherished moments from your progeny instead of the intermittent dependency and instability of my siblings. I feel you two have been dealt a grave injustice by the quirk of fate I wish I could change ...

At the moment, I live in despair, hoping and praying for a change as this is like living in a slum doing a filthy job, even though it is on a professional level. We call our section of huts "Watts." You might compare it to some of the huts landscaping highway 80 in Mississippi. I will eventually move into an air-conditioned Quonset hut…

… I am averaging one flight a day and have earned my first air medal.

"Your son in Nam", Terry

I did not mention the moustache I was growing, the first and only one I ever had. My blond hair from youth was now pretty much brown but my moustache barely showed up. I was also working on a tan by sunning at the beach as often as I could but had to be careful with that. I burned easily and quickly, which I attributed to my fair skinned, Scandinavian heritage. I didn't mention the white dotted rash I was getting on my abdomen. I assumed it

The author in the doorway of his Southeast Asia (SEA) hut in Chu Lai, Vietnam, sporting the only moustache he has ever had. The photo was taken by one of the author's peers.

was heat related and had Doc Bouvier working on it. Everyone wrote me at first but some eventually tapered off. I kept a separate epistolary dialogue going with my dad containing chess moves and our ongoing discussion about college campus happenings, etc. The war zone heightened all my senses and I examined myself, considering my mortality, and cogitated on world affairs. It was inevitable and unavoidable but often led to depression.

Brown and I launched on our afternoon soft ordnance close air support sortie. We headed west to the A Shau Valley. The A Shau was always a hotbed of enemy activity for a variety of reasons. It was near the Ho Chi Minh Trail and Laos. The valley was thickly wooded with a high canopy and enemy forces were difficult to track and fight, as was the case this day. Our controller had us on target right away. I was wary because of our proximity to the border and kept my eyes peeled for evidence of triple A. We put our bombs on target and quickly set up for rockets. After Dash Two was on and off target, our controller told us to hold so he could put down another mark. He was seeing something we could not. After firing our rockets, we headed back to Chu Lai. I was glad not being on the ground but also glad to be in "Brownie's" back seat. We missed chow and headed to the club. The conversations at the club ran the gamut with nothing off limits. The brass garnered their share of the negative commentary and there were no repercussions. What were they going to do, make us lieutenants and send us to Vietnam? It was too early to mark off days, but I was marking off weeks; this was my fourth.

The next afternoon, Brown and I flew a close air support sortie up near the DMZ with napalm and twelve 250-pound retardant fin bombs. Our wingman's plane was configured with a 20mm Gatling gun pod and rockets. It was excellent ordnance for lower altitude delivery to which the target area was conducive. Marines were heavily engaged with enemy forces near Dong Ha. For the first time, Brown and I had trouble obtaining a visual of our airborne controller. We couldn't see him because he was well below us. Once he acquired us, he was anxious to get ordnance on the enemy's position and threw down a mark. He gave us an east to west run-in heading so we wouldn't get into the DMZ during our downwind leg. Apparently we were right at the demarcation line. That was no surprise; the enemy pretty much ignored the de-militarized zone restrictions, day and night. Our controller called us in hot and Brown pulled our plane into a 10-degree dive. Our napalm lit up the ground. On our downwind leg, I watched Dash Two hit the controller's mark with rockets. Brown and I followed with our 250-pounders and waited above the target for Dash Two. Our controller changed our wingman's hit information and I watched him spray bullets across the designated target. He joined up and we flew back to Chu Lai.

Our next two hops were two back-to-back night escort hops. We were escorting Air Force Phantoms specially equipped with high speed cameras under the nose (with straight down and side-looking lenses), often infrared. The reconnaissance Phantom was photographing bomb damage, troop movement, and any recent build ups or potential targets across the borders into North Vietnam. We never saw the reconnaissance plane; he was just out there ahead of us or way off our wing. Our escorting Phantoms flew clean planes so we could intercept any MiGS coming after him. The flight was a little scary due to SAM sites and the possibility of dog fighting MiGs; but flying blind at low altitudes and very fast speeds (often supersonic) was a rush. The photos were processed before dawn and disseminated by HQ to all appropriate Intel units.

Phantom units were also tasked with escorting B-52 bombers, the mail plane, an occasional transport plane, and VIPs (Very Important Persons). Our second escort was very late and culminated at dawn. The flight back to the base was during a beautiful sunrise with large thunderhead clouds over the ocean, reaching as high as 40,000 feet. Escort flights earned two points towards air medals. The next afternoon, Brown and I had a CAS hop in the Hoi An, drawing enemy fire and that night we had a Steel Tiger sortie at the border of Cambodia. My anxiety rose prior to the Steel Tiger sortie but, fortunately, it wasn't nearly as dramatic as my first one. I ended my fourth week in Country with this flight and had earned enough points for my second air medal. I thought things were going along smoothly until I saw the Read and Initial board. It was notifying me to contact Admin the next morning. Damn it, I wondered what the hell I had done now?

I showed up at 0800 hours and was surprised to find out I was assisting fellow RIO Knudsen, combined with two ground officers and two enlisted personnel, to collectively be a committee to put together and get published a cruise book for the squadron. It would cover our most recent organization and Vietnam deployment. I couldn't have been happier. I was not scheduled to fly for the next five days while our group organized a game plan, developed potential book and page layouts, and photographed the majority of the personnel in the whole squadron. Knudsen and I took advantage of not being scheduled to fly and worked eight to five, more or less. I had already been taking shots suitable for the book. During the five days much had been accomplished and much was assigned and lay ahead, including trips to Okinawa.[18] Knudsen and I were ecstatic. I never knew why I was selected. We divided up photo assignments and took our cameras along on more flights. Our project was ongoing until completed.

Knudsen ended up getting into the Ville with Doc Bouvier and got up to Okinawa numerous times. I never got there regarding the cruise book project but I made several trips through Okinawa, including one very memorable one. On the fifth day I was scheduled with Brown for a Steel Tiger mission at

Photo reproduced from the VMFA-232 *Cruise Book* showing the author in the rear seat of a Phantom jet next to a revetment wall of their flight line at Chu Lai, Vietnam.

dusk. I was a little more comfortable with a pinkie than full dark and was now becoming more comfortable with Steel Tiger hops. The hop went fine and I presumed our ordnance was accurate and destructive. After chow, I went to my hooch instead of the club. I wrote a long letter home. While I was writing this letter, it was unusually quiet. While laboring over words, I decided to venture out from my hooch to see the source of light from one of the other ones. Harlow and his hooch mates were entertaining fellow aviators with projected "blue movies." I watched for a while and then decided to return to my letter. The movies weren't necessarily offensive to me but porn films were highly erotic and being horny was not on the top of my list of desirables. Food additives, if we were being fed them, weren't working after the images we saw and sexual arousal at Chu Lai was counterproductive. Some of my letter went like this:

Your foreign despondent is doing just fine. I have earned my second air medal …

All of your pastries have made it here and were delicious. Notice the past tense there. You have received many compliments in addition to my own. I will try to get something to everyone for Mother's Day. Mom, don't worry about me catching Malaria. I've been inoculated for every disease known to man. There's probably a few here they haven't discovered but I'll stay away from those. Our flight surgeon is right here with us …

Practicing religion here is difficult. I have doubts about our Chaplain. He even seems pessimistic …

The name of our newspaper is the Pacific Stars and Stripes. It is informative but is selective and slanted …

Operations are fine and I now have less than 12 months to go …

The weather here is always variable but nearly never clear, mostly due to billowing clouds and some manmade bomb smog. The nights are cool and refreshing so far. But everyone says hot weather is coming …

One thing this trip has done is made me appreciate the little things in life. It has also strengthened my religion. It has made me take a long look at myself, my purpose in life, direction, goals, ambitions, aspirations, talents and accomplishments. I appreciate that I've come from a pretty good family …

My morale has lifted a bit since receiving a tape from Jan but our mail has gotten a little sporadic due to rocket attacks in Da Nang. It comes through there. "They" are looking for an offensive in the near future here but I am not so sure. It seems to me the war is slackening on both sides. The consensus of opinion is that the war is over everywhere, except officially. Your incurable pessimist doesn't think so. I also, pardon my pun, don't think we are making an impact here. I believe our effort is an exercise in futility. We are helping our troops and maybe destroying some enemy but is there a positive effect? The war machine is well tuned when left to the tacticians …

Dad, I have been making rough plans for a house that I want you to design for me, more on that soon …

Love, Terry

I recalled that I had written home to my folks and Jan about command minimizing operations and hinting that U.S. forces were having a very positive effect in the war and that real progress was being made. But in truth, I saw that was just a big lie. The Intel briefings at the group and squadron levels were more telltale, not many enemy killed and not any extensive BDA tallies, with bullshit statistics that included meters of trench destroyed, etc. One curious BDA got mentioned during a brief. Warrant Officer Steele listed five water buffalo with packs. Without packs they didn't count, but with packs, they were considered tactical and could be counted. It wasn't even comical it was so absurd. Some dark humor began to emerge: "Don't you just love the smell of napalm in the morning" and referring to enemy killed with napalm as "crispy critters."

On May Day afternoon, Brown and I had a Steel Tiger hop near the Laotian border. We were one of many on target. Muzzle flashes weren't real evident during the daytime but the black puffs of smoke filling the air near us were unmistakable. Just waiting to be on target was unnerving. Finally we were called in hot. We rejected our controller's first run-in heading. It was too close to the heading of the flight that just came off target. We asked for a new target mark. The controller re-marked the target, gave us a new heading and cleared us hot. On our second run we changed the run-in heading somewhat and jinked during the dive. Jinking is moving around some (deviating from straight in) during the dive before settling into a constant prior to release of ordnance and sometimes while pulling out of the dive. The constant part was the time the pilot needed to get his sight picture. I was glad when we pulled off the target and headed back to Chu Lai. "Mayday" is an aviation emergency distress call. I never had one in the F-4. This May Day ended happily for us but probably not for many enemy combatants.

Late the next evening, near dusk, Brown and I were out at the same location leading another flight against AAA sites. The darker it got the more brightly the muzzle flashes appeared. Once again I was uncomfortable. This time the airbursts seemed erratic and no location seemed worse or better than another. Evasive action was pointless and I prayed for none of the airbursts to be close enough to hit us. We were quickly on and off target with two deadly accurate runs and headed back to our base.

I broke my string of Steel Tiger missions the next day when Brown and I had a close air support near the Marine outpost of Khe Sanh. Khe Sanh was located in the northwestern province of Quang Tri just south of the de-militarized zone and not far from the Laotian border.[19] Though the "battle of Khe Sanh" happened October 1967 through February 1968, its location continued to make it a hotbed of skirmishes with enemy forces. We were on target quickly with napes and snakes to quell the enemy attack. As we pulled off target, the next flight was quickly in hot. We were never given a body count for this flight. It was sort of like a sniper's official (confirmed) kill count. We would never know an accurate, actual count but we knew the number was way more than we were credited with.

Brown and I were on another Steel Tiger sortie the next day near the Cambodian border just south of Laos. This day we were loaded with ten 500-pound Yankee Daisy Cutters. Brown got us briefed and we launched and headed west. When we checked in with our controller, the air traffic was busy, both radio and in the air, so I was careful to scan outside the cockpit. After we held awhile, we were called in on target and given our run-in heading.

For these sorties, I now loved the 45-degree delivery dive angle. We came in high, were on and off target quickly, and headed back to the base in short order. Ironic, I thought: I had dreaded these flights while training back in the States. Hostile fire always changed things. We weren't given a BDA but I had no doubt the Yankee Daisy Cutters were deadly.

Brown and I had a Steel Tiger and a close support the next day. By now, Brown and I, and the whole squadron for that matter, were seasoned aerial combatants. I had over thirty flights at this juncture but wasn't keeping score and didn't know anyone else's tally. Since we had to verify and sign off on our flight logbooks, I did a quick count of mine out of curiosity. Our close air support was right after noon and we dropped napalm and 500-pound bombs with retardant fins on an enemy in the A Shau Valley again. I knew the Marines' encounter with the enemy was hellacious in the thick jungle and prayed for them. I hoped all the platoon had to deal with after we left were crispy critters. That night Brown and I headed west with secret weapons to attack AAA on the Cambodian border again. Once again, the muzzle flashes were unnerving as we headed in on target but once again our first run diminished their number. We varied our run-in heading some, dove down at the target, and pickled the remaining ordnance with pinpoint accuracy and devastating effects. I was aware of our own U.S. forces' weekly body count and I hoped our sorties garnered many enemy kills to help minimize them. On the way back to the base, I knew I was changing mentally.

Brown and I had a CAS and Steel Tiger mission again the following day. Our afternoon close air support was west of Hue City assisting an Army unit that had come under enemy fire. Our controller was anxious to get ordnance on the enemy's position from the "get-go." Both our Phantoms had bombs and rockets. After being assigned our run-in heading, we were cleared in hot and obliged the controller by quickly and completely covering his mark. Often, we never knew our effectiveness or the outcome of the air support. This was especially true if other aircraft were on target after us. It was happenstance, not an intentional omission. I didn't expect thanks or praise. Gratification came from a job well done, hoping we were lessening the deaths of some of our military combatants satisfied me.

Close-up photo of the author in the doorway of his SEA hut in Chu Lai, Vietnam, looking serious after numerous combat flights. He sustained the cut on his forehead getting into the bunker during the previous night's rocket attack. The photo was taken by one of the author's peers.

After dinner, Brown and I headed to our Steel Tiger briefing. As I walked, I realized being scheduled frequently for them didn't make them routine or any less emotionally draining. We briefed at 1830 hours to be on target, after dark, back at the Cambodian border. Brown and I performed flawlessly in spite of muzzle flashes and airbursts. The flight went fine and I assumed the results were too. I was curious why so many Steel Tiger hops were being scheduled at that particular time. Apparently they were effective but "carpet bombing" by B-52s later on was even more effective and well suited for this mission. Brown and I conversed as we flew back to the base. We had bonded well and were a good team. I liked him as a person and pilot. There was a certain amount of comfort in that and I had his six, literally.

The next morning we had an intelligence briefing. The crowning jewel of this day's brief was that a Vietnamese barber, who cut officers' hair at the Exchange barbershop, was captured while he was helping enemy forces gain access onto the base through the perimeter fence early that morning! Everyone in the briefing gasped at that one and immediately acknowledged that not knowing who the enemy was might be part of the problem. I felt things were escalating at all the borders because we were flying so many Steel Tiger missions into Laos and Cambodia. I thought we needed to fly those missions all over, including just above the DMZ.

I was scheduled with Berger for a CAS right after the meeting and another that afternoon with Brown. During the morning sortie with Berger, we were in a tense close air support flight with the enemy in close proximity to the friendlies and began to receive a barrage of small arms fire with visible tracers. We dropped our ordnance on target and were lucky our planes did not sustain any hits. Not long after that flight, Berger refused to fly any more combat missions. He was assigned to the group and flew the mail plane everywhere but mostly between Chu Lai and Da Nang. Ultimately, Berger was killed when his plane impacted a hill near our base while dropping flares at night. All aboard were killed, including Sergeant Bunch, one of the squadron's best maintenance NCOs. He was just along for a ride. It was truly a sad day. I liked both of them. It was an unfortunate part of the war's ugliness.

Brown and I flew a close air support in the Hoi An River basin that afternoon with soft ordnance of napes and snakes delivered at low altitude and the engaged enemy real close. Our controller, Lapdog, set us up, gave us a run-in heading of 100 degrees and put down a mark. He called, "Love Bug lead, from my mark, hit six o'clock at 30 meters." I called us in hot and Brown and I put our napalm right on the target. Lapdog told Dash Two to hit 12 o'clock at twenty meters from his mark, clearing him in hot. As our plane flew downwind in the pattern we went over the Hoi An River and that's when I noticed tracer rounds whizzing past my canopy. Knowing you might be taking fire and seeing it are two totally different things. I told Brown that I was seeing tracers. Brown said, "Call it." I called over the radio, "Lapdog, Love Bug lead, we are taking fire and it seems to be coming from the small island in the river." Instead of changing the set-up or at least our run-in heading, Lapdog casually came back with, "Roger Lead, we always take fire from there; drop your bombs at twelve o'clock at 50 meters from my mark." Brown called in hot and I read off airspeed and altitude with my blood boiling because of the controller's blasé attitude. I was ready to get the hell out of there.

Dash Two dropped his bombs and Lapdog radioed, "You've got 'em on the run. Do you have anything else?"

Brown came back with, "Roger, we have some Zuni rockets with high explosive heads."

Lapdog said, "I'll take 'em; I'll throw down a new mark." As Brown and I and our wingman set up for the Zunis, Lapdog put down a new mark and said, "Hit my mark, at eleven o'clock at 20 meters, no forty meters, they're runnin' like bats outta hell."

Brown called, "Roger, one's in hot" and fired our Zunis on my mark.

Lapdog called, "Fantastic Lead, you scored a direct hit. I can't give you a kill because there's no body; you vaporized him. Dash Two hit at 12 o'clock at 75 meters." Dash Two fired his Zunis and came off the target. After the runs, Lapdog told the flight the tracers might have been leaflets since a lot of them are dropped in the area.

I asked Brown, "You believing that?"

Brown said, "No."

I barked at Brown, "Why the hell doesn't a controller have us blow that little island off the face of the earth?" Brown didn't respond. Our flight cleared the area and headed back to Chu Lai.

Back on the flight-line, during post-flight inspection, I asked Brown to come back to the tail section, where I pointed out a dent that was an obvious bullet strike. It did not pierce the horizontal stabilator but it was definitely a hit. It might have been serious if it had penetrated somewhere else on the plane but was a non-issue where it was. It was my first time in a plane that was hit. The Hoi An River basin was living up to its reputation and I chose a "good" flight to audiotape. Nothing else was said between Brown and me even during debrief, but we both knew we had a close call. We would have others. That night there was live entertainment at the club. It was a group of Korean girls imitating American Rock 'n' Roll. They weren't attractive and they weren't that good but they were loud and entertaining. It was a nice break from the war.

I took my still or movie camera on about half my flights but frequently the flights were too intense for me to take my attention off the situation at hand. My close air support sortie the next day with the skipper was just such a flight. Our ground forces were engaged with the enemy at just thirty meters, 100 feet. There were casualties between our troops and the enemy that needed to be recovered. Fortunately we were armed with napes and snakes for low delivery. On target the controller was very nervous about the proximity of the friendlies. It was an intense situation. Hutchins and I and our wingman, Billison, with my friend Carpenter in his back seat, could not immediately drop our ordnance. We made repeated dives at fifty feet over the enemy, without dropping ordnance, to make them keep their heads down. Due to the circumstances on the ground, established standard operating procedures for this flight were totally abandoned and our aircraft were dangerously exposed at that altitude. We made as many as twenty runs; I lost count. The U.S. forces took advantage of the aircraft's suppressing runs to deliver heavy fire on the enemy and repel them. The controller put down a mark and our flight delivered napalm and bombs with deadly accuracy. At the end of the flight, our planes joined up and were about to check out of the area when the ground commander came up on our frequency. This was the first time for me that this happened in Country. Oddly, the commander was also Red One and told the flight thanks, "You saved our asses down here."

Later that day word came down from Group HQ that the Red force had a body count of thirty-five KBMA for the CAS hop. It was one of our squadron's higher body counts. There was talk of writing the skipper up for a single mission air medal. To my knowledge that never happened. I never received anything and there weren't any accolades for the skipper or anyone else. Everyone moved on to the next flight, which I had that afternoon. That same day, word was getting around about P.J. Allen's close air support flight at the Rockpile with 334 pilot, Major Scafe. When he and Scafe pickled their bombs over the target area on their second run, a secondary explosion from an underground cache of arms and munitions blew numerous holes in the belly of their plane. Their right engine was fodded by dirt clods and they immediately diverted to Da Nang to make an emergency single engine landing. Allen and Scafe were unharmed but it was another close call and another averted disaster.

Writing nothing about that close call or any of mine, my next letter home went like this:

I was wrong about the slackening. Things seem to have picked up a little and we are flying more close air supports, sometimes being scheduled more than one flight a day. The department of defense has an armada in the Sea of Japan off Korea right now. But, we have huffed and puffed before without taking any action ….

Mom, I got the banana nut bread and it is delicious! Thank you …

Dad, those are some interesting educational observations and intellectual stimuli. I have a couple thoughts; 1.) In our society today, nonconformity is a type of conformity, and 2.) In Texas for sure, students today are intellectually and emotionally ill prepared for college, hence their shock when they start. Regarding the protests trying to end poverty and discrimination. They have existed since the beginning of time and are archaic complaints, they are an example of man's inhumanity to man. I think Christianity could solve the poverty problem and would if it was better supported but there are too many hypocrites supporting things other than with words. Obviously action is the answer, it speaks louder than words. Discrimination is another story. It is inherent, in human nature. It will never be completely eradicated. Just as we Yankees in Texas, who already practiced integration, were severely ostracized for moving to the Lone Star state from Wisconsin. Prejudices will always exist, maybe discrimination will lessen. Time will tell …

Our chaplain just walked in smoking a cigar. He is a dynamic individual, a good sport and a morale booster. I wonder about him though, if he really has the right attitude …

More soon,
Love, Terry

The next week on a close air support near Chu Lai base, 232 pilot Stokes had control issues with his Phantom (it went inverted) as he rolled in on the target and he and his RIO, Devere, had to eject. They were picked up by a Search and Rescue (SAR) helicopter in less than fifteen minutes. The only injury sustained was a riser burn to Devere's neck. The plane, however, was a total loss. Stokes and Devere were very lucky not to have been captured. Pilots and aircrew seldom survived enemy capture in South Vietnam. In fact, they didn't always survive ejection even though our squadron was currently averaging 100 percent. If aircrew ejected over North Vietnam and got captured rather than recovered (the norm), they were generally taken to the Hanoi Hilton. But in the South they were deadweight and a mouth to feed where food was minimal. Therefore, downed aircrew in South Vietnam who were captured were usually tortured and killed. They were lucky if they were just shot to death. One such pilot was captured, and he was horribly tortured by having his skin stripped from his body while he was still alive, then castrated and disemboweled. This information was presented in a lecture preparing us for our Vietnam tour and the reason I had spoken to my brother as I did. I planned to put a bullet in my head before I would let the enemy torture me to death.

The afternoon of the same day as the lost plane, Brown and I were on a CAS on the wing of Executive Officer Zych, who had Steele in his back seat. We were delivering bombs first, then 2.75-inch rockets in 30-degree runs. Everything was progressing normally in the flight until Zych and Steele headed in on their rocket run. Zych obviously forgot to switch from bombs to rocket dispense on his weapons selection control panel because when he pickled, no rockets fired. Instead of having a devastating impact on the enemy, two rocket packs loaded with nineteen rockets each plummeted to earth unfired. It was like handing the enemy explosives, which might be turned into booby-traps. Brown and I rolled in and put ours on target. Zych apologized to the controller and the flight returned to Chu Lai. This quickly swept through the unit and Hutchins took imme-diate action. He transferred Zych to headquarters in Da Nang the next day. Zych never flew with the squadron again, which was fine with me, of course.

I now had lots of stuff I couldn't write home about; but, instead, for some unknown reason I wrote this:

Equality is virtuous. I hope it gains acceptance and is universally practiced. I am returning your Martin Luther King article, it was enlightening. He led an inspiring life to say the least...

.... I don't see an anti-intellectual society [advancing] but I do see mass media playing an ever increasing role. In fact, it is replacing books, newspapers and weekly magazines. A little mass media goes a long way and I'm afraid it has become infiltrated with a lot of useless garbage and often erroneous information. It may even be slanted like our Stars and Stripes but the danger for the public is the media being biased.

Tonight I am standing the air to air hot pad. It requires a 15 minute alert to get airborne. If launched, we would escort other aircraft, most likely B-52s. Reference Steel Tiger missions, they are classified secret and like a good boy I was hush-hush about them, but Newsweek Magazine spilled the beans and we can now write home about them. We are also using secret weapons, a CBU bomb and Rockeye. On the air to ground hot pad, we drop hard and soft ordnance—napalm, bombs, rockets, and sometimes utilize a 20mm Gatling-type machine gun. This represents 60 percent of our missions.

Over here, life's philosophy has a way of lingering just beyond the present thought. I'm not attempting to be philosophical; I'm trying to explain a personality trait in play due to the mental strain of war. I don't feel I'm going to die but the possibility exists and prevalence thereof is difficult to suppress. I have told Jan this in so many words. I have flown almost every mission variety they have here; all I must do is pass the time a year involves. And I hate that a year of my life has to be spent in this manner. But I do it for the sake of my country, which is to say, all Americans and that includes my relatives.

Many personalities have changed since arriving in Country. Many in our squadron have begun to show their worst side. I, fortunately, have retained my sense of humor and consequently carry on in a dignified fashion ... It's sad what stress can do to a person. This is indeed a rare experience. Mom, I guess you coined it when you said, "living your religion." I think that is hard anywhere you are. I just happen to be here. I could refuse to fly but I must live with myself regarding every decision I make. We must have faith in our fellow man—for earth's problems are manmade and must be man solved .... Our society is searching for answers. I hope that they are found before we destroy ourselves.

My thoughts reference the college campus demonstrations remains the same, abuse it and lose it ....

I'm doing just fine in health and state of mind and don't need anything but sure enjoy getting mail ...

I have jungle survival training soon. I will fill you in on that later. It is in the Philippines and I will get Mother's Day presents there that you will receive after the fact ...

I'm in the Post Office doing my customs inspection thing as I draft this letter. I'll pop it in the mail before I leave.

Love, Terry

P. S. It's hot. But I hope the war is cooling off. I think, I hope!

Without thinking, I had told my parents just about everything that I was doing and thinking and how I really felt. After mailing the letter, I regretted putting as much and the type of information in it that I had and hoped my parents didn't make the wrong assumptions about anything I wrote. Too bad I was so damned honest all the time.

My next sortie was a close air support with Major Schnippel. I hadn't flown with him since we left the States, which seemed a long time ago. He briefed the flight and we launched towards Quang Tri City up near the de-militarized zone. A joint Marine and Army camp there was under enemy fire and suffering casualties. Our controller indicated the enemy was pressing from the north side of the camp and put down a mark for us to hit. Schnippel called in hot and we dropped napalm first and on our second run, fired 2.75-inch rockets. On the way back to the base we were able to talk a little. I asked him how he thought things were going and he said, "Squadron wise, I think very well." He continued saying, "You seem to have adjusted very well. I'm proud of you."

I expressed my appreciation for his comments and told him, "I have come far and love being in this squadron."

My close air support mission that afternoon was with a visiting pilot from the group, Captain Franks. Lead pilot, Major Logan, briefed 10-degree napes and snakes at 30 degrees. I was still leery of flying in the back seat of visiting pilots. It wasn't fear, just the unfamiliarity factor. We launched and headed towards the Laotian border near A Shau Valley, where an Army unit was engaged with enemy forces found transporting munitions and supplies on a tributary of the Ho Chi Minh Trail in Thau Thien Province. After contacting our controller, we set up for our runs, Franks took interval, and our target was marked. Logan was cleared in hot and began his dive. I began seeing muzzle flashes. Franks called in hot and we were cleared hot as I read off airspeed and altitude in the dive. As Franks pulled off target up and to the left, I saw our napalm hits explode in a huge fireball. We climbed to our run-in altitude and circled around to drop our bombs. After they were expended we joined up with Logan, flew back to Chu Lai, and entered into the break. Franks was a good stick and I wasn't hesitant to fly with him again.

Brown and I had a deep night BARCAP that night with a 0200 to 0400 time on station. After about an hour, all quiet, and bored as hell, I was practically falling asleep. The silence was broken by our shipboard controller saying, "Love Bug 4-5-2, harmonica check." I had no idea what that was or how to respond and was about to ask Brown what to say when the controller repeated his message, "Love Bug 4-5-2 would you like a harmonica check?" I was now really confused but responded, "4-5-2, Roger." And following a slight pause, Brown and I were played a professional sounding tune on the harmonica. It was exactly what we needed. I was now wide awake. I occupied my time in the back seat, not reading comic books or girlie magazines as some pilots jokingly accused us of doing, but painting targets with my radar. I eventually hit on a suspicious low altitude target and called the controller, "Love Bug 4-5-2, I've got a low altitude bogey at 320 degrees at 20 nautical miles."

The controller responded, "No you don't."

I replied, "Roger that, how about another tune?" We were serenaded with a few bars of "Moon River."

My BARCAP flight in Brown's back seat the next night went a little differently. I ate a leisurely dinner at about 1800 hours at the Officer's mess and then went to the club to kill time until my 2230 brief. I ran into one of my flight instructors, Captain Morrison, who taught meteorology at Pensacola. Morrison was an R-I-O who had just joined the F-4B squadron, VMFA 115. We had a long conversation and then I socialized with my other squadron cronies until time for my brief. I and my fellow RIOs, Harlow, Knudsen, Allen, Foltz, and Carpenter, all shared similar concerns about flying with 334 so often. I nursed a couple Cokes during the evening but they did not settle my stomach. Before I left, most of my peers were getting pretty lit. Maintenance Officer Villarreal, who was seated across from me, started a familiar quip, "Who fired that shot?" The immediate response from Admin Officer Nagelin was, "Nobody, I farted."

Brown and I briefed, launched, and made our BARCAP midnight time on target. By then I was really sick to my stomach. By 0100 hours I mentioned it to Brown and indicated that it may have been my dinner. Just before our time expired at 0200 hours, I asked Brown to go cold mic. By then, I felt like crap, my stomach was aching, and I was sweating profusely. That's when I vomited, something I hadn't done since I left the United States. I felt a little better but was glad when we got back to the base. My first time to throw up in the combat zone was due to food poisoning! I would throw up one more time from food poisoning several weeks later. The two food poisonings would account for one-half of the total times I threw up in Vietnam. Back at my hooch, I had some water, a small snack, and a couple of my mom's cookies and hit the rack. I was awakened the next morning by Admin personnel going from hooch to hooch notifying all squadron personnel that the fuel and water lines were breached at the same time near the hangar, causing the fresh water to be contaminated. We had to get drinking water for our canteens from a "Water Buffalo" (a marine mobile water carrier). After repairs, the fresh water could be used but not consumed. It smelled like JP5 jet fuel for about a week or so. The standing joke was no smoking in the shower, no kidding.

Brown and I were on our way back to Chu Lai from a close air support sortie the next afternoon. We were receiving landing instructions when our tower transmission was interrupted by this one, "Chu Lai tower, this is Army Lima 1-6-2-1, requesting landing instructions. I've got a code 3 aboard, over." It was another busy day at Chu Lai and flights were lining up.

The Chu Lai tower controller, a Marine corporal or lance corporal, continued broadcasting to us, "Love Bug 4-5-4, report the initial, you will be number five in the pattern."

Right after that transmission the Army plane came up on the tower frequency again calling, "Chu Lai tower, this is Army L1621 with a code 3 aboard, requesting landing instructions, over."

Chu Lai tower responded. "Roger L1621, the runway is 16, altimeter 29.95. Proceed to the 10 nautical mile fix on the zero one zero degree (010°) radial and do a 360."

The Army pilot came back, "L 1621 copies, 010 at 10 miles and hold."

Visiting VIPs were given code numbers to identify just how important they were. Code one was the president or other very high-ranking person like a senior Senator, ambassador, Commandant of the Marine Corps, or Commander of Western Pacific Command. A code two was a high-ranking dignitary like a senator, etc. A code three was probably a general, celebrity, or other significant politician. I had little use for brass and neither did most combatants and other squadron personnel, including this corporal (or lance corporal) in the tower. VIPs were distractions. They were usually just taking a look at things but were always made a big deal out of. In the meantime, two A-4s had landed and two A-6s were cleared to land with two other F-4s ahead of my Love Bug flight. Before I reported the three-mile fix on final approach, the pilot in the Army plane came back up on frequency, "Army L1621 is reporting the 10 nautical mile fix at 010 degrees."

The tower responded, "Roger, L1621, do a 360." The two A-6s landed as the two F-4s ahead of Brown and me were cleared on final.

L1621 came up on the tower frequency sounding really aggravated, "This is L1621 with a code three aboard; do we have an ETA on getting in the pattern?"

The tower came back, "L1621, I copy your code three, do a 360."

"L1621, copies," was the response.

Another flight of F-4s checked in and was cleared into the pattern as number four. We were expecting to be cleared on final next when L1621 came back up on frequency with all kinds of attitude in his voice, "Chu Lai tower, this is L1621, I've got a code three aboard. WHEN are we going to be cleared to land?"

Before responding, Chu Lai cleared another flight of F-4s into the pattern. The Army pilot emphatically came back, "Army L1621 ..." This transmission required a tower response. All this was going on while my Love Bug flight was getting down and dirty (gear and flaps), in preparation for landing. The tower came back, "Love Bug 4-5-4 Dash One and Two, you are cleared to land, L1621, go ahead."

The Army pilot being given permission to transmit, chimed in with obvious anger and volume, "L1621, WHEN ARE YOU GOING TO GET MY CODE THREE ON THE GROUND?"

The tower came back equally aggravated and probably totally pissed, telling L1621 what all other aviators in the pattern thought: "L1621, I COPY your CODE 3 [heavy emphasis], now do another 360, these boys are coming home from the war!" L1621 had no choice but to comply. We landed and switched to ground control as we came off the runway. I hoped the corporal or lance corporal didn't get into trouble. All tactical aircraft needed to get back on the ground to get their planes turned around for their next flight. I watched the Army plane finally land as my Love Bug flight was taxiing back to our flight-line. I opened my canopy, disconnected the right side of my oxygen mask and smiled hugely. It was poetic justice: the general flying circles while I got preferential treatment. I loved it. It was a good day and I thought "to hell with the general; I AM coming home from the war."

I thought my next letter home should be more upbeat and less factual. Indeed, my mom and dad had been very moved by what I wrote. My dad had trouble concentrating at work for several days and my mom didn't sleep for two nights straight. Finally they read and re-read the letter and surmised that I was being honest and trying to show what my daily routine was and that

I was okay. They prayed for me while I prayed God would ease their mind and He did, especially when they got this letter:

My apologies if my last letter was too informative. I know you can't help being concerned for my welfare. Please know that there are plenty of non-dangerous things here. I've been sunning and collecting shells at the beach. I get time off occasionally, plus, I have my mundane collateral duties to attend to and I read a lot....

Here's a Polaroid picture for you. It shows the squadron Administration office in the background. I work here some when I am not flying. If you are marking the days until I am out of here, try 19MAR70. I am going to Okinawa soon to get our cruise book started. I am also going to jungle survival school in the Philippines at the end of the month ...

Mom, got your cookies yesterday. Boy, are they good. You have had a ton more compliments...

I have a safety meeting this afternoon. It'll be dull. (I'm back. It was)

I shaved my moustache off. I may not have told you I was growing one but it was getting long, was not dark and was not regulation. Oh well.

Today I taped a close air support mission. I think you will enjoy it very much. It'll give you an insight into how much work is involved in flying and all the radio transmissions which occur ...

Not much news to report. Tonight is steak night at the club. I missed lunch and I'm probably down to 150 pounds again. Fifty percent of my diet is liquids and I usually wake up starving. So, I now eat breakfast when I can.

Love, Terry

Friday, May 16, would be another day I would never forget as long as I lived. The day started out simple enough. That morning, Brown and I had a close air support sortie near the A Shau Valley. That afternoon we were on the skipper's wing on a CAS that received small arms fire. After the hop Brown and I went by Ops to check the flight schedule. Major Schnippel was looking for a pilot and RIO to volunteer to stand the hot pad 1800 hours until 0600 hours due to the illness of a pilot and RIO. Brown and I volunteered

Reproduced Polaroid photo of the author next to the VMFA-232
Headquarters sign in Chu Lai, Vietnam. The photo was taken by one
of the author's peers.

because it seldom launched. Not two hours into it, just after the sun set at
1907 hours, a call came in for an emergency close air support sortie. Brown
and I launched with Forney and Matzen. I was pretty sure it was 232's first
night emergency soft ordnance CAS. As our flight took separation preparing
for our runs, we could see small arms fire being exchanged. The controller's

brief indicated the enemy was also using mortars on the good guys' position. This concerned me because there was always a chance of a mortar hitting our plane. I also didn't like diving towards the ground at lower altitudes without being able to see it. I checked my topographical map to verify our pickle altitudes were safely above the ground for pull out. The controller put down a mark and then a flare to light things up pretty good as we headed in on the enemy. I stayed uncomfortable until the hop was over. I knew our flight was receiving fire and didn't think two points was enough for this mission.

When I got back to Chu Lai, I had a Coke and a bag of potato chips and lay down for some rest. I had already flown three flights for the day and it wasn't even midnight. I didn't rest long. Intel was requesting an escort for their reconnaissance plane. It launched at midnight. We recovered a little over two hours later and I lay down again. In less than two hours, the phone rang. The Air Force was requesting a B-52 escort. I had heard about Arc Lights but had never seen one. The B-52s flew out of Guam or U-Tapao Royal Thai Air Base in the Gulf of Siam. These required escorts to ward off any MiG fighter planes. B-52s were vulnerable because they were big and reasonably slow but they carried a huge load of bombs and could travel great distances for delivery. The huge number of bombs they dropped was referred to as carpet bombing. But when viewed at night, the almost continuous explosions made it appear from altitude like a welder's torch moving along the ground, hence, its nickname, "Arc Light."

Brown and I launched, were vectored into position at 35,000 feet and directed to hold until the B-52s were finished and cleared the area. I never saw the B-52 plane nor did we fly formation on them. I had seen plenty of them in Fort Worth at Carswell AFB. But the Arc Light was impressive and I was glad to have witnessed it even though it was my fifth flight in less than twenty-two hours. I was totally exhausted. After I computed our approximate location off a TACAN reading, I could see the B-52s were bombing along and just inside the Cambodian border heading northerly, most likely into Laos. They were obviously attempting to eradicate pesky AAA sites. That was fine with me. It was the only Arc Light I ever saw.

It was almost dawn when our Love Bug flight was cleared. I realized that we were actually not that far from the DMZ as we turned east and headed "home." I decided I wouldn't trade the experience for anything but I was ready for sleep. I relaxed a bit. Half focused, as the tip of the sun was just beginning to rise on the eastern horizon, my attention was grabbed by an image in my right mirror that sent me into absolute horror. There was a plane rolling in on the flight's five o'clock position and closing. I thought the next thing I would see would be a missile fired at us and called to Brown in an excited voice, "I've got a bogey in range at five o'clock and closing." Instead of instantly calling the flight into a combat defensive posture or making an evasive maneuver like hitting afterburner and pulling into a climb and separating (what I fully expected), Brown said calmly, "Roger" and did nothing. I acutely focused on the plane and hoped it was friendly since he had his acquisition lights on. After several agonizingly long seconds without a flash, the plane peeled out and headed west. I let out a huge sigh of relief. I assumed it was an Air Force plane that wanted to "play." I was glad our flight wasn't blown out of the sky. Had there been a flash, it could have downed both our Phantoms. I didn't relax until after our plane landed at Chu Lai.

After debrief, Brown and I headed to Ops to inform them of our five-flight marathon. We were both given the day after off, but this day was not over yet. To my knowledge, no other pilots or RIOs ever had five flights in a twenty-four-hour period. I headed off to breakfast and then hit the rack. I could hardly roust myself out of bed for my napes and snakes CAS that afternoon. I was not familiar with the area, Dong Ap Bai, but the controller had us hitting the top of a hill of strategic importance currently occupied by enemy forces. It was a difficult delivery and putting the ordnance long would have wasted it in the adjacent valley, while putting the ordnance short endangered the friendlies. We were successful all the way around and headed back to Chu Lai. I was surprised to find out later our target had been "Hamburger Hill" (#937). Back at the base, I looked ahead to my day off, the next day, a Sunday. I had earned it. Later on, after consulting my flight logbook, I realized those five flights tallied up ten points, earning me half an air medal in one day!

I went to church and then did some sunbathing during the day. I was beginning to get a pretty good tan. I never relaxed so much that I would've fallen asleep for fear of getting a sun burn. Getting sun burned was a court-martial offense and had happened to numerous enlisted personnel. I could've partially forgotten I was in a combat zone if it weren't for the Huey (Bell helicopter UH-1) gunship that regularly patrolled the beach. That helicopter had a distinct sound called "mast bumping" that I would recognize anywhere, forever, without even looking at it. I could do the same for C-130 Hercules aircraft because of their four turboprop engines. Being from Texas never meant heat didn't bother me. The truth is I hated it. I never got used to it in Texas, being a Wisconsin transplant. It wasn't conducive to sleep either. I returned to my hooch, showered, and wrote letters home.

My parents' letter read:

Well, I'm going on jungle survival May 22nd, so your Mother's Day gift will be further delayed. I'm not going to Okinawa at all. I am still on the project however, but pissed about it all and will tell about it another time.

I have the hot pad tomorrow. Flying has been fine and I am already on my way to earning my fourth air medal. Hasn't been my week but at least I didn't stub my toe on my way into the bunker this time.

Sorry I missed a visit with Lucy and Dale. Guess y'all had a lot of fun talking about old times in Wisconsin. Y'all must have been a sight looking for an armadillo …

Glad RutheAnn is doing better. Tell my sister to get her act together and that I'll write her soon. I've enclosed a letter for Tommy. How is he doing?

Today has been a good day. I went swimming …

I am reading the May National Geographic's article about the Apollo 8 voyage. What a fantastic venture. I wish I could do it.

Love, Terry

I mailed the letter and headed to the club.

Chapter 18

War Is Hell

When I arrived at the club, it was unusually quiet. I got my food and sat down next to Harlow. He asked me, "Did you hear about the 115 bird that went down last night?"

"No," I said, "I had the day off after having flown six flights in two days, five of them in less than a twenty-two-hour period."

Harlow continued, "One of their Phantoms flew out over the ocean to dump their unused bombs and inexplicably disappeared. Both the pilot and RIO were lost and presumed dead. I don't remember the pilot's name but the RIO was Captain Morrison."

"Morrison?" I exclaimed, "I just had a conversation with him two nights ago when he first arrived. He was our meteorology instructor at banana school."

Harlow replied, "I know, I can't believe it either."

"I really liked him," I offered in dismay and consternation. I could hardly eat my food as I sat in a funk. After a long period of silence, I asked Harlow, "How's your ass?"

He replied, "It hurts." Then the two of us slipped back into silence, absorbed in our thoughts. Back at my hooch, I had trouble going to sleep. While lying in my rack, I couldn't get Morrison out of my mind. What a waste, I thought, while contemplating other things, including my mortality. There seemed to be no rhyme or reason to any to it, especially the war part.

An alert RIO could save a pilot in a variety of ways without having any control over the plane. I felt I already had. Something went terribly wrong. How could they just disappear without a trace, emergency transmission, or an explosion? No explosion was reported. Nothing was recovered. There was no evidence of a crash and no radio beacons (from ejection) were heard. They just mysteriously vanished. They were never found and were officially listed as MIA but were obviously lost, dead. Lots of scenarios were proffered. I didn't believe any of them for two reasons: instruments and our extensive training on them, including night flying, and secondly, the radar intercept officer. I hoped Morrison died quickly without suffering and then hoped the same for myself if I died here. I said a prayer for the Morrison family as exhaustion took over and I went to sleep. There was no rocket attack that night. It was a good day gone bad.

I was really looking forward to Jungle Escape and Evasion Survival Training (JEST) school in the Philippines and being out of the combat zone for three days. It was mandatory training for aircrew in the Far East Theater. I had a daytime close air support hop with Brown back at Hamburger Hill (the assault was almost over) and a night CAS with Schnippel. The next morning I flew with twenty-two other 232 aviators to Cubi Point for jungle training. We were bussed into the jungle and trained by Filipino Negritos. They were masters at it and could get fresh water from just about anything. I bought a Negrito knife, a hammered steel pipe blade with a water buffalo horn for a handle. It was basically a small machete. The training was good and extremely appropriate considering the area of the world we were conducting operations in. It was also an X in the box, satisfying a training requirement, albeit over six weeks into our tour of duty. I had been battling sinus problems for days prior to JEST training and now had a sore throat so I paid a quick visit to the flight surgeon. He diagnosed an inner ear infection and grounded me from flying for one week. I was ecstatic. I had a whole week away from the war in the Philippines. I didn't care who was pissed about it. It was my "Catch-22" (paradoxical situation) and I was going to enjoy it. I did some gambling and called home to Jan and my parents a couple times during the week. I bought and shipped home some monkey pod Filipino hand-carved wood items: a set of NFO wings, a multi-tier Lazy Susan, and a coffee table with the entire surface depicting a rural indigenous scene.

I met two Navy aviators at the Officer's Club who were furloughing off the aircraft carrier the *Bon Homme Richard*, nicknamed the "Bonnie Dick." The three of us decided to go into Manila and while there I was able to pay a short visit to the wife and daughter of the minister who had officiated my wedding. They were missionaries there and glad to see someone from the States. Manila was a strange mix of large city high rise and affluence, and poverty, much of which I would describe as squalid. The city was a flurry of activity and was colorful due to the large number of "Jeepneys," World War II surplus jeeps left in the Philippines that were converted into taxis. They were brightly, obnoxiously colored and the tops were festooned with bangles hanging down from the roof.

That night the three of us rode one of those taxis into Olongapo, truly sin city. It was a collection of clubs, bars, eating and entertainment establishments, tattoo parlors, brothels, and souvenir shops. Prostitution was rampant

Author's photo of Jeepney taxis (colorful conversions of World War II surplus Jeeps) on a street in Manila, Philippines.

as were sexually transmitted diseases (STDs) that couldn't be cured. I had never and would never patronize a prostitute. I planned to remain celibate. I thought I'd just have a beer and enjoy the floorshow. We chose a strip club based on our driver's advice. It was a nasty place. All three of us ordered a beer. I was leery of even putting my hands on top of the table. I never liked beer but considered it "safe." When the cocktail waitress delivered the beers, she handed the other guys theirs. She took mine, lifted up her skirt and shoved the neck of my beer bottle into her vagina for a few seconds and then handed it to me. That disgusting act pretty much characterized Olongapo. I didn't know if she was offering her services or just being as nasty as the entertainment. The girls weren't attractive but they were available and many servicemen indulged because they just wanted to get laid. Some of them paid a high price with the after effects. I watched the show for awhile without drinking my beer and then headed back to the base. I slept well in the Philippines until it got close for me to return to Chu Lai.

The next day our trio headed out early to Lake Taal, which had an active volcano in it. We took a bus from the base into Manila and then a bus to the lake. That bus ride was identical to a scene I later saw in the 1984 movie, *Romancing the Stone*, in which actors Michael Douglas and Kathleen Turner rode a bus in Columbia from the airport into the countryside instead of Cartagena. Our bus to the lake was the same color as and resembled a typical American school bus (without air-conditioning). It was full of indigenous people who were carrying a variety of things from small packages, groceries and kids to live chickens. It made its way up into the mountains along narrow, curving dusty roads, coming dangerously close to the edge of steep drop offs. The ride was bumpy, hot and smelly with many stops. Our stop ended up at a small open-air market, where indigenous people were selling mostly bananas and other locally grown fruits and vegetables. Nothing looked clean and the vendors appeared impoverished.

After a short walk down a trail, we stood at a vista overlooking Taal Lake. It was a beautiful setting with a crater in the middle of the lake. There was no smoke this day but a week after our visit, it erupted and smoldered for days. While waiting to catch the bus back to Manila, I bought bananas at the fruit stand, overpaying for them, and once on the bus, gave them to some of the passengers. During our ride down the mountain road the scenery included two thatched huts on stilts, with barnyard animals and dogs standing and lying around in the yard. Near them a man was guiding a water buffalo harnessed with a "sleigh" for hauling while his wife stood not far from him holding a baby. It instantly reminded me of the carved scene on the coffee table I had recently bought and quickly snapped the picture. I lamented over their poverty and felt very blessed to be a citizen of the United States, "The land of the free and the home of the brave," though the brave part was a little unnerving at the moment.

The week had flown by and the second group of aviators from 232 arrived at Cubi Point for their JEST training. I met up with Knudsen at the O club pool. I started diving off the pool diving board. Knudsen was impressed and shot movies of me with my camera. I loved it because my dad had won ribbons for his diving abilities while on the University of Wisconsin swim team. I asked Knudsen if I had been missed. He said there were some grumblings but, no, everything was cool. Knudsen asked me if I had heard what happened to Terry Ewing, a helicopter pilot who was at banana school with us. I told him I hadn't. Knudsen said while inserting a recon team into a landing zone (LZ) with his Huey gunship, Ewing's chopper took enemy fire. His co-pilot was killed and the helicopter sustained so many hits that it crashed right there, inverted. Both Ewing's wrists were broken and he couldn't undo his shoulder harnesses or his lap belt. He hung in his seat watching the enemy advance. The Recon team repelled the enemy with Huey Cobra air support, saving the day and Ewing. He was in a Da Nang hospital recovering. I found out later, he turned in his wings and returned to the States. I totally understood hanging upside down, non-ambulatory, with a clear view of an advancing enemy shooting at him. In my mind he had earned a trip home. It seemed eons since the Ambassador Hotel in D. C. and his drunken escapade. I never confirmed the story but I never heard about or from Ewing again.

My peaceful interim was over; I had my "up" chit from the flight surgeon and was on the returning flight to Chu Lai. I had to endure a little kidding but no one was an asshole about my absence. Besides, I felt that my six flights in two days paid for it in advance. I got right back into the flow and was scheduled with Brown for a close air support the next day, June 1. It seemed to me that things were heating up, and not just temperature wise. And, when it rained, it did not cool things off. It just got steamy. The next day, at the end of our CAS mission, we landed in a downpour. The landing was a little tricky and I was glad to be on the ground. I could not open my canopy so I got busy in the back seat packing up my stuff and pulling the refuel probe circuit breaker. When I pulled my head up and looked out through my canopy, I saw the last apron at the end of the runway. I hollered at Brown and that was enough to catch him from going off the end and into the mud. There was never a dull moment in military aviation but this time a maintenance nightmare had been averted.

Brown, whom I often called Brownie, and I had two close air support sorties back to back the next day. Our first one was near the Hoi An River basin with napes and snakes. Enemy fire was guaranteed. One of our Marine units was in a skirmish with the enemy across the river. This was not good for the enemy since it gave air Ops a clear line of demarcation and spacing between them and our friendlies. What our Marines were experiencing was mortar rounds. Our controller put down a mark and we were in hot. Brownie and I, as well as our wingman and his RIO, were deadly accurate and the Marine unit's threat was eliminated. Brownie and I squeezed in lunch before our next brief and got to visit a little. I felt lucky to have him as my pilot, though now flying more often with others.

Our afternoon CAS was south of Chu Lai west of Tam Ky City, just inside Quang Ngai Province. That was about as far south as we flew sorties. The area was relatively flat. We prepared to drop our twelve 250-pound bombs with retardant fins and then fire our rockets. This enemy kept retreating into spider holes. Our controller marked them and we were in hot. Apparently we weren't as accurate as our controller wanted us to be. He didn't understand why we couldn't put one of the bombs right into one of the holes. We were good but that was an unreasonable expectation. (Laser guided bombs weren't developed yet.) We fired our rockets and returned to Chu Lai. I ate dinner at the club and relaxed.

I had a close air support flight the next day in the back seat of Wayne Flor. We were Dash Two on the wing of Major Ezell and his RIO. The mission went fine, but I got airsick because Flor was still not a smooth pilot. I threw up before we landed. A couple days later, I was scheduled with him again and once again got sick before the hop was over. I'd flown over sixty combat missions and hadn't thrown up on any of them except for food poisoning. I went to Ops and met with Major Schnippel and requested not to be scheduled with Flor again. After my explanation, Schnippel agreed. In a few weeks it became a moot point.

There was an awards ceremony on the hangar deck later that week at 1300 hours. Messages were passed back and forth about how to dress. The last message I got was utility sleeves rolled up and showed up that way. For some reason, I failed to notice that everyone else had their sleeves rolled down and nobody bothered to bring it to my attention. The skipper was presenting along with acting Executive Officer, Major Cagle. Promotions were handed out first by Hutchins and then congratulations ensued from Cagle. After those were done, Hutchins and Cagle did the same with air medals for the aviators. As Hutchins faced me to present me my air medal, he was congenial and complimentary. I saluted him and he moved in front of P. J. Allen to my right, putting Cagle in front of me. Cagle quietly lit into me. He asked me what the fuck I was thinking by showing up as I did. While berating me, he asked if I considered myself an exception to the rules. I couldn't believe my ears; I was shocked and totally embarrassed. I had absolutely no defense for it. I had screwed up. Though priding myself on being squared away, somehow in the middle of my squeezed schedule and sleep, I committed a huge no, no in front of the squadron hierarchy.

As Cagle moved on, I first became angry with myself, then just angry. I thought it was all a bunch of crap. Except for the embarrassment, I really didn't give a damn. In the middle of an auspicious occasion, I felt miserable. To me, this whole war thing was a total waste. And then, of course, I thought, what were they going to do, make me a lieutenant and send me to Vietnam? Too late! Later that day, I learned that two of our RIOs, Foltz and Feiring, had been permanently transferred to 334. I knew that meant there would be other transfers and that RIOs would fly more often, more missions, and be scheduled more frequently for duty assignments. It all sucked. After the ceremony, it was business as usual, flying, duty, etc. At the O Club that night, I was introduced to a new pilot who was joining VMFA-542, another

F-4B squadron on base. I welcomed him aboard. The floorshow that night was good for a change. The entertainment was a female comedian. She was hilarious. One of her skits was performed while wearing a huge cloth diaper which had a large safety pin over the crotch area with a padlock on it. Laughing out loud was cathartic.

The following night I had a BARCAP with pilot Owen. I hadn't flown with him since August of '68, ten months prior. It was a deep night flight that lasted nearly three hours. That gave us lots of time to talk. He pretty much had the same opinion of the war that I had. I liked him as a person and pilot and felt he would have been a good second choice for me. Though the flight was long, there were no contacts, missteps and, sadly, no harmonica tunes. However, we were fortunate to have missed a rocket attack while airborne.

A couple days passed with everything and all flights going smoothly. There was no food poisoning, no rocket attacks, no extra duties, and I even got mail from home. I flew an early close air support hop with a new pilot, Lieutenant Colonel Braddon, who was joining 334 and would eventually become their commanding officer. Prior to our flight brief, Warrant Officer Steele gave an Intel briefing. He summarized the previous day's stats and gave the BDA, which did not include any enemy killed. Then Steele brought up some bad news.

"I regret to inform you that Cowboy and Indian were killed." He paused and then said, "Yesterday, the gooks won." It all hit home for me. I was angered at Steele at first and then realized he was just the messenger. Though I was genuinely and deeply saddened by the news, I was irate because he was right. Though depressing, the reality was, not just people on the ground were dying. I was despondent during my flight but focused and performed as I had on all my others. It was difficult to carry on and difficult to accept. I hoped they knew how well liked they were. I loved those guys and all the effort they put into my sorties.

Two days later, I launched in Braddon's back seat again on a close air support near the de-militarized zone. We were supporting troops who had been forced off a road branching off the Ho Chi Minh Trail by heavy enemy fire. The large unit of U.S. troops took refuge in the jungle east of that location.

The road was heavily used by friendly and enemy forces. Several vehicles had been abandoned in the road, including the commander's jeep at the rear of their entourage. The flight was briefed by the controller for low passes and soft ordnance delivery on the west side of the road where the enemy was and he put down a mark. Then the controller added, "Do not hit the colonel's jeep." Lead came back with, "Roger that." Lead called in hot and was cleared. On the first drop, he annihilated the jeep. It didn't matter what our ordnance hit after that, as long as it wasn't friendlies! The remainder of the flight went fine and our runs on the target devastated the enemy forces.

As the flight headed back to Chu Lai, I smiled. I figured if the colonel didn't want his jeep destroyed, he shouldn't have left it in the road. But it wasn't just a bad day for the colonel. When our flight got back to Chu Lai, there was a really dark cloud hanging over the unit. I asked what was going on and Schnippel informed me that a new VMFA-542 pilot (the one I had met at the club), during his fam hop, flew through the left wing of the aerial hot pad KC-130 tanker while two Phantoms were taking a drink. He and his experienced RIO were killed instantly and their Phantom lost. The KC-130 spiraled into the ocean in a fire ball, killing all six crewmen aboard. The pilot and RIO in the Phantom refueling on the port side of the tanker ejected because of damage and lost engines. They were recovered by a SAR helicopter. The Phantom on the starboard wing limped back into Da Nang on one engine with the refueling drogue and about twenty feet of hose still attached.

The experienced RIO probably had the fam pilot looking at the ground and forgot about the restricted area. Their Phantom was probably flying with its port wing lowered some and in a slight nose up attitude when it hit the tanker. The refueling Phantoms would have been very preoccupied and never saw it coming. The KC-130 didn't have a chance flying at approximately 250 knots and being impacted at about 500 knots. I stood there speechless. It was one of the worst airborne disasters of the war to date. Eight Marine air crewmen were dead in the blink of an eye. Over 13 million dollars (1966, '67 and '68 budgeted) of aircraft lost due to pilot error and not a direct result of enemy action. It wasn't just a lousy day; it was catastrophic and devastating. I was awestruck and overwhelmed emotionally. I vowed anew to be alert, maintaining an edge and go by the book. Again, I felt sorry for the families of the lost. It was almost as bad as being killed by friendly fire. I hoped my parents hadn't heard about it and worried I was involved; I could have been, just wasn't. We were all somber for days and mediocre floorshows didn't help, however, for some, alcohol did. I realized for the second time that someone I had just recently talked to had perished in the war. Once again, meaningful sleep was thwarted as I dwelled on the fortunes of the war.

None of us could become preoccupied with the disaster or dwell on it for long; our next flights were already scheduled. The next afternoon, Brown and I had a CAS with napes and snakes and took fire. After landing back at Chu Lai, we taxied our Phantom off the duty runway onto the apron to allow one of the ordnance personnel to check the racks. I watched as an ordnance lance corporal came out of the shack and walked towards our plane. Right away I knew something was up. He was in no hurry to get to the plane. In fact, he looked as if he was walking in slow motion and I swear his feet were barely touching the ground. I got Brown's attention on hot mic and said, "Hey, would you look at this guy. He's got to be high on something." Brown prevented him from approaching the plane by immediately powering up the engines and taxiing away from him. As we taxied, I saw the guy casually turn and saunter (lope) back in the direction of the shack. I came up on the radio and told ground control to get someone out there quick before someone got killed. I radioed Dash Two and told him to skip the ordnance de-arming check and both planes taxied to our flight-line.

I got on squadron common frequency while taxiing and asked for a representative from ordnance to meet us just off our flight-line. Once in the maintenance hangar, Brown and I told Ordnance Officer Lackey about the incident. I never knew the fate of the lance corporal, but I knew the outcome wasn't good. Two days later, at 0500 hours before shift change, all available lieutenants in 232 conducted a shakedown of the enlisted barracks. Not that much contraband was found; however, in one of the hooches, wedged between some plywood sheeting acting as a ceiling covering the corrugated steel roof, I found a large plastic bag of marijuana. It was about six inches in diameter and over a foot long, probably weighing over a pound. I knew a court-martial was coming for some unlucky Marine and I knew it would not be the last court-martial while in combat. The Marine deserved whatever punishment he got. The risks of mistakes due to an unclear head in combat were too high.

Later that day, I had occasion to call ordnance out to the runway. Brown and I were providing close air support in the same area we had been two days earlier. We dropped our twelve 500-pounders and rolled in on the target to fire our five-inch Zuni rockets with high explosive heads. For the first and only time in a run, I was distracted enough to lose track of our current/correct altitude. As my attention came back into the cockpit, I read off altitude and airspeed to Brown. Just before calling, "Mark, mark," something clicked, probably the fact that we were going below two thousand feet. I realized immediately we were too low, well below the 2400-foot minimum for high explosive heads. I panicked and quickly told Brown, "Skip it, skip it, skip it." Brown pulled off the target without firing. Before Brown could ask what the deal was, I said on hot mic, "My bad, let's make another run." We did, accurately firing on our target from the correct pickle altitude. As we pulled off target, I gazed out of my canopy to scan the horizon. As I looked right, the tip of an unfired Zuni rocket caught my eye. It was another "holy shit" moment.

With panic in my voice, I called it to Brown's attention. The high explosive warhead of the Zuni rocket extended about two feet beyond the leading edge of the right wing. The motor had obviously misfired for it to be lodged the way it was. Any damage to our plane was unknown. We told Dash Two not to join up. There was no sense losing both planes and crews from an explosion. It was an intensely serious situation and a pucker moment that would not ease until Brown and I were back on the deck away from our plane. I cleared us out of the target area and got the flight on squadron common frequency. Brown told Dash Two to keep a two-mile distance and then started a dialogue with 232 Ops on our way back to Chu Lai. It seemed an eternity getting back to the base while staring at the nose of that rocket protruding in front of the wing. I prayed hard it wouldn't explode. We ruled out diverting to Da Nang and declaring an emergency. The pattern was cleared by Chu Lai tower as Brown made a straight-in approach and the smoothest landing that he had ever made and softest I'd experienced in an F-4.

I lifted my ass off the seat as Brown deftly kissed the runway and we rolled out without deploying the drag chute. I remarked to Brown, "Beautiful," as I looked to make sure the rocket had not moved. We pulled off onto the apron at the end of the runway and shut down the engines. Brown and I egressed as quickly as possible, jumped into a waiting ordnance truck, and were driven to the maintenance shed. The further we got from the plane, the more I relaxed. I looked at Brown and said, "Superlative landing. That was tense wasn't it?"

Brown said, "Sure was, I'm glad it's over."

I said, "Me too, sorry for the altitude miscue on the second run on target."

Brown, totally unconcerned, said, "Forget about it, no big deal. You caught it and that's all that counts." I never messed up another pickle altitude.

Our emergency ordnance disposal personnel took care of the rocket without incident and the plane was prepped for the next flight. Brown's debrief was short and included verification of the way the two of us handled the emergency. During debriefing, I thanked God for our safe return and the failsafe safety features in rockets and missiles. After debrief, I was told to go to Admin. It was good news and bad news. I got new living quarters, an air-conditioned hooch. "Hallelujah," I thought since the weather was really getting hot. The bad news was my roommate was Tokyo Bob. Of all people in the squadron, how the hell did I end up with Snyder? I finally had something to write home about and some creature comforts of home. Cohabitating with Snyder was another story.

Early in June, I wrote this home:

Today was my day. I got your batch of fudge cuts and four letters. I got your cookies yesterday. Thanks again, Mom ...

I guess Mickey [my close friend since junior high school] has been over to see you by now. I envy him. [He had been discharged from the Army after serving in Germany.] But it won't be that long for me as the time is passing fast. I also become eligible for R&R next month ...

Dad, Happy Father's Day when it comes. I cannot think of anyone who deserves it more than you. Have a great day. Here's a great quote from RFK, "Our future may lie beyond our vision, but it is not completely beyond our control." Sorry I haven't written in a while. This letter should catch me up and answer your backlog of questions ....

Japan is looking more like it will happen, maybe in September. I sure hope so. Jan is looking forward to Hawaii (R&R) and also Japan if it happens. I can bring her there for two months, according to regulations ...

All the squadron members are rotating back and forth to Cubi Point to participate in a missile shoot. I will not go because I had a week there, gratis. However, I am sending my movie camera with a pilot who is going to film some footage for me from the front cockpit. I have been taking movies from the back seat of some of our Vietnam missions. Speaking of missions, things just plod along about the same here ... We didn't have good results from bombing yesterday. Lack of progress here is not due to the lack of bravery nor American offensive effectiveness. I believe the U.S. political arena has misjudged the nature of this war. We have sought to resolve, with our military might, a conflict whose issues depend on the will and conviction of the South Vietnamese people. We ought to withdraw because Saigon's government has let us down ...

Good news. I am moving into air-conditioned quarters. Please buy Jan some flowers from me for our anniversary (June 25). I will pay you back. Just let me know the amount.

Quote of the day, "The Marine Corps is a four and a half year tour in civilian appreciation."

Happy Birthday to Tommy.

Let me try to minimize my recent letter which I consider to have been more than a little extreme and I hope I didn't lower your spirits. Let me clear the air and recap everything, putting it in its proper perspective. Naturally there is the possibility of death. But that albatross is on everyone's neck. My problem here is not facing death, not owning up to my duty, not lack of courage or persever-ance. It is merely maintaining the proper state of mind. I accept all things the way they are. My greatest problem, which is temporary, is loneliness. For the first time in my life my efforts to change my environment, to resolve the situation I am in or alleviate dissatisfaction, are futile. On what then can I lift my morale? There is nothing concrete. But I have come to a state of mind I would describe as hopeful. In short, I realize that after this low point, which has few merits, but indeed there are some, I shall endeavor to never again be subjected to stagnation and degradation. I cannot dispel the fact that I have accomplished something. That is my reward. Not honor, nor peace, nor worldly goods, nor prestige, nor heroic deeds I have accomplished; but I have accepted, received and survived humiliation and mental torment for my patriotism. Thus when I can, I will leave the service with a job well done to the best of my ability and an education in just exactly what the hell the military is all about. I am convinced that there is a better world to see. Presently my vocation is not an avenue of approach, but rather a one way street of reactionary necessity. Soon, I hope to be back to creativity, not destruction.

About Hamburger Hill (hill #937 on our topographical map), I had two close air support sorties there and then went to Cubi Point in the Philippines. It was over before I returned to flight status. For us, in the air, it was pretty much business as usual. For the ground troops, it sounds like it was pure hell. I have much empathy for them. Pray for them. Ground troops are far worse off than me. They look pathetic every time I see them in the exchange.

Hope you got the gist of all this. Do not let it affect you adversely. I was trying to say I'm lonely but my spirits are still up and I'm fine. Tell everyone hello from halfway around the world.

Love, Terry"

When my parents received this letter, my state of mind could not have been clearer. It did not put them at ease but it made them realize that fate would take its course and they, too, would have to accept it. My mom cried. My dad consoled her and said, "Let's be positive; he is. It sounds as though he really has it okay."

My mom said in reply, "Tom, my heart aches for him. He doesn't deserve this."

My dad said, "No one does. But our country exists because men, and women, accept the call. I am so proud of him."

My mom replied, "Me too," then cried. Later that day, they read about me receiving my air medal in the local newspaper. I read it about it a week later, receiving that local paper for free.

I moved into my air conditioned hooch that Monday. My reception from Tokyo Bob was cool. I didn't care. It was the cool temperature I was interested in. Our interaction was minimal due to schedules and things seemed to be okay. I relished the cool temps and semi-privacy. There were rumors going around about Snyder, rumors beyond his womanizing. More correctly stated, it was an extension of his womanizing. He had reportedly taken a nurse from the Cubi Point hospital for a nighttime back seat ride in an F-4 while at the missile shoot in the Philippines. It was a real no, no and he might've gotten away with it if he hadn't had her make the call to the tower for landing instructions. She tried to make the call that all RIOs make but it broadcast over the tower frequency something like this, "Cubi tower, this is, oh Bob, I don't know what to say." I never did understand how he thought he would get away with a feminine voice transmitting from a Phantom. Everybody knew what the motive was and Bob would pay a high price for it. Bob and I were roommates less than two weeks when his punishment was assessed. He was sent out to a ground unit as a forward air controller (FAC) for a month. Fellow RIO Josh Carpenter from Louisiana became my new roommate. We became good friends and were roommates for the remainder of our tours in Vietnam.

I had the twenty-four-hour duty the next day. While we were hanging around Admin, the squadron received our copy of a released Headquarters Marine Corps (HQMC) all-Marine message stating effective immediately, all Marine Vietnam tours would be twelve months long instead of thirteen, the same as the other branches of service. While I was relishing this information, one of my unit's lance corporals came to me and claimed his boom box had been stolen and that he knew who had it and could identify it. We recovered it and gave the theft incident over to the Group JAG, Judge Advocate General. The guilty young Marine was reduced in rank. As I wrote everything in the duty logbook, I wondered why the thief committed such a petty act and why he thought he could get away with it, especially knowing it would tarnish his military service. I thought it a reminder of one of the differences between officers and enlisted personnel, and then I reflected on Snyder, thinking maybe some weren't that different after all.

Once relieved from duty, with the day off, I bought a small refrigerator and soft drinks, and I headed to my hooch. After sleeping for awhile, I headed to the beach. Even with a good tan, I still had the white spotted rash on my chest and stomach and it was not responding to medication. The sun wasn't killing it either. Being allergic to certain soaps, I thought maybe it was related to the detergent used by the indigenous personnel who did our laundry. That thought increased my hatred of the place. I saw Doc Bouvier once again and he switched ointments. I paid dearly for my day off. I was scheduled for three CAS hops the next day starting at dawn. The first one was with visiting pilot Bliss and then two in a row with Brown. On my first close air support with Brown, our refueling probe inexplicably came out shortly after takeoff. The actuating switch was non-functional and I pulled the circuit breaker so it wouldn't do anything else. As the probe oscillated in the air slip, we burned off fuel, headed out over the ocean to dump our bombs and landed safely. We took on a ground-directed bombing Steel Tiger sortie and had our night hop changed to a Steel Tiger sortie near the DMZ.

My stomach was upset and while on this level flight ordnance drop, I threw up. I didn't know if it was food poisoning again or stomach flu but this time vomiting didn't help much. By the end of the flight I was exhausted, still had an upset stomach, and was feeling a little dizzy. After debrief, I headed to my hooch feeling like crap. The Cokes I drank did not help my nausea. I was only scheduled for one flight the next day, another nighttime Steel Tiger with Brown, and was able to sleep in. I drank a little water hoping it would settle my stomach and "hit the rack." Carpenter woke me up the next morning. I must have looked like shit because he asked me if I felt okay. I answered, "Better than last night but not the best, what's up?" Carpenter told me I needed to get to Ops ASAP; Schnippel was looking for me. I asked him if he knew what it was about and he said no. It was 0900 hrs.

I got there at 0930. Schnippel told me that my Crypto wheel wasn't turned in to the S-2 at the end of my previous night's flight and asked if I was aware of it, had it, or knew where it was. I told him that I was certain that it had been turned in, but would verify it. I still wasn't feeling well. I didn't have time for this shit but knew it had to be tended to immediately. Luckily, I was not scheduled for a flight until that night. If a Crypto wheel went missing for over twenty-four hours, it was assumed compromised and all classified codes for all of WestPAC, had to be changed. The proverbial hammer would fall on the skipper who Schnippel said I needed to report to next. Hutchins was in a really shitty mood. I protested my innocence, saying I was certain I'd returned the wheel after my last, late hop. Hutchins chewed me out real good. He said in no uncertain terms to locate the wheel that day before close of business or it would be my ass and I would suffer the consequences. "Yes Sir," was my reply.

I headed straight for Intel. Sure enough, the log had not been signed and it showed as not returned. I couldn't believe it. I went to flight equipment thinking that maybe I left it in my nav bag where I always put it and had simply forgotten it during my impaired state of mind. I rifled through the bag. Damn, no wheel! I started to panic. I didn't know where the hell it was and went to the on-duty flight equipment NCO and asked if a Crypto wheel had been found. His answer was no. I was really starting to sweat. It was noon and the wheel was nowhere to be found. During this worrisome distraction, I didn't have an appetite even though I had thrown up the night before and gone without breakfast. Had I been hungry, lunch was way down the list of priorities. I was terribly distraught, almost in tears. I went back to trace all my steps, starting with the plane I flew in the previous night. I asked Brown and then went back to S-2 and flight equipment. No luck. I didn't know where the hell it could be. I started looking in places I had already looked, even back in the plane. I knew if an aviator found it he would turn it in. I started getting sicker to my stomach. I went back to my hooch. I didn't find the wheel but ate some of mom's cookies.

I went back to Ops and obtained the bureau numbers of the other two planes I flew in the previous day. No luck. I was stymied. I went back to the hangar and asked around, no luck. It had seemingly vanished. I wondered what the hell else I could do and realized the shit was going to hit the fan soon. It was mid-afternoon. I didn't want to face the skipper but had to admit soon that the wheel was lost. My deadline was fast approaching and things were looking bleak, plus I had a flight that night with Brown and needed to get something to eat. In my quandary, I never thought of God's help but I think He gave it to me anyway. Totally deflated, I went back to the hangar again. I looked everywhere and then went back to flight equipment. I tore through everything with no luck and then went back to Lance Corporal Jones at the desk. I asked him if he had been the NCO on duty the previous night. The response was, "No Sir." It was Corporal Smith. I rushed over to Smith's barracks only to find out that he was eating at the enlisted mess. I ran there with my adrenaline pumping.

I found Smith. He had found the Crypto wheel and realizing its importance, locked it in the desk drawer at flight equipment! I could have kissed him. I thanked him profusely and rushed back to the hangar and had Jones retrieve the wheel. I thanked him, headed back to the S-2 and got the wheel checked in. I told Schnippel and then headed to the skipper's office. It was 1600 hours. I told the skipper that the flight equipment NCO had found the wheel near my nav bag and locked it in the desk drawer where it remained until just a few minutes earlier when I retrieved it and checked it in. Hutchins was less than enthusiastic and told me that I had everybody on edge all day and that I needed to do a better job of taking care of my business. I mentioned my three flights and being sick. He wasn't interested in excuses.

Hutchins said, "Never let this happen again," to which I replied, "Yes Sir." And then Hutchins said, "Now get the fuck out of my office, Lieutenant!" I turned and left. I was relieved but somehow felt it was not over yet. It was a fuck up that just sort of happened. It had been preventable but given my mental and physical being at the time, I felt it was forgivable since no harm was done. Starving, I headed to the chow hall.

Brown and I had our Steel Tiger hop later that night. It went fine. I had no idea that it would be our last flight together and my last flight in VMFA 232. The next morning Hutchins transferred me to 334 permanently, ordering me to report to 334 the next day. I left Hutchins's office totally dejected and angry. It sucked the big one, putting everything in a state of flux. How would I explain this to everyone back home? I was heartbroken and embarrassed, uncomfortable having any interaction with my 232 comrades until some time had passed. I spent the rest of the day checking out of the squadron. My GSE personnel said they were sorry to see me go and I told them I was proud of them and would be available if any of them wanted to contact me. As I thought about it all through the day, I took some solace in the fact that two of my fellow RIOs, Foltz and Feiring, had already been transferred to 334. Having flown with the squadron and knowing some of the pilots and RIOs, including my two RIO friends Leist and Yorkoff, eased my anxiety some. I had flown sixty-nine combat missions in the Red Devil squadron, earning almost six air medals. It was the end of an era for me, but my tour wasn't over. I was now a Falcon.

Chapter 19

Trading My Horns
for Talons

At 0800 hours the next morning, June 21, I reported to 334 Administration. (See Appendix D for VMFA-334 history.) Everything was heating up: the temperature, the war and my anxiety. I was anxious about my duties and whatever other changes I was in for but as it turned out, most of what I worried about was unnecessary. I kept my hooch quarters, flight equipment, top-secret clearance, and other items associated with, and issued by, 232. I met Commanding Officer, Lieutenant Colonel D'Angelo, Executive Officer Bond, and Operations Officer Pieri. I gave Pieri my updated flight logbook. Pieri told me I would be scheduled the next day. When I checked into Administration I found out it was my new collateral duty. I tried to be enthusiastic but couldn't manage it. I resented being transferred and was nervous about 334 pilots. I hoped a few flights would resolve this issue. After familiarizing myself with all of the ins and outs of 334, I headed back to my hooch. I wrote a long letter home explaining everything. I was evasive rather than untruthful and upbeat rather than pessimistic, maybe even overly optimistic. When Carpenter arrived at our hooch, the two of us talked and then got on top of our bunker and had a yoyo contest. Several minutes into the contest, we both started laughing so hard we couldn't continue. I wiped

The author's photo showing fellow RIO and hooch mate, Josh Carpenter, taking a break from the war to relax in their air-conditioned quarters on Chu Lai Base.

the tears from my eyes and told Carpenter to take movies of me. We then went to dinner and the club, chuckling on the way.

My first flight as a 334 RIO was a close air support with pilot Ricketts and it went fine. Before I headed back to my hooch I checked Ops for the next day's flight schedule. Shit, I thought, as I glared at the schedule. I was scheduled for three flights, all close air support. My pilots were Tyson, Braddon, and Hajduk. I didn't say anything to anyone and wondered what I had gotten into, but already knew. I thought I might fly a little more often in 334 due to their manning level but this was bullshit and survival crept into my mind. I went to dinner and the club. At the club I ran into Brown, who said he missed me. I never knew who took my place, if anyone. We had a special bond. I missed him too. We talked into the night. Brown and I were not drinkers, but those who did drink were getting after it. That kind of escapism was unhealthy in our environment. Pilots who were less than 100 percent made me nervous. However, most of them were likable. Doc Tyson was likable but quite inebriated by the time I left the club.

As I arrived at my 0530 close air support brief the next morning, Tyson was already there and looked like hell. We were lead aircraft and I was sharp and attentive. Apparently something in my gaze elicited a response from Tyson, who knew I had observed him at the club the previous night. Tyson said he would snap to when he got in the plane and on pure oxygen. The statement wasn't much comfort to me but I hoped he was right. On target, unpredictable winds were affecting our flight's ordnance delivery. Tyson's drops were not very accurate. When I checked out with the controller, Tyson apologized for his inaccuracy, telling the controller, "Sorry, couldn't hit my ass with either hand today." I kept silent; I had to move on mentally. I had two more flights that day.

My next flight was with Lieutenant Colonel Braddon, who would become Commanding Officer of the squadron. After launch, we were directed north to Quang Tri Province and bombed with soft ordnance near the "Rockpile," south of the DMZ. The Rockpile was a solitary rock formation outcropping and was called Thon Khe Tri by the Vietnamese. The Marines knew it as Elliot Combat Base, near Dong Ha airfield.[20] This landmark was not very far from the Khe Sanh outpost where I'd flown numerous sorties already. More often than not, missions near the de-militarized zone turned intense. As soon as we rolled in on target, we started receiving fire from the enemy forces the Marines were engaged with. Our napalm quieted them down. After dropping our bombs, we headed back to Chu Lai. No BDA was given but I knew there were lots of KBMA.

My third CAS, with pilot Hajduk, was cancelled while airborne. Vice Squad converted it into a ground directed bombing mission. Upon checking in with that controller, he informed us he had "a tree park down here that would make a good target," and we dropped our 500 pounders there. Basically we bombed the jungle to keep from dumping our bombs in the ocean. It was a huge waste of taxpayer money.

The next morning I flew a close air support mission with Operations Officer Pieri in the Hoi An River Basin and once again there was enemy fire. I now understood how and why so many aircraft were lost there and didn't want to be one of them. A profusion of visible tracer rounds had me on edge. After our napalm drop, we changed the run-in heading and dropped sixteen 250-pound bombs with retardant fins getting as close to the ground as practical. It was an intense, nerve-wracking CAS even though our actual flight time was less than one hour. Once we cleared the area, another flight was quickly over the target area. I relaxed on the short ride home. After Pieri's debrief he said to me, "Welcome to the squadron." I thanked him, feeling I had successfully assimilated into the unit.

My first flight with pilot Captain Trachta was a "routine" ground directed bombing sortie the next afternoon near the de-militarized zone. It was routine including the growl of the "inactive" SAM site. Being "painted" by its radar was unsettling and I couldn't wait to clear the area. On the way back, our plane had a single generator failure. The other one performed flawlessly and we landed without any problem. That was my first mechanical issue in Country and this day, it was a nonissue. Maintenance personnel were doing a good job on our planes and so far, things were positive with my pilots.

I flew a close air support sortie per day for the next two days and except for receiving ground fire, they went fine. Then I was scheduled for three flights in one day again, two close air supports and a Steel Tiger. My morning CAS with Pieri started with a 0700 brief. Pieri led us on a priority soft ordnance napes and snakes sortie near Hue. Marines who were engaged with enemy forces west of the city were taking casualties. By now, this had an all too familiar ring to it. I contacted our controller and he had us in hot right away. We dropped our napalm with deadly accuracy and set up for bombs. We put our bombs on target and cleared the area. As our wingman joined up, I waited for a BDA, but another flight was already on station so we cleared the area and we headed back to Chu Lai. Often our BDA came in later and frequently we shared kills with other flights that had been on target.

My 1100 hour CAS briefing with Major Potenza, who would become Executive Officer, was a sortie north of Quang Tri City right at the DMZ, not far from the coast. I got our flight airborne and on target. It was my first sortie this close to the de-militarized zone and we had to be careful not to fly across this invisible line during our runs or we would be accused of a border violation. Using an east-to-west run-in heading, we dropped our ordnance on target and returned to Chu Lai over the ocean down the coastline. Flying over the Gulf was reasonably safe. After dark, I had my Steel Tiger hop with pilot Rath. I had already flown with numerous different pilots and that would continue the whole time I was in 334. Our lead pilot, Storm, whose call sign was "Stormy" of course, led us over the target and told us to take interval. It was eerily dark. After Storm's drop, the AAA sites opened up and the ground was ablaze with muzzle flashes. Rath and I were cleared in hot and as we dropped our bombs, airbursts started going off but, happily, they weren't close to us and there were fewer muzzle flashes on our second runs. Surprisingly, but undoubtedly due to adrenaline, my ass wasn't dragging after the three hops. After landing, I headed to the club, pleased with the day's outcome and glad my airsickness thus far was concealed in 334.

On the last day of the month, I launched on an early morning CAS in pilot Johns's back seat. Johns and I were wingman to the X. O. and his RIO, Foltz, my friend from 232. We were out again near the Hoi An with Marines heavily engaged during an enemy assault. As we dropped our napalm from a low altitude ten-degree dive, we started receiving fire. We changed our run-in heading and jinked some during our higher altitude bombing run. We got a "thank you, your hits were great" from our controller as we climbed back up to altitude and flew back to Chu Lai.

After an early, leisurely lunch, I went to Admin to put in some hours on my new collateral duty until time for my late afternoon close air support hop. I had much to learn about administrative duties and due to my heavy scheduling of flights since joining the unit, I'd spent little time there. Flights took priority because my MOS was Naval Flight Officer, numerical designation 7587. At 1600 hours, Major Noggle briefed our close air support sortie in the A Shau Valley. I was nervous about the flight with Noggle, but apparently he hadn't forgotten his last flight with me and had his shit together. We boomed out of Chu Lai and headed west. This flight was very close to the Laotian border. The skirmish was near a branch of the Ho Chi Minh Trail extending into South Vietnam from Laos. We dropped our soft ordnance with pinpoint accuracy and headed east for home.

My June flights were over and I headed for the club. Most of the conversations were about the very active rumors about transferring to

Japan. According to the most popular one, which I prayed had credence, both F-4J squadrons, 232 and 334, would transfer to Iwakuni, Japan, and VMFA 323, the "Death Rattlers" currently at Iwakuni, would transfer in Country to Chu Lai. I felt being in Administration gave me a leg up on headquarters' correspondence and started spending as much time in Admin as possible. I wrote home about the rumor, cautiously. I was elated about this prospect because being in 334 would get me out of Vietnam a few weeks sooner. I mentioned again in a letter to Jan about going on R&R and her meeting me in Hawaii for a week. It was all tentative based on the actual deployment to Japan. Jan's response letter was ambiguous. I wondered what was going on. My sister knew, but wasn't saying yet. July entered like a lion.

On July 1, I had a night Steel Tiger sortie with Tyson. Tyson was good on this flight. The enemy seemed to be more subdued and there were no airbursts near us. On the way back to the base, on tower frequency during a rare moment of relative silence, a voice came up on the air and said, "I pushed the wrong rudder." Then there was a moment of utter radio silence, which I had not experienced since coming to Vietnam. That moment was broken by the same person who was even more startled by his goof-up saying, "Can you believe it? I pushed the wrong rudder." His transmission was soon followed by an unidentified voice declaring in aggravation, "Well push the right button!" I broke the silence that followed by requesting landing instructions for my Love Bug flight. I reflected on the errant radio transmissions, both major faux pas, and felt, "Somebody just earned a new nickname." After the flight was over, Tyson headed to the club. I headed for Ops to check the schedule and Read and Initial board. The rumors were true: we were transferring to Japan! I would wait for official notification and orders to express my joy but tonight it was time to celebrate. At the club I ran into Harlow.

He said, "Today isn't all good news. Do you remember Dennis Peek?"

I said, "Of course I do, since the beginning of OCS when we were stranded at Baltimore Airport."

Harlow said, "He died today. He rolled in on target in his A-4 Skyhawk and flew straight into the ground."

"Damn it," I said, "I hate this war." I was melancholy the rest of the night. Peek was a great guy, great Marine and pilot, handsome and intelligent, with a great future ahead of him. What a waste.

As I began to feel more comfortable on 334 flights, I started taking my camera again. The next day, I had a close air support with pilot King. We were on the wing of Trachta and his RIO. When the flight came up on the controller's frequency, the controller sounded really excited and said, "The bastards are shooting at me. I can't believe these crazy bastards are shooting at me. You guys can blow the shit out of 'em for me." And with that, the controller threw down a mark and cleared us in hot. Apparently our Love Bug flight did "blow the shit out of 'em" because we were credited with eleven KBMA. I thought to myself, there's another one for Cowboy and Indian as Dash One had us join up. Our two Phantoms proceeded out over the ocean east of Quang Tri and headed south for the base, not at altitude but fifty feet off the ocean. Trachta had the flight go into burner and we were causing rooster tails flying just above the water. It was exhilarating but it was also dangerous. I had heard of pilots "dicking" around after their mission was over. It was often an emotional release during a brief state of euphoria following an intense adrenaline rush due to a particularly hairy or scary mission.

Our flight was barely subsonic and all of a sudden I saw a couple of dark things in a blur pass by on the right. I asked King, "What was that?" Without response, the flight throttled and popped up. I could now see what was behind us that the pilots probably had acquisition of due to their forward visibility. Helicopters were flying low towards land from atop the deck of an LPA, a landing platform that basically was a small helicopter carrier. Our flight had flown through them. I thought, too close for my comfort zone. Many a good pilot has been killed by "hot dogging." I recalled the old adage, "There are old pilots and bold pilots, but there are no old, bold pilots." I preferred to play it by the book. Back at the base, I headed to Admin to see if there was more information on the Japan transfer.

As my flight returned to the base from a close air support the next day, I called the tower for landing instructions. Our Love Bug flight was number three in the pattern. As the first flight landed and cleared the runway, the second flight was cleared to land. As we approached the initial, Chu Lai base came under rocket attack and the tower controller obviously dove into his bunker without saying anything over the air. The lead Phantom of the second flight got to the end of the runway and blew a tire on shrapnel as he barely got onto the apron. His wingman blew both his tires during roll out and fouled the deck a little past halfway down the 8,000-foot runway. His RIO notified everyone in the air that the deck was foul even though the rocket attack seemed to be over. That closed Chu Lai airfield to traffic temporarily and all aircraft diverted to Da Nang, until further notice. At Da Nang, we refueled and waited a couple hours until Chu Lai was available again. Fortunately, tires were the only casualties. This time, the controller on duty deserved to have his ass chewed off. I totally understood him trying to save his butt but he could have cost others theirs. Our Love Bug 457 flight got back in time for dinner.

The Fourth of July passed without much fanfare or celebration in the combat zone. Our fireworks were airborne and on the ground. However, many individuals celebrated with alcohol. That night, while I was relaxing in my hooch, I heard a loud bloodcurdling scream. I grabbed my .38 revolver and ran out the front door hoping the base had not been invaded. Captain Bracken, a 334 pilot who lived in a hooch across from me, while inebriated, decided he was going to drive his Negrito knife through the front door of his hooch using an underhanded motion. The knife didn't pierce the door, it just lodged in it. Bracken's hand continued along the blade to the door nearly cutting off the four fingers of his right hand. Bracken was sent back to the States after several days in the hospital.

We were flying mostly CAS and Steel Tiger missions, commensurate with the operations of the war and U.S. forces being continuously engaged with enemy forces. On my next close air support sortie, my plane had a single generator failure, my second in Country. That caused the flight to be canceled but I was quickly re-scheduled. Other than an occasional radar malfunction, I never had another airborne problem or emergency. Missions were a different story.

I began a whole string of close air support hops for what seemed like days on end. From July 7 through July 16 (ten days), I flew fifteen sorties; thirteen of them were close air support missions. The string began with a morning close air support mission in Lieutenant Colonel Braddon's back seat. We launched with soft ordnance to hit enemy forces that were attacking the Phu Bai Combat Base of Army and Marines, located south of Hue. We were not the only ones on target and once multiple air strikes were completed, the enemy ended their assault.

The same afternoon, I flew in pilot Hajduk's back seat on a close air support sortie. I liked Hajduk. We were on the wing of Ops O Pieri, who led our flight back up to Dong Ha near the DMZ with napes and snakes. Amidst enemy fire, we put our ordnance on the controller's mark and after joining up over the Gulf, headed to Chu Lai. I was scheduled as lead RIO about as often as Dash Two; either was okay with me.

The next day I had a close air support flight with an on-target time shortly after dawn in the back seat of pilot Woody. We were Dash Two, briefing in darkness and launching at sunrise. Our planes were loaded with hard ordnance (six 1000-pound bombs) to do some damage to enemy forces (possibly PAVN) in the A Shau Valley. Nobody anywhere near was able to sleep in. The bombs worked very well on a target covered with the thick forest canopy. Our bomb concussions were visible as they exploded. For some reason, most controllers had ceased providing immediate bomb damage assessments. Sometimes days passed before we knew results or heard them at subsequent Intel briefings, if we heard them at all. By then we had already flown more flights so the reports lost their luster. Once I realized bomb damage assessments were padded, BDAs became irrelevant and certainly not worth the number of lives lost and the amount of tax dollars wasted. There was no doubt our flights were devastating to viable targets, so I clung to the premise that we were saving some American lives.

That night I had a nearly three-and-a-half-hour-long BARCAP flight with Rath. Fortunately, we had a 2200-hour time on target. By the time we got back to Chu Lai, my ass was sore and dragging. I flopped into my rack just before the air raid siren announced incoming rockets. For the second time, I donned my helmet and flak jacket and hit the floor without rushing into the bunker. I might have fallen asleep right then and there but the desire not to be a meal for the lizards was strong enough for me to crawl back into my rack.

I rousted myself out of bed for my morning CAS mission back in the A Shau Valley and then had another close air support in the afternoon near Khe Sanh. The war was NOT slackening. Both close air support hops went fine and though both received fire, each had great results. I went to bed early knowing I had another early brief. I'd made chow but hadn't been social at the club in days. In the middle of my string of close air support sorties, July 12 happened, another day I would never forget.

I completed a daybreak ground directed bombing mission, spent time in Admin, and after lunch, headed to my early afternoon CAS brief with Lieutenant Colonel Braddon. The close air support sortie was for an Army unit in the Hoi An River basin. I contacted the airborne tactical air controller and things were interesting from the get go. We had a 20 mm Gatling-style machine gun pod and sixteen 250-pound retardant fin bombs (D2a—delta two alphas). Dash Two had napalm and 500 pounders. We had briefed for 10-degree runs. The airborne controller indicated an Army unit had casualties on the ground requiring medical evacuation, but the enemy was too close (just thirty meters!), and had our friendlies pinned down. The controller was very nervous about the proximity of the friendlies but the situation was getting desperate to remove wounded. Braddon suggested that we make some passes to suppress the enemy fire with our machine gun. The controller conditionally okayed this. He said he would only clear us if it looked good and then threw down a mark. Our run-in heading could not be in over our troops even though their location was well defined. Braddon and I were cleared in on the target. We were not cleared to fire on the first run but just flying over the enemy at fifty feet had an effect. On the next run Braddon unleashed several deadly accurate bursts of the machine-gun. I knew immediately we were not making a few runs and heading back to the base. It was turning into a nail biter. Braddon and I rolled in on target, making run after run, sometimes shooting and sometimes not.

The enemy now became preoccupied with the flight and I was certain they were firing at our plane. The friendlies were engaging with automatic weapons fire, forcing the enemy into breaking contact. At that point, the medevac helicopters swooped in to snatch up the casualties. It was a very intense flight, a total adrenaline drain. The friendlies were still relatively close, but falling back as my Love Bug flight set up for its napalm and bombing runs. Our planes made repeated runs, dropping our bombs in pairs instead of clusters until we expended all our ordnance. The enemy disengaged. What was supposed to be a simple close air support sortie lasting less than an hour, turned into a very harrowing, emotionally and physically draining mission lasting over two hours. Making over twenty runs on the target area violated all kinds of standard operating procedures. I never knew the enemy body count but felt elated that our ground forces were removed from harm's way by Marine aviation. It was a very rewarding moment. Braddon and I were both written up for an award. I was awarded a Bronze Star for my air medal and I've never known what Lieutenant Colonel Braddon received. My citation reads:

For heroic achievement in aerial flight while serving with Marine Fighter/Attack Squadron 334, Marine Aircraft Group 15 in connection with combat operations against the enemy in the Republic of Vietnam. On 12 July 1969, First Lieutenant Thorsen launched as a Naval Flight Officer aboard the lead aircraft in a flight of two F-4 Phantom aircraft assigned the mission of providing close air support for the emergency medical evacuation of casualties from a United States Army unit which was heavily engaged in combat with a large hostile force south the Hoi An in Quang Nam Province. Following a briefing on the ground situation by the Tactical Air Controller (Airborne), First Lieutenant Thorsen provided precise flight data which enabled his pilot to execute a strafing run on an enemy machine gun emplacement and silence the hostile fire. When the proximity of the enemy to the landing zone precluded the delivery of heavier ordnance, First Lieutenant Thorsen, undaunted by the intensity of the hostile fire directed at his aircraft, skillfully monitored his instruments and provided a continuous flow of vital information which enabled his Phantom to be maneuvered on multiple simulated bombing and strafing runs which diverted the enemy fire to his flight while the transport helicopters entered the precarious zone and extracted the casualties. When the extraction aircraft lifted out of the area, he expertly and rapidly computed navigational and ordnance delivery data as his pilot executed repeated bombing runs and delivered all of his ordnance on the target with pinpoint accuracy. First Lieutenant Thorsen's courage, superior airmanship, and unwavering devotion to duty at great personal risk were instrumental in accomplishing the hazardous mission and were in keeping with the highest traditions of the Marine Corps and of United States Naval service. Presented on behalf of the President by H.W. Buse Jr., Lieutenant General U.S. Marine Corps, Commanding General, Fleet Marine Force, Pacific.

Due to the slowness of military bureaucracy, I actually did not receive this award until I was back in the United States. In retrospect, the award rather glorified the mission. I actually felt it was for Braddon and I just happened to be in the back seat, though it was one hairy flight. I also resented the fact that GIBs were awarded something less than pilots for the same mission. RIOs believed "Same day, same way"; in other words, whatever the pilot gets, the RIO should get. Years later the policy would change to that but there were no retroactive upgrades. I thought of the casualties as our flight returned to the base, low on fuel but out of harm's way. I inspected our plane back on the flight-line and was amazed there were no bullet holes. Maybe the enemy was too busy keeping their heads down or, better yet, being killed by Marine Air! Truly God was watching out for me.

I finally got to the club for some down time but could not clear my head. Braddon and I did not talk about the mission that night; in fact, we never talked about that mission. I never even knew we'd been written up for a medal. It came after the fact and our next missions were already scheduled. The trend continued; CAS missions were the order of the day. I briefed with pilot Rath the next morning for napes and snakes and we headed out for a close air support northwest of Da Nang, where suspected enemy had been firing rockets at the base. While waiting our turn on target, I took movies of two Air Force Phantoms dropping napalm on the side of a hill. When it came our turn on target we did the same and headed back to Chu Lai. We did not receive enemy fire that I was aware of. The numbers and types of flights were now creating a little delinquency in my letter writing, so I wrote some shorter ones and spaced out mailing them to make up for it. I didn't want Jan or my parents to worry. I was certain they did anyway and rightfully so. Little did they know.

My afternoon close air support mission was a little more "spectacular." Pilot Ahrens and I were on the wing of Lieutenant Colonel Braddon back out in the A Shau Valley. The flights ahead of us must have been numerous or very accurate because we were no longer needed. No suitable substitute target was acquired, so we proceeded out over the ocean east of Chu Lai to dump our bombs. Ahrens, after release, surprised me by hitting afterburner and pulled the nose straight up. I had my camera with me and took a photo of a small island in my right-hand mirror just before we leveled off, then we "dicked" around along the coast for a while before landing.

My close air support mission the next morning with pilot Rath (again) was back out in the A Shau Valley where Ahrens and I had been dismissed the previous day. Apparently the enemy hadn't had enough of our air power and was causing hell once more. Some napalm and our 500 pounders quieted them down. At dusk, Tyson and I had a Steel Tiger mission at the Laotian border not far from my morning sortie. There was nothing special about the flight, our target or delivery and recovery, but there was something significant. It was a milestone that I didn't realize until days later. It was my hundredth combat sortie. I received a 100-mission patch and had it sewed on my flight jacket. Though proud of the patch and my personal accomplishment, I was fully aware that our presence in Nam wasn't amounting to a hill of beans and how many more combat sorties I would fly was unknown. But with this milestone, an incredible thing happened to me during flights. I relaxed. It was a place I had never been. I was not uncomfortable with it, just amazed at it. It was something I never expected to happen and had no idea where it came from. Even though I relaxed, I never let down my guard nor modified my conduct or behavior in any way. I just seemed to be at peace with everything. I knew God was in this too.

Chapter 20

The Rumors Were True!

No more scuttlebutt; we received the news we'd been waiting for. Official word came that both F-4J squadrons, 232 and 334, were transferring to Japan. It was even written in the *Stars and Stripes* "rag" paper. The event was billed in the States as de-escalation. But the truth was that the new F-4s, the J model with pulse-Doppler radar systems, were going to Japan to assist the Air Force in being a deterrent against North Korean aggression. Squadron 334 was relocating the end of August with 232 following in September. I didn't care what the reason was or exactly when it happened, as long as it did. And based on past history, I wasn't going to hold my breath or believe it until I was on a departure plane. That was not the only news that day. News of the Ted Kennedy, Chappaquiddick fiasco was circulating through the squadron. I thought Kennedy was another womanizer getting his just desserts, his ass in a sling. My thoughts were with the Kopeckne family. I didn't give a damn what happened to Ted. Political discussions and dialogue, in letters between my father and I, never waned. There was no love lost for me with Washington ilk. I wrote this in a letter later that day: "You don't have to be very old to know the difference between political rhetoric and outright lying; campaign promises are usually only that."

My next close air support sortie was in the back seat of Major Oliver from the group. I had never flown with him before nor even heard of him for that matter. I've never forgotten him. Of course, we were Dash Two on Captain Trachta's wing because visiting pilots couldn't lead any of our flights regardless of rank. We were back in the Hoi An River basin with napes and snakes in ten-degree runs. The area was hot and the enemy was giving U.S. troops holy hell. Over the target area, while getting set up for our runs, Oliver informed me he preferred fifty feet level for napalm release. I was in shock. No pilot had ever disregarded what was briefed, other than for a state of emergency. I didn't like it but couldn't do or say anything about it. Before I could gather my wits about me, Oliver called in hot and our Phantom headed in on the target. I called off airspeed and altitude, even though altitude was irrelevant. This run was all visual. Apparently, Oliver didn't think jinking was important either. Jinking, when dropping ordnance low and slow, was always a good idea so we wouldn't be an easy target. In my mind, it was imperative to survival, especially in the Hoi An. Our napalm was on target but I was getting real uncomfortable in the back seat and couldn't wait to finish our next run.

I saw trees closer up than I ever had seen before and it really was pissing me off. Dropping bombs forced us to a higher altitude delivery, thankfully. Dash One was on and off with their second run and Oliver called, "Dash Two's in hot." I read off altitude and airspeed. At "mark, mark," Oliver pulled up off target and I assumed we would join up with Trachta and head back to Chu Lai. Before I could breathe easier, the controller came up on the radio and said, "Dash Two, negative on your drop." So Oliver called Trachta and said, "Dash One, Two's going to make another run." Trachta responded, "Roger that," when he could have told him no and to join up. So much for the two-run restriction. My surprise came when Oliver, on the downwind leg, came up on hot mic and asked me, "Lieutenant, how do I re-arm the racks?" There was no Weapon Selection Control Panel in the back seat but I knew how to do it.

I said to Oliver in an aggravated voice, "Go to rocket dispense and then back to bombs cluster or ripple." I wasn't about to mention the option for single or pairs but they were plainly labeled on the selection dials right in front of his control stick. I hoped he selected cluster. I was ready to get the hell out of there. Then I heard, "Dash Two's in hot" and the controller cleared us hot. Once again Oliver used the same run-in heading, altitude and airspeed with no jinking. I called "Mark, mark" at the appropriate altitude and did something I hadn't done before.

I looked out of my canopy directly at the ground and then looked in my left mirror as our plane pulled up. Everything was going by fast but I could see muzzle flashes. I didn't care if they were friendly or not, I had had enough. The controller reported no drop again and Trachta told Oliver to join up. Oliver's response was quick and matter of fact, "Negative, Two's making another run." I was incensed. Trachta did not respond but held at altitude circling the target. At this point, I was just along for the ride but the problem was if Oliver killed himself, I'd be dead too. Oliver called in hot again and was cleared. Once again, there was no jinking, no alteration of the run-in heading, altitude, or airspeed. I had no choice but to give Oliver flight data because my ass was just as vulnerable. At pickle altitude, once again, our bombs did not release. Once again, Trachta said "Join up" and once again Oliver emphatically said negative and set up to make another run. I was livid. I knew without any ordnance going off the enemy was using us for target practice. I told Oliver I thought any further attempts were hopeless and that we should abandon the target and join up with Dash One. I barely got the words of my mouth when Trachta, again, told Oliver to join up. Oliver repeated negative and called in hot. I did my job and started praying. Oliver didn't jink and the bombs didn't drop. I held my breath praying Oliver would come to his senses and realize the bombs were never coming off. After the run, as our Phantom was climbing back to altitude, Oliver said to me, "I guess they aren't coming off."

My anger could not be disguised as I replied, "Obviously."

At this point I didn't care what Oliver thought of me; my opinion of him was solidified. We joined up with Dash One and returned to the base. I notified squadron ordnance personnel we were returning with bombs and Oliver made a silky smooth landing. Back on the flight-line, during the visual inspection of the aircraft, I found out why we couldn't drop our bombs. The electrical connection (called a "cannon plug") to the rack was completely disconnected. The bombs would have never come off. The racks with the bombs attached could have been jettisoned in an emergency, but the bombs could not be dropped armed to explode. That made me angrier at Oliver for risking our lives in an exercise of futility. What I found next and pointed out to Oliver was a bullet hole through the port wing flap, just inches aft of the wing. The wing had an internal fuel cell and the bullet was perhaps only a millisecond from hitting it, which could have caused it to explode. Oliver made no response; I could have killed him. In debrief, Trachta brought up the violation of SOP, stopping short of calling it insubordination. Oliver made no apologies. I went straight to flight scheduling and told Major Pieri that I would never fly with Oliver again and didn't.

I checked the bulletin board. There was a luncheon for General Buse, Commanding General of the Fleet Marine Forces in the Pacific, at the officer's mess at noon the next day. All officers were to attend. I had a close air support that morning and hoped it would run long so I wouldn't have to attend. Buse was brass and I couldn't have cared less about his presence but was curious why he was coming. My CAS went fine and I was not able to miss the lunch but the flight did make me late. To my chagrin, the only seat available was right across from the general. I had arrived in time to eat and the menu, amazingly, was steak and lobster. I had never had a meal of this caliber before and never would again while in Vietnam. I made small talk without divulging my real feelings. I wanted to tell him about my utter disdain for pilots receiving higher medals than RIOs for the same flight. I spent most of the time feeding my face without speaking to the general at any great length. When I did, I was cordial but all the while thinking we weren't accomplishing anything good while in Vietnam and the bombing of a "tree park" was evidence of it. I feared screwing up my chances to go to Japan, so I was civil and enjoyed a great lunch. I left as soon as I could and went back to my hooch unaware that I would be in Nam just five more weeks.

I was in the back seat of another visiting pilot, Lieutenant Colonel Wilson, on a close air support the next day. The leader of this flight was Captain Trachta again. The ordnance was 500-pound bombs and Zuni rockets. The controller briefed our target, a small village of about twenty-two thatched huts along the side of a river. The controller indicated that there was reportedly automatic weapons fire from this location. The controller put down a mark even though one was not needed: The village stood out like a sore thumb. Something just didn't ring right for me. As our flight took separation for our runs, I told Wilson, "With all due respect, Sir, I don't think we should hit this target."

The colonel replied, "Lieutenant, your objection is duly noted," as Dash One was cleared hot and Wilson and I soon followed suit.

I read off altitude and airspeed and then, "Mark, mark." Just like that, the village was destroyed and we returned to Chu Lai. I was not chastised for my remark. It was never mentioned, but I never forgot it. Collateral damage was inevitable.

I went to lunch and then checked my mail. I got a letter from Jan agreeing to R&R in Hawaii. It was not difficult to set up; I was an officer in Admin. I scheduled it for August 8. Also going that same week were 334 pilots Hajduk, Ahrens, and Frost. We were all excited and really looking forward to it.

But not everything was rosy. Sadly, the next morning a lance corporal in another squadron accidently died when he tripped a lanyard wire during routine maintenance on the ejection seat of an F-4 and promptly ejected himself into the roof of the maintenance hangar. It was another reminder that aviation pay was hazardous duty pay and war was hell. I was glad not to be their ground safety officer. I hoped to get out of hell soon. But the real history for this day, July 20, was made in the States, or more accurately, in space. Apollo 11's Eagle had landed at Tranquility base and Neil Armstrong walked on the moon. I lamented over being in the Vietnam hell hole and not being able to witness it firsthand as millions around the world had. But I was nonetheless proud of my country and NASA's accomplishment and once back in the States I watched every other subsequent NASA event that I could. Even though they were all good, except the shuttle disasters, nothing filled the void my Vietnam tour had made.

Later in the day, I had a hard ordnance close air support near the "Interdiction point," the junction of North and South Vietnam and Laos at the west end of the DMZ. This was always a very hot area, close to the Ho Chi Minh Trail, and saturated with anti-aircraft artillery. U.S. ground forces were fully engaged with the enemy and suffering heavy casualties. Numerous flights had already been on target before I checked in our Love Bug flight. We were told to hold and I observed as much as I could on the ground while two other Phantoms finished their runs. The radio traffic was fast and furious and the situation on the ground was critical. The controller wanted all the air support he could get and got our flight on station quickly. We had bombs and rockets with high explosive heads. The controller gave us a run-in heading and threw down a mark. The controller also said the area was very hot, but requested multiple runs—in other words, not pickling everything off at once. As my pilot set up for our first run, I scanned the horizon and the ground and then my instruments. Then Rath called us in hot. Our controller replied, "Roger lead, you're cleared hot." As our plane dove toward the deck, I fixed on the instruments, calling off airspeed and altitude. At "mark, mark," Rath fired rockets with deadly aim at the target.

As our plane pulled off target, my attention was drawn to the APR-25 scope on the left side of my front console. The screen of that round scope, smaller than the diameter of a tennis ball, displayed each AAA site that was tracking our plane. Radar guided AAA sites (probably 57mm, 37mm, and/or 22mm) were represented by a line on the scope, indicating the direction of the site from the plane's location/heading. The triple A site didn't have to be firing artillery shells; it could just be tracking. The caliber didn't matter; any one of them could be deadly. I once again looked at the ground for muzzle flashes as Dash Two called in hot and was cleared. The controller was varying the drop instructions, clock position, and distance from his mark. He obviously was seeing something we couldn't. Due to the brightness of sunlight, I wasn't seeing airbursts at that moment. Dash Two was off the target and Rath and I were cleared in hot. Again, the position and distance from the controller's smoke, which was beginning to dissipate, were adjusted. After firing additional Zuni rockets, while our plane pulled out of the dive and began to climb, my attention was again drawn to the scope.

There were more lines on the scope and I was beginning to see puffs of dark smoke in the air. I was glad to hear my pilot request a new run-in heading as we came off target. It was granted and the controller put down another mark. I looked at the APR-25 scope as my banking plane called in hot. There were more lines on the scope. I called off altitude and airspeed, then, "Mark, mark." On this dive, we released our first two bombs. My eyes immediately went back to the scope. There were more lines displayed. The lines were numerous and even though the scope was not full, some of the lines nearly overlapped. The triple A literally seemed to be all around us, coming from every direction and there was more smoke in the sky from the airbursts. In fact, the sky was turning gray and, in some cases, black with the smoke. At that moment, I did something I never had done before and never did again. I reached up and turned off the scope. I didn't want to see it.

Our flight made several more runs until all our bombs were dropped and we cleared the area. The next flight was on target immediately. I breathed a sigh of relief and when we got back to Chu Lai and out of the plane, I was sopping wet with sweat. The BDA was not received for days. It revealed that many of the AAA emplacements were disabled or destroyed and the body count huge. I thought Arc Lights would be more effective and less dangerous for this mission and then my thoughts turned to Japan, home and Jan, R&R, and Hawaii. I felt that none of it could come soon enough and hoped it would come, period.

There was a live floor show at the club that night. For a change it was not a group of ugly female Koreans playing and singing lousy rock 'n' roll imitations. The entertainment of the evening was a young round eye: a U.S.-born, decent-looking, redheaded vocalist who had a good voice and band. Marine Aircraft Group 15 Commanding Officer Colonel Rash's favorite floorshow was here again for the weekend. It was rumored that Rash and the redhead had a thing. I didn't care about that, just that the show was decent. Everyone was enjoying the performance when suddenly the base came under rocket attack. There wasn't enough bunker space for the large number of personnel at the club. Fortunately, the rockets weren't near us. At the all-clear, the show went on. Obviously, the colonel had connections. Not long after the attack, "Puff" showed up and began working over the suspected origin of the rockets. Puff was an AC-47 modified twin-engine prop plane that had a sophisticated, highly effective, Gatling gun mounted to shoot out the side door like the Huey gunship. The gun's rounds looked like a flame shooting out the airplane door. It made a whirling sound like a strong wind, until it quit. Then it made a unique mechanical sound like a huge metal wheel or saw blade, with a chain attached, coming to a stop. It was another sound that I would never forget. There were no more rockets that night as the show continued.

I had the duty the next day (the twenty-fourth) and did not fly when Apollo 11 splashed back down. It was a bittersweet moment. To me, this great feat of technology and bravery for the United States was somehow ironic in lieu of the fact that it occurred as war raged. And it was raging. To me, victory now seemed impossible. I thought it all a moot point and a total waste. I felt that the warmongers and fat cats were benefiting, because no one else was. I, like most other combatants, knew the U.S. was losing an average of 125 male youth per week, a great many of them black. That total didn't include those who died later or were maimed and/or scarred for life, including mentally. I was saddened by the precarious situation of the ground troops.

I went to Admin to check on my R&R status. It had not yet been approved. It was pouring down rain as I headed back to my hooch. Once the rain quit it was hot and humid again, like a hot August day in Texas. I drank a Coke and played my guitar. I was improving but wasn't really good. I just enjoyed it and it was a small temporary escape. I wrote home, telling my folks the moon shot made me feel patriotic and that my military service in some small way contributed. But the truth was I didn't believe it. I also wrote that I thought the Ted Kennedy thing sure sounded suspicious. I told them that I only had another month of combat flying based on when the squadron would depart for Japan. I thanked my mom again. Then I wrote in response to my dad's comment about incompetence and corruption at high levels: "What will ruin the U.S. is for the factions who are trying to destroy America by corruption and chaos from inside (trying to break down our basic institutions—family, education, religion and government), to be successful. And believe me the leak in the dyke has long since started. The solution is simple to say but difficult to accomplish and that is for each person to improve their own lot, with particular attention paid to his/her progeny." I also told my dad that the "Peter Principle" was alive and well in the military. I omitted everything about my missions.

The next day I had a soft ordnance close air support mission in Captain Rudy's back seat, with Frost and Foltz on our wing. The enemy was once again near Hamburger Hill. It was a difficult target. I had my movie camera with me but due to the intensity of the mission, couldn't take any footage. As we headed back to the base, Frost decided that he was going to do a canopy roll over our plane. I started my camera and Frost started his roll from our starboard side. His F-4 going over our plane looked good while filming him through the canopy and then it all fell apart on the port side as Frost ended up not next to our plane but way left, lower and aft. I laughed. It made a pretty good movie but it was so-so in the technical execution department. It didn't matter. Once back at Chu Lai, we headed into the break. After the hop, I headed to admin to see if there was progress on my R&R request.

As I crossed the road towards the hangar, there was a loud whoosh and bang and then dense black smoke slowly rose above the revetments on the flight-line. Somehow, while testing ordnance on one of our squadron F-4s, the ordnance technician had inadvertently launched a Sparrow missile. The missile impacted the revetment across on the other side of the flight-line. Two fortunate things occurred preventing a huge disaster and most likely loss of life and at least one plane. The rocket had not traveled far enough to arm and therefore did not explode. The second lucky thing was that the revetment it impacted was empty and did not have a fully loaded, fueled plane parked in it. It was all very fortuitous. The avionics technician learned a very valuable lesson and lived to tell about it. He regained his hearing days later. Once again, I was happy I wasn't the ground safety officer. My R&R was approved. Now I had to get word home. I wrote Jan a letter explaining everything and that she would receive a packet from the government with a voucher for her plane ticket. But I knew the timing was not good (potentially too late) and there was a very real possibility she would not get her packet in time.

Aircrews, one at a time, were getting a little break in the action by being scheduled for a flight late in the day, near the Laotian or Cambodian border. After the flight, they would divert to Thailand (Ubon or Udorn AFB) overnight for a little time in town. Some guys bought jade and some bought time with women. I was scheduled for my flight the next day when word came down from the Group HQ saying they were wise to our unauthorized R.O.N. (remain overnight) and to stop them that day, until further notice. I never made it to Thailand. I thought, they can cancel Thailand but they cannot cancel my R&R. That was authorized by HQMC and paid for by the government. Because of the Japan certainty, I got some negative vibes from some of my peers for going, but I didn't care. Army and Marine personnel going on R&R stood down for two days before departure, so I would get nine days away from the combat zone and would leave for Japan within a few weeks after R&R. The reason behind the new policy of standing down before R&R was that a Marine pilot was killed the day before he was to leave to meet his wife in Hawaii and she was already on her way, only to get there and get the news he was dead.

My thoughts were of Jan and our week in Hawaii. It was August 1. I got nervous about the R&R plans, knowing I couldn't totally rely on the government or postal system to get the packet and her ticket on time. I felt I should somehow personally contact Jan with the details and let her know about the R&R schedule and the arrangements to meet. There were no phones like there were in the Philippines. There was, however, a short-wave radio station that could make a hookup. I arranged a call to my parents and gave the details to them to relate to Jan. Basically, she was to get her own ticket at her expense, if necessary, and fly to Honolulu on the eighth, if she hadn't received the packet. I would meet her at the airport. I was not aware that pilots of two major airlines were threatening to strike and had no further communication with anyone back home.

That night, an enemy rocket hit the ammunition depot in Da Nang, causing a huge explosion, tremendous damage, and numerous casualties. The smoke was visible at Chu Lai. For a time it looked like it might affect personnel who were going on R&R that week. I felt sorry for the families of the casualties but now started feeling anxious about R&R. This was my only window. If I missed it, it was gone. Things settled down over the next few days and my R&R orders were honored. At the club that night, Doug Harlow told me about his BARCAP flight the night before. He said he and his pilot, Cliff Lowry, had been on station about an hour when they were given a target, an aggressive MiG in the area. Doug said things got tense when the controller began an intercept. Once "painted," the MiG headed for Hainan Island, China's territory. Going supersonic, Doug vectored their plane in for a kill and requested permission to fire. Both planes were about to go feet dry over land, a border violation for us that would have caused an international incident, when the controller said, "Skip it, skip it, skip it." Cliff immediately got them back into international waters. Doug was extremely disappointed knowing they could have had a kill and lamented over it for days. He missed a chance to accomplish exactly what we had been trained to do. In a sense, the incident epitomized exactly what the war effort was: a waste of time, money, and American talent.

In a few weeks, if everything went according to plan, I would deploy to Japan and most likely not return to Vietnam. That was the best I could hope for and I prayed hard for it. I had three more days before I stood down. On a close air support hop near the DMZ the next day, the "viable target" issue was evident. Our flight was taking small arms fire from within the de-militarized zone and as I pondered our inability to strike on our own volition, in a bold move my pilot decided to use rockets against this enemy. Faulkner and I rolled in and sprayed the area where the fire was coming from. Instantly the codeword for border violation came up on the guard channel. It took me a minute to realize that it was us. I said to Faulkner, "Hey, that's us."

Faulkner's reply pretty much summed it up, "Who gives a shit?"

I responded, "Roger that." After the run, no more fire came from the area. There would be no KBMA for the sortie. There were no repercussions either. On my close air support sortie the next morning, we were west of Khe Sanh where the enemy threatened to overrun the Marine outpost. We hammered them with napes and snakes while they shot at us, and then quickly headed back to Chu Lai. At dusk, I had another ground directed bombing mission near the interdiction point where we recently received heavy fire. It was docile this time. I stood down for R&R after this flight.

The next afternoon, I flew to Da Nang. My orders authorized civilian attire but I got dirty looks when I wore them. As we landed in Da Nang, I could plainly see the smoke still rising from the hollowed-out ammo dump. Hajduk, Ahrens, Frost, and I were all in good spirits. We stayed overnight in the BOQ in Da Nang and then took our flight to Hawaii the next day. We traveled overnight but it was still Saturday and due to my anxiety and anticipation I slept very little. All four of us had reservations at the Hawaiian Princess.

I got a rental car and checked into the hotel. I had been nervous the whole time after leaving Chu Lai. I had no information on Jan. I didn't know if she got the government packet, was going to be able to get a flight or if she was even coming, and if so, when she would arrive. I crashed and slept.

When I got up I phoned the airport and asked when the last flight from Dallas, Texas, was due to arrive. With the information, I headed for the airport. If she wasn't on this flight, plan B was to call her parents. I arrived at the gate, bought an orchid lei, and waited. In those days, some of the airlines were still using steps to act as a ramp from the plane to the tarmac. As the last plane from Dallas arrived and the people started to disembark, Jan was the first person off the plane. I couldn't believe my luck. I was ecstatic things had miraculously worked out. We rushed to each other and embraced.

Jan asked me how I knew which flight and I said I guessed. Jan said she never got the government packet and just bought a first-class ticket. Wives who didn't, were delayed in getting to Hawaii because of two airlines' pilot strikes. Some, sadly, were delayed so much that their flights arrived after their husbands' flights had already left to go back to the combat zone. This onus was on the airlines and not the government but it was a travesty to many, especially the patriotic servicemen at that time. I felt sorry for any of them who were seriously affected but for the moment I was jubilant. Jan couldn't believe how brown I was. Unbeknownst to me, that great tan was probably the trigger for a skin cancer that surfaced on my forehead years later. Jan and I went to dinner on the strip of Waikiki and then back to the hotel for sex. To me it was great; to Jan it was an effort. I had no idea what was going on with her back in Texas and she wasn't saying.

The next morning we went to breakfast on Waikiki. It was there we saw the headlines about Sharon Tate and the whole week we were in Hawaii, the headlines were about the Tate, LaBianca murders. We planned the week out with a mixture of sightseeing and privacy. We went to places like Blowhole and snorkeled in Hanauma Bay. We drove to Pali Lookout, then Diamond Head and watched the sunset on Waikiki. We went to a bird sanctuary and a sealife park. We went to the Polynesian Cultural Center, based on a recommendation of one of Jan's friends. The bus was nearly full with other tourists and most of them well on in years, while we were twenty-five and twenty-three years old respectively. We definitely felt out of place. The cultural center was great as was the evening entertainment but on the bus ride back to the hotel, an elderly woman began to sing the song, "What the world needs now, is love, sweet love," and several others joined in. It irked me to no end. How ironic, I thought: in a few days I would leave paradise and go back to killing people again. My ire instantly turned into sadness. While together, we discussed our separated activities. Other than work, Jan was a little vague. I candy coated most of my missions, but in the end, a week was not enough. It had flown by. Each day in Hawaii was overshadowed with the dread of going back into combat. Jan's flight was earlier than mine and amidst a lot of tears she departed on her plane. It had been wonderful, but surreal and brief.

While waiting for my plane, I had time to think. Things with Jan were different. And then I thought, it wasn't just her; I was different too, but not for the same reasons. I would eventually dread the knowledge of Jan's activities while I was deployed. If there was a silver lining to any of this, it was that my time remaining in Vietnam was short. I prayed hard for strength, Japan, and just about everything else. Outside my plane's departure gate, I joined the three pilots. We all were pretty glum. We talked about Japan. In a few hours, we were back on the plane headed for Da Nang. I tried not to have somber thoughts as the plane headed west to Vietnam and this time crossing the International Dateline was unceremonious and inconsequential. In less than twenty-four hours we were back in the combat zone flying sorties. I had two the next day.

The first one was a pre-dawn ground directed bombing sortie with Trachta. A week in Hawaii didn't change my opinion of the war. I hadn't lost my edge and got right back into the swing of things but my sleep schedule had changed due to the time zone difference. My 0430 brief was very difficult to wake up for. The hop up near the de-militarized zone was perfect for getting me started and probably woke up some other folks as well. We were back in time for breakfast. It was August 18 and the squadron was a hive of activity now that planning the transfer to Japan had begun in earnest. By this time, I had come to know most of the 334 aircrew, flown with lots of them and liked many, including Trachta. Many of them were looking forward to rotating home within days of getting to Japan. I felt sorry for them in a way. The military was obligated to get them back in the States on the one-year anniversary of the tour deployment date. Consequently, they would not be able to see the sights I was about to see. Before my afternoon brief, I spent time in Admin. In the midst of my busyness, I found out I was put in charge of the rear echelon. The word "transfer" did not only mean moving from Vietnam to Japan; it meant a large number of original squadron personnel were at the end of their tour and rotating back to the States. And that meant numerous new members were joining the unit to replace them, putting Administration on overload.

That afternoon I launched on my close air support with Major Pieri. We were back out in the Hoi An River basin with napes and snakes and as soon as we rolled in on target we started drawing fire. Now that I was short, taking fire had new relevance, heightening my awareness. At the beginning of my tour, with lots of missions to fly, it was something worth noting because it determined the points toward my medal count. Now, with the end in sight, it was beginning to cause me great angst. I never worried about enemy fire during missions unless I saw it and even then it didn't affect my focus. I was never preoccupied about it before flights either. I still wasn't; I just didn't want to die this close to the end with Japan in sight. Our close air support ended without incident and with good bombing results. Pieri and I were a good team. I was scheduled for two similar sorties the next day.

My early morning CAS, in Tyson's back seat, was near the interdiction point on a tributary of the Ho Chi Minh Trail where an army unit was pinned down. Once we headed in on the target all kinds of ground fire erupted. I guessed at this point I was going to get shot at all the way up to my final sortie. Tyson was on his game and the napalm from our plane, and that of our wingman, was on target because a bunch of the ground fire melted away after our first run. We dropped our deadly bombs and departed the area, assuming the bad guys had had a bad day.

My nearer-to-noon than afternoon close air support mission was switched from a sortie near the Cambodian border to a soft ordnance hop not far from our base. Our Americal Army unit was in a skirmish with a large enemy force at Quang Ngai and was suffering heavy casualties. When we checked with our controller, another flight was still making bombing runs, so we circled at altitude waiting our turn. It was a "no brainer" that we'd get small arms fire during this hop. I watched the other flight on target and paid close attention to the ground forces activities. I was certain that when we were through with our runs, all the army personnel had to do was clean up but mostly I hoped U.S. deaths were minimal. Very often U.S. and ARVN forces fought together, both suffering casualties. We rarely knew who the forces were and mostly only knew we were assisting friendly forces. Once pilot Oldham and I were cleared in hot, we and our wingman dropped our napalm and bombs with pinpoint accuracy and then headed home. The flight was so brief, I made it back to the base in time for another organizational meeting before Admin shut down for the day.

The squadron's preparation for deployment moved at lightning speed. Fellow RIO George Menk was assigned to assist me with the troops in the rear echelon, which meant neither of us would be in the back seat of a Phantom when we left Vietnam. I didn't care as long as I got out in something propelled by jet engines. The transport plane we would be on fit that criterion. We had to attend many miscellaneous meetings and all preparatory meetings, including some in Da Nang. I hoped this might limit the number of sorties I would fly the next few days. When the flight schedule was circulated, I had two more flights the next day. The number and types of flights I was flying made my air medal count rapidly rise. I had not checked nor did I care about the count, just survival. After a late meeting was over, I went to chow and then the club where I ran into pilot Frost. We reminisced about our R&R and Frost joked, "now that I'm back from Hawaii, the waitresses here look ugly again." They were. There were many unfamiliar faces at the club that night. Most turned out to be part of the VMFA 323 advance party. Many of those faces looked pretty long. I had no difficulty relating to their plight.

My next day's close air support flight with Captain Johns started with a 0900 brief. Nearly all my CAS hops recently were "hot" and I anticipated the same on this one, back out in the A Shau Valley. When we checked in with our controller, he wanted all the airstrikes he could get. Charlie had been active all through the night against one of our Marine units and some of their mortar rounds had been pretty accurate. Helicopters were having difficulty evacuating wounded. It was a fluid situation with many negative elements. All we needed was a good mark to do our thing. I hoped for the ground unit to be able to repel the enemy. My hope for us was to annihilate as many as we could and give the unit the advantage or a reprieve. This day, on our controller's mark, we dropped 500-pound bombs and fired rockets. Once our ordnance was expended, our controller indicated we had received enemy fire but did not provide bomb damage assessments and we flew back to Chu Lai.

My second hop was a late afternoon Steel Tiger mission near the Laotian border with Tex Cagle, who was now Executive Officer of his squadron—VMFA-115. I didn't know why he was flying with our unit but was glad to be in his back seat. Cagle was talkative. I guess he didn't recall his tirade at the promotion ceremony. I still liked him and not just because he was from Texas. I told him I still resented having missed his party, which was now forever ago. Cagle asked me how things were and I surprised myself by saying, "Very good." Of course, I was going to Japan in less than two weeks and had just returned from R&R in Hawaii. The flight lasted barely an hour but our interaction was very amiable and our mission went very well. Cagle wished me luck in Japan and I wished him the same with his career. He said maybe we could hook up in the States sometime. I said that would be nice but I never saw him again.

The next day Frost and I were on a CAS sortie near Tam Ky, close to Chu Lai, not far from the Hoi An or the Gulf. Our lead plane carried napalm and 250-pound fragmentary bombs with retardant fins. Our plane had rockets and a 20mm machine gun. It was the perfect ordnance for our mission, all delivered up close and personal in ten-degree runs. Our run-in heading was north to south so our downwind took us near the ocean. An army unit was engaged with enemy relatively close. Lead started things off with napalm and we followed with our machine gun. I watched our lead pilot's pinpoint bomb run and our controller indicated the enemy forces were on the run and quickly put down a new mark for us. While he was doing this, I looked out the right side of my canopy at the coastline and once again thought how beautiful this land could be if it weren't war torn. Then we were in hot on our second run impacting the controller's mark with rockets. As we pulled off target, Frost radioed the controller saying, "I've got more twenty mike mike if you want it." I knew the controller wouldn't turn it down and anticipated a third run, not worried about enemy fire at this point. If we had some at the beginning, it was gone now that the enemy was trying to save what asses they had left. We rolled in and ripped up the area the enemy was escaping through. The awesomeness of this weapon was almost euphoric to me. Back at the base, I had the rest of the day to assist with the extensive administrative task at hand. Japan was a lot closer than it had been just weeks earlier.

Obviously the war was not winding down, but 334 operations were. I had a morning close air support with Trachta near Khe Sanh at the Laotian border. The heavily wooded area furnished the enemy with good cover. That, however, would not protect them from Marine air. Our ordnance was 500-pound bombs and five-inch Zuni rockets with high-explosive heads. As I checked our flight in with the controller, he informed us that the AAA sites were active but U.S. troops were in dire need of close air support. It was an all-too-familiar scenario. Run-in headings were limited and I hoped we could stick to our two-run limit. The sky was overcast and threatening to rain. I'd had very few weather-related issues during most of my sorties but the overcast ceiling this day, at this location, pushed us lower to the ground to fulfill our mission. That wasn't something new; it was just unnerving and not something I wanted to do. That did not give the enemy an advantage but it did give him an opportunity. I'd had all the encounters I wanted with triple A. Our dive angles and release altitudes were recalculated and we were cleared in hot with our run-in heading. Our drops were good and our Phantoms joined up to head back to Chu Lai before many more airbursts went off. After lunch, I wrote a quick letter home and headed to Admin. Flying and working was helping the time pass quicker. It was August 22. For the moment, my two-point flights continued.

I was scheduled with yet another close air support the next day. Doc Tyson and I briefed the flight for a CAS in the A Shau Valley again. Our planes were loaded with hard ordnance to be delivered at 1100 hours. We launched and proceeded west. I contacted our controller who had us hold at altitude until the flight on target concluded its runs. Once again things were hot and heavy and AAA was apparent but it also seemed just out of reach. As we circled, I prayed for our ground forces, knowing I would soon be out of the combat zone and their hell was not over. We were called in and quickly put our bombs on the enemy location. Before we cleared the area, the next flight was cleared on station. As we headed back to Chu Lai, it was evident to me that our tactical efforts were effective but this war was not. I continued these thoughts during lunch. I didn't know it at the time but that hop was my last close air support sortie. Though transfer preparations were still meticulously being reviewed and revised, the end for us was near. I was scheduled for a BARCAP flight the next night. I wrote more letters home, all upbeat.

Pilot Storm and I briefed the BARCAP hop for a 2400 to 0200 hour time on target. We launched on the twenty-fourth and recovered on the twenty-fifth. The flight turned out to be routine with no incidents or plane issues. The biggest problem I had was staying awake. Fortuitously, it was my last combat mission. The VMFA-323 squadron was now operational and our squadron stood down from the war. I had flown a total of 123 combat missions. I had accumulated enough points for ten air medals. I received a Navy Unit Commendation for both VMFA 232 and 334 and got a Bronze Star Award for my mission with Lieutenant Colonel Braddon. All this was in addition to the usual medals and ribbons for being in the Vietnam Campaign and I still had six months left on my overseas tour. I had no regrets about leaving the combat zone. I regretted that our U.S. military was still in it.

After getting very little sleep, Menk and I went up to Da Nang for two days of planning. As the Officer in Charge of the rear echelon, I received my roster of personnel and itinerary. After the last brief, Menk and I had some free time before our flight back to Chu Lai. He suggested we go into the "Ville." I reminded him about the strict orders not to go into town, off base. Menk quickly dismissed that and talked me into going. In flight suits, armed with our snub nose .38s, we walked out of the front gate and crossed the bridge into downtown Da Nang. We got strange looks, especially when we went into one of the bars. Instantly, Vietnamese hookers tried to get us upstairs. I was already uncomfortable and very nervous about possible attempts on our lives, but being caught by the MPs would be worse. After some time and a couple beers, I convinced Menk we should get the hell out of there. We wandered the streets for a while, then headed back to the base and flew back to Chu Lai without incident or reprimand. We met with the troops and put out the word. Basically it was get your shit together and staged by the twenty-ninth and be in uniform, ready to go early on the thirtieth. We were flying to Iwakuni and having lunch on the way in Taipei, Taiwan. At Iwakuni we would all receive orders, quarters, and assignments.

On August 30, the plane was on the flight-line. It was a Navy plane resembling an airliner. It was the first time I truly allowed myself to believe we were leaving. There was always so much uncertainty with the military. (Years later, after I joined the reserves at Naval Air Station Dallas, nothing had changed.) Menk and I conducted roll call and all were present and accounted for. Apparently, no one wanted to stay in Vietnam. Many Navy personnel were also leaving on the same plane, mostly medical and dental personnel. A lot of them had been commissioned straight into the military. I knew all about protocol, rank-and-file, and was well aware of Navy rank, whether it was on their sleeves or their lapels. When the time came to board, I ended up boarding ahead of a couple of dentists who were Navy lieutenants. That pissed off the pilot (it was his ship) and he dressed me down for it. I let it go but was thinking the whole time, "Does this shit ever end?" I was in command of the Marine personnel; did it really matter one iota as we left Vietnam? But I apologized and went on. The dentists probably didn't care even if they noticed.

The plane got to Taiwan, and landed at an Air Force base near Taipei. I got off the plane to meet the Air Force liaison officer. Soon, a lieutenant colonel walked towards me. I saluted and introduced myself while he, looking around me towards the plane asked, "Where's your commanding officer?" I replied, having fun, "I'm the commanding officer," and continued, "Where's the mess hall?" After lunch, our plane proceeded to Iwakuni. I boarded after the medical staff, of course. At Iwakuni, everyone got their barracks and berthing assignments. I was surprised when I got to my BOQ. It was a four-plex. My fellow residents were Knudsen, Harlow, and Griffin. That night, I got the best night's sleep I'd had in six months. The next day, I found out that indigenous persons, local Japanese nationals, were the maids, whom we called a "house mouse." There was one per four-plex. Things were looking up. There was much to do to get settled in and flight operations were starting in two days. The squadron mission was changing. We would transition from mainly air-to-ground operations to mainly air-to-air operations. Our aircrews and those in 232 would become highly trained in air combat maneuvering and would soon assist the Air Force in standing the hot pad alert at Misawa AFB on the northern end of Honshu.

To keep current on air-to-ground work the squadron would periodically deploy to the Philippines. That sounded good to just about everyone but me. I got the sickest on ACM flights. But there was other really good news. The squadron was reverting to a five-day workweek and personnel would have weekends off unless standing the duty. Fantastic! It was heaven compared to where we had been and I called home to tell my parents and Jan. My parents were elated and began to relax. My mom was practically in tears. Jan was a different story. She seemed distant and her joy was only moderately expressed.

Chapter 21

Fox One

The next Monday morning, Commanding Officer D'Angelo addressed the squadron. He did not mix words. He told all hands to not incite the natives, to obey the law of the land, and respect their space and property. He cautioned us all not to end up in a Japanese jail. He reminded us that "Yen is money" (the exchange rate at that time was 355 yen to the dollar) and "There is no such thing as love," hoping to dissuade his young enlisted personnel from taking a young Japanese woman home to mom. After mentioning drunkenness and being unruly, D'Angelo generically outlined the squadron's new mission. Administration focused on base services, activities and privileges, uniform requirements and restrictions, local etiquette, liberty and the Ville, warning of safeguards, and utilizing common sense. Operations had the flight schedule already printed for Tuesday and informed aircrews that our 1300-hour briefing would review base ops, local FAA, and international flight rules. Maintenance indicated they were up and running for the next morning's hops. I studied the high altitude charts and took notes on the base nav aids and communications. After a brief time in Admin, I headed to my BOQ room and wrote another letter home. I wrote in part:

We actually got Labor Day off, my first holiday in over five months. I guess they thought we'd earned it. A group of us went up to Hiroshima, not that many miles north of our base. I forgot to buy postcards, so I'll just have to send you some photos. Hiroshima has been re-built and there is a beautiful park at ground zero ....

I am buying a motorcycle, a Honda 90 (cc) and getting an international driver's license. A bunch of us are doing it. I plan to see as much of the country as possible ...

The Officer's Club here is beautiful and the food is good, prepared by locals. The Exchange is fantastic, complete with all the "made in Japan's" you could want; so, send me a list. All I can say is this will probably be the best time of my life so far. "I'm lovin' it."

I certainly enjoyed your letter, Dad. I hope you turn to the pen in retirement. Your comment about the "Japanese seem to be able to simplify design, beautify the product and build it cheaper but durable," is all around me. Ingenuity at its best.

I'd forgotten what good music was until I put my ear to the radio stations here. They are comparable to Seattle or St. Louis. Or, maybe everything just sounds better now that I am out of the combat zone. Machs Nicht!

Mom thanks again for the letters and goodies. I don't think you realize the magnitude of the positive impact of your loving, caring, thoughtful, gracious act to me and those I shared with. Do not hold Christmas for me. It's Christmas everyday here. Jan will be coming here and we will have it together. We'll do my part of the Thorsen family celebration in March when I get back to the States.

Our Mamasan does our laundry and keeps our rooms. The government pays their salaries. I like it here!

Love, Terry

After the letter, I headed to the club for dinner with peers. The food was excellent. Everyone was in great spirits.

Flight Operations began on September 2 with a boom. I had a morning aerial combat maneuvering flight with Baird. The hop went fine. I was nauseous near the end but didn't barf. After touchdown, for whatever reason, Baird requested to be cleared onto the high-speed off ramp. The tower denied the request, so our F-4 Phantom continued to roll out and decelerate to the end of the runway. I busied myself with pulling the IFR probe circuit breaker, etc., and when I looked up out of my canopy, to my surprise, the last exit ramp from the runway was going by, which meant the plane was about to roll off the end. I had no idea what Baird was doing but he was so distracted he didn't have his eyes outside the cockpit. I was so caught by surprise that momentarily I was at a loss for words until I, for the lack of something better, blurted, "Whoa!" over the hot mic. Baird braked so hard that he locked the brakes and sheared off so much tread from both the main tires that they blew and the plane stopped right there, just off the runway.

"Shit!" he exclaimed. I remained silent for a few seconds and then called the tower to tell them that our plane was down with flat tires. We were a beached whale and going nowhere.

I called maintenance on squadron common and requested a crew to come install two new tires. The tower inquired if there was foreign object debris on the deck and I responded, "Negative." The tower called the deck foul and put out the word to all aircraft in the pattern. I knew the embarrassment had only just begun and felt sorry for Baird, not accepting any responsibility at the moment. The runway itself was clear; only the north end was involved. Even so, the tower told a flight of two Navy aircraft, who were calling for landing, that the deck was foul and that no landings were allowed until further notice. It was a perfectly clear day, so the Navy planes asked what was up. Eventually they were cleared to land due to fuel considerations. Baird and I were transported back to 334 Ops via a follow-me truck and the plane was towed back to the flight-line after two new tires were installed. I thought, "Welcome to Iwakuni. What an entrance." I never asked Baird what he was doing or why he didn't see the end of the runway approaching. Nothing about the tires was mentioned in debrief and I thought that was it. I was wrong.

I had two more flights that week that went well and without incident. Flying in Japan was fun. It was now Friday and I looked forward to my first whole weekend in Japan. It would begin with Happy Hour at the O Club. Iwakuni was a Marine Corps Air Station with at least two Navy squadrons stationed there. The O Club was well attended by naval officers. As the evening progressed, while I was socializing with my peers, a Navy squadron officer got up on stage and took the microphone. He called Baird and me up on the stage. As Baird and I stood on the stage he began a humorous satirical poem lamenting our flat tires while two other naval officers brought the two tires up onto the stage. At the end of the poem there was a toast and with that, Baird and I had been ceremoniously embarrassed. It was more humorous than pathetic. Though ridiculed, we took it in good stead. The tires remained on stage all night and the embarrassment faded away as alcohol was consumed. I left the club early and headed back to the BOQ and crashed. I fell asleep with ease.

On Saturday, Harlow, Knudsen, McInerney, Griffin, and I all went into Iwakuni town. We wandered up and down the streets and in and out of shops and then had lunch. During lunch, we all agreed to buy a motorcycle to get around in Japan. After lunch, we did some more window shopping and I decided to get some tailor-made suits while in Japan. After perusing shops, several in the group wanted to go into a local bar called Club Sorrento. Sorrento's was an upscale place to get a drink or a girl. I was not interested in a girl, but several of the Josans (prostitutes) were reasonably attractive. After a few drinks, we left. There was something magical about the town of Iwakuni. It was quaint and Kin Tai Bridge at the west end of town added to its charm. Compared to Vietnam, it was heaven. Things looked bright. Except for ACM hops, I loved being stationed at Iwakuni.

I was not flying every day but occasionally flew twice in one day. I had two air combat maneuvering flights that Wednesday and threw up on the second one. My airsickness nemesis was no longer a secret in 334. My forty-five-minute airsickness tolerance for just about any type of flight broke down with that second hop. The typical ACM in Japan was identical to the scenario in the States. For us RIOs, it often meant not knowing what was coming next with G-forces on and off the plane quickly and rapid, violent turns, often rapidly reversed. The pilot was frequently in and out of afterburner when extra thrust was needed, often sending the plane into supersonic speeds. RIOs attempted to obtain or maintain the bogey location during this "wild ride." I frequently lost track of the horizon and had to grab a quick glance of the "meatball" (ADI) to know the attitude of the plane, often inverted, while my

G-suit pressed hard into my gut. Every movement is enhanced by not being able to see straight forward of the plane.

Attitude is all relative in the three-dimensional environment. Safely obtaining the six o'clock position of the bogey for a kill was all that mattered. I was now very comfortable in the three-dimensional environment; it was my inner ear that was not. Fortunately, not all flights were air combat maneuvering hops. I prayed to not have two in one day. I took two Dramamine before every ACM and did my best. That weekend I bought a Honda motorcycle and passed the test to obtain an international driver's license.

The next week I had two ACM flights on Wednesday again. And again, I vomited on the second flight. I still refused to ask for any special consideration. The next week was the same thing, two flights on Wednesday. I got very sick on the second and wasn't much help to the pilot. The following week, our squadron began the mission we had been training for and the reason we were in Japan. I was paired with Captain Baird. A flight of four planes and crew flew to Misawa AFB on northern Honshu. After landing and parking on the flight-line, the eight of us were escorted to one of the many underground bunkers. Upon arrival we entered into a situation room. It was a room with a huge oval oak table surrounded by chairs. In front of each chair was a red phone. There were maps everywhere. As I took all this in, I got the impression I was in a James Bond movie. No one sat down. Before I had completely absorbed this sight, a lieutenant colonel came in and asked for our senior officer. Captain Baird spoke up saying, "I am, Colonel." The lieutenant colonel seemed surprised by his rank. I wasn't that familiar with the Air Force but knew they were heavy with brass. The lieutenant colonel conducted a brief and we were escorted to our quarters.

We began operations the next morning, taking turns manning a five-minute alert hot pad through the week. If a launch occurred, it would be against North Korean aggression because it was needed. There had been tension ever since the USS *Pueblo* and EC 121 reconnaissance plane incidents. We were a deterrent. It was apparently working. Each hot pad alert was with two planes and two crews. Aircrews from 334 and 232 rotated in and out of Misawa every few days. I never launched on a flight. Sitting around was pretty boring except for knowing any launches could be one-way trips.

The mission distance could mean returning to Misawa was not feasible. Making it to Seoul, South Korea, or refueling were options but even those were iffy. By the time our mission ended months later, only one 334 flight had ever launched. The flight was given an eastern vector after launch. It was just a test. North and South Korea and China all lay to the west.

When I returned to Iwakuni, I had a message to report to X. O. Bond. He informed me that I would be the new squadron Administrative Officer and I would begin my duties on October 1, the next week. I was ordered to team up with the current Administrative Officer, Captain Tilly, immediately in order to ensure a smooth transition. The X. O. said the order would be written up that day and I would be given a copy. Then he added, "By the way, there's going to be a change of command next month and you will be the adjutant in charge." I was speechless. I was being ordered to fill a ground officer billet. I wondered how I was going to fly and do admin too. I responded, "Yes, Sir, I'll start tomorrow." Then Bond added, "Go to Ops and reduce your flights according to your needs. I'll inform Major Pieri." While walking back to my BOQ, I wondered if this was punishment for my airsickness, or was I just in the right place at the wrong time. I vowed to do my best. Admin turned out to have its advantages. I had never been in charge of a military event before and started preparing.

After a few more flights, I drastically reduced my flight time while planning the change of command. I worked closely with the squadron and group brass and very closely with Master Sergeant Castle, who was Sergeant Major of the squadron. Reducing my flight time was inconsequential; newly joining aviators were hungry for flight time. During planning, I met daily with my Admin Staff NCO, Gunnery Sergeant West. "Gunny" West confided to me that his rotation date back to the States was the end of the year. I recognized that West's expertise and experience spearheaded and sustained the unit. I knew he was an asset I couldn't do without. Surmising my Admin deficiency, I went to my boss and requested his tour be extended until March 1 to cover me until I rotated back to the States. My request was granted. I promised West high marks on his next fitness report. He was promoted before we returned to the States.

The X. O., Gunny West, Sergeant Major Nelson, and I started meeting daily and the change of command of outgoing Lieutenant Colonel D'Angelo and incoming Lieutenant Colonel Braddon took shape. I began rehearsing my role as adjutant. Basically, I was the person who physically directed the conduct and sequence of the events. I would do this using audible commands and by the exchange of the flags between the two lieutenant colonels. As Administrative Officer, I was gaining a lot of general knowledge about the Marine Corps, procedures, and the day-to-day functioning of MAG-15 and VMFA 334. It was a lot more than I ever wanted to know. For our government, military included, autumn was a very active time of year. There was the Change of Command ceremony, the Marine Corps Ball, pro and con marks (evaluations) for enlisted personnel, and fitness reports for officers and NCOs. And there was something else I was planning. Numerous other officers and I were bringing our wives to Japan.

All one-year tours were unaccompanied but spouses could join military personnel in an authorized non-combat location for a maximum of sixty days. It would be at the individual's expense and base housing could not be used. Those of us bringing our wives to Japan had to live off base, complying with all the restrictions and requirements imposed by the government. Fred Griffin, Terry Foltz, Doug Matzen, Rusty McInnerny, and I, along with about a dozen other pilots and RIOs, planned to bring our wives to Japan for the full sixty days. Fred, Terry, Rusty, and I all planned to have ours fly into Tokyo the first week of November so that they wouldn't have to fly home until just after New Year's. As the Admin officer, I was in charge of tracking spouses who joined their husbands. In the end, I did not keep track of spouses' arrival or departure dates. I relied on the honor system. That I knew of, no one violated the sixty-day restriction but even if they had, I wasn't going to blow the whistle.

My administrative duties were steadily increasing. Maintaining any kind of flight schedule was becoming increasingly difficult and I removed myself from being scheduled until after the change of command. I hated to see my friend Jerry Leist head back to the States. We had become close since I joined 334 in Chu Lai. His wedding in California and the day we first met were distant memories. We vowed to stay in touch. I had much respect for him. He had flown over 450 combat missions and earned more than twenty air medals, twice as many as I had. During September a huge influx of personnel was assimilated into the squadron. The new batch of pilots and RIOs changed the complexion of the unit. They were rotated into the flight schedule right away. Planning the annual Marine Corps Ball was also underway and some of the details were ironed out on the golf course. As Admin Officer, one of my duties became Public Information Officer. I coordinated with my group counterpart, a female Marine named Sergeant Beck. I also assisted the local Japan news network, NHK, with a news story about 334 moving to Japan and invited them to our change of command.

The day before the change of command, an all-Marine message came through which I immediately took into the C.O.'s office to discuss. The message was from the Commandant and it addressed discrimination in the military. D'Angelo said he would take care of it. That afternoon during rehearsal, with the entire squadron assembled, the commanding officer addressed the issue this way. After speaking about last minute details and general and menial things, he announced, "There will be no discrimination in this unit." That was it. If there was or had been, it was never mentioned. On October 1, 1969, I worked through the morning at a feverish pace and attended to every detail of the change of command until noon and then I sat down and rested. At 1245 hours, dressed extremely squared away, I went to the hangar and checked to verify that all the media and dignitaries were seated and comfortable. Then I visited each of my four "platoon" commanders. It was all perfunctory because my preparation and chain of command appointments were as squared away as I was.

At 1300 hours sharp, in a loud, deep voice I commanded, "A-ten-hut" and all squadron personnel on the hangar deck snapped to attention. It was sharp, it was a spectacle, and it was perfect, down to the passing of the flags and straight through dismissal and on into the reception. I thought to myself, I should get a good fitness report for this and then relaxed and enjoyed the after festivities. I visited with the media and then had a brief interview with my new commanding officer. My high bled over into the evening and that night at the club.

After the change of command I relaxed and began to totally enjoy Japan. I was immersed in administrative duties and well entrenched in the squadron upper echelon. I was included in the majority of the executive meetings and briefings and took the lead on all administrative matters, including all officer meetings. The new fiscal year saw our squadron with a new commanding officer and a deployment later in the month to Cubi Point, Philippines, for air to ground operations. Fitness reports and pros and cons were due. Pros and Cons were evaluations, primarily affecting promotions. It would be a busy month and November was coming. For Marines, November was a hell of a lot more than Thanksgiving. The Marine Corps had a day even more important to them than Veterans Day: the Marine Corps birthday and ball. I was in charge of coordinating the planning of this event. I, of course, would not be in attendance. Fred, Terry, Rusty, and I would be in Tokyo picking up our wives, spending three days with them there before heading to Iwakuni. A letter home partially read:

> Still lovin' it here. I played 36 holes of golf this weekend. I like the game. Next weekend we're going on a motorcycle trip to see some sights …
>
> I've definitely changed some. I suppose war does that to a person. I don't think I've changed much, just certain attitudes and realizations and the way I see things, of course. This is not to say that I have given my life any new direction, just that I have modified some of my thinking …
>
> I am conserving money for purchases here due to the extraordinary values. So, start dreaming up your Christmas list and if you want anything else from the Philippines, I'm going there again next month …
>
> Can hardly wait until Jan gets here. It really hurts to see wives here now.
>
> Doing great,
>
>   Love, Terry

By now, all of us who wanted a motorcycle had one and nearly every weekend, a group of us headed out on excursions. I always took my camera. It was fantastic with so much to see, especially since the fall colors added an extra appeal. One Saturday several of us headed south and west of the base. We passed through a fishing village named Tokuyama, where we saw a man casting a net into the water. I saw a Japanese woman pushing a Japanese man (probably husband) in a wheelbarrow. She hurriedly pushed into an alley so I couldn't get a photo. Japan was a staunch patriarchal society and a hard-working people as evidenced by the three women who were walking down a mountain road carrying firewood in bundles on their backs. Numerous shrines dotted the landscapes and I loved the Japanese architecture. Much of the cultivatable land was tiered for growing a variety of crops, including rice.

We stopped in a small village and had lunch in a small café. The food was strictly native and the male owner did not speak English. We made it through the language barrier without difficulty and had great food but the laughable thing was the John Wayne Western movie that the owners were watching on a small black and white television mounted up on the wall. John Wayne's speaking part was voiced over by a Japanese male with a high-pitched voice. It was truly comical. No matter where we went, the Japanese people we interacted with were very down to earth, gracious, and hospitable. On another Saturday, Fred Griffin and I broke off from the gang and scoped out some of the countryside north of the base and into the mountains. After a few miles along a mountain road, we discovered a quaint inn. We made reservations for the weekend before Thanksgiving as a surprise for our wives after their arrival. This trip would coincide with a visit to Miya Jima National Park off the coast near the road to the inn. Miya Jima was famous and a tourist destination for both American and Japanese. The Torii in the ocean at the entrance to the park was on many travel brochures.

Weekend treks weren't enough for me and I began taking short jogs after work even though the days were getting shorter. I was able to leave work about 1600 hours and venture off into Iwakuni town or take photos around the base and visited the lagoon dotted with small boats at the end of the runway that I had seen from the air on approach to the base. These small boats were used by indigenous villagers. The sunsets in Japan were beautiful. The cloud formations, mountains, and ocean made things very picturesque. I was totally captivated with the scenery, people and their heritage and culture, including the art and architecture. It contrasted sharply with the lack of tradition and culture in the United States.

That ancient architecture absolutely fascinated me and I couldn't get enough of it. Like Europe, Japan has a long and rich history, a distinctive

The author's photo of the Cenotaph in Peace Park in Hiroshima, Japan, near ground zero. The super structure of the building destroyed by the atomic bomb that represents ground zero is visible through the monument.

A photo of the author in a flight suit on his motorcycle in front of his berthing quarters at MCAS Iwakuni, Japan. He was a first lieutenant at this time. The photo was taken by one of the author's peers.

architectural style, and traditional dress. Kimonos, which they didn't wear that often, were especially delightful. On Sunday, our motorcycle gang went back to Hiroshima and Peace Park at ground zero. It had a profound impact on me. I photographed everything: the skeleton of the building at ground zero, the Cenotaph, cute and darling little Japanese children, the pigeons and men playing a game of Go. It was both interesting and gut-wrenching to tour the memorial museum. Yes, it was horrific and sad, but it prevented a prolonged and agonizing Japanese defeat and reduced the war atrocities Japanese soldiers inflicted on NATO forces all over the Pacific and Asia.

Most Japanese, especially the older ones, readily accepted Americans and American soldiers. They knew the United States was helping rebuild their country but it was obvious that the country was rapidly westernizing, especially the youth who were not very fond of the American military at all. I saw evidence of juvenile delinquency everywhere and the young men especially loved playing Pachinko, a type of vertical pinball machine often used for gambling. On one of my outings, on a mountain peak where I could see the ocean in both directions, I found a weather worn tree. I waited until the sun was low in the west, climbed two small, unstable trees and positioned myself for a photo. I tore my shirt getting down, arriving back at the base well after dark. The award-winning photo was worth it. Good photos were more than being in the right place at the right time. (When I got out of the Marine Corps, I became a professional photographer.)

Chapter 22

Mach 2

I was now flying very little; administrative duties were too demanding. However, one day I ended up in the ready room playing Ace Deuce with P.J. Allen, losing of course. While conversing as we played, I caught wind of a test flight. It was my chance at a Mach 2 run. I bumped a junior lieutenant to get scheduled for the flight. Pilot Renton and I took off from Iwakuni and headed southeast in our clean bird, climbing up to 20,000 feet out over the ocean. After leveling off, Renton asked me if I was ready. I replied, "Roger that." Renton pushed forward on the stick slightly, went into full afterburner and the plane instantly went supersonic. As the plane accelerated toward Mach 2, there were no other indications of anything; it was just quiet and smooth. According to the NATOPS manual, the F-4 Phantom was not thrust limited, meaning it had unlimited power. That was a half truth.

Anyone who has studied physics knows that everything ultimately reaches terminal velocity. The F-4 reportedly was capable of Mach 2.3. Our plane labored to reach Mach 2 and barely rolled to it from 1.99 before the canopy overheat light came on in Renton's cockpit. That was one of the F-4's limiting factors. Air friction would eventually melt the canopy in prolonged supersonic flight. If the canopy failed, the pilot and RIO would be incinerated. Renton backed off the throttles, turned 180 degrees and headed back to the base. The experience had been somewhat anti-climactic. When the Phantom (or any supersonic jet) goes from subsonic to supersonic, the altimeter and air speed indicator fluctuate while trans-sonic (breaking the sound barrier). Once the plane is supersonic, the fluctuations cease and there is no other sensation when Mach 2 is reached. However, it took a lot longer to get back to the base because of how far we had flown while attaining Mach 2. It was another aviation milestone I've never forgotten. We had flown over 1400 miles per hour. Very few people ever do. I was proud of my Mach 2 feat and pinned the Mach 2 pin on my flight jacket next to my 100-mission patch.

The squadron was due to deploy for two weeks the latter part of October and all evaluations were due into Administration before they left. It was my job to review and audit the results. It was pretty typical, if not characteristic, for Marines to be overrated in order to help their careers, especially for promotional purposes. I was pretty much okay with things until two different Marines in maintenance were rated with perfect tens. I thought about that a minute and then called Gunny West into my office. I said, "Gunny, you know you're going to get an excellent fitness report. But I am not accepting these enlisted pro and con marks. No one is perfect and according to these submittals we have, not one, but two perfect Marines in the squadron. I am trashing them. Help me draft a memo to all section heads to have them re-evaluate and resubmit their marks with a deadline of before the squadron deploys."

"Yes Sir," the gunny replied. I thought that would be the end of it.

At the completion of the project, with the gunny in my office, I said, "Gunny, close the door."

West closed the door and said, "What's up?"

I replied, "We have some irregularities, no, falsifications in the pros and cons. Look at this. One of the corporals in our Administrative section has obviously changed his pro and con marks." The inks were dissimilar and it was very obvious when looked at closely. After some time investigating, West and I discovered several changes and it appeared two Marines in our Admin office had made them. "What do we do?" I asked. The gunny said we should involve the Commanding Officer. Braddon began a formal investigation, handing it all over to the Group S-1. I kept all the evidence under lock and key and temporarily assigned the two corporals elsewhere until a lieutenant colonel from Guam, representing the JAG, came aboard to investigate. The two corporals were ultimately found guilty and summarily court-martialed. They were transferred because they couldn't continue to work in 334 Admin. Those strokes of the pen were certainly costly to them and the Corps.

October was moving along swiftly. I flew some but mostly spent my time keeping Admin squared away. I rented a small new house in Iwakuni town for Jan's visit. I was cautiously excited about it. The contract for the house included a clause requiring all persons to remove their shoes upon entering, a Japanese custom that was strictly enforced. The house came complete with a small cabinet for shoes just outside the door.

The majority of the squadron deployed to Cubi Point, Philippines, for air to ground work. I was perfectly content not going but had to be payroll officer for all deployed squadron personnel. On October 23, I went to disbursing and withdrew $43,000 cash and placed it in a metal ammo box. Prior to sunrise the next morning, Captain Baird and I pre-flighted our plane. I questioned the wear on the two main landing gear tires. Several steel cords were visible and I felt the tires should be replaced prior to launch. Baird blew it off and said it would be okay. The flight launched without incident with the ammo box between my feet. At 30,000 feet as the sun rose over Kyushu and Shikoku islands, I took photos. We headed south and landed at Kadena AFB on Okinawa. Once refueled, while pre-flighting the plane, I again questioned the worn tires. Baird blew it off again. We taxied toward the duty runway and on the apron before taxiing onto the duty runway for takeoff, the right main tire blew. The plane listed to the right and wasn't going anywhere.

We opened our canopies and Baird shut the engines down. As we sat on the apron like a crippled duck waiting for a tire change, I couldn't believe what taxied by—an SR 71 Blackbird. The Air Force pilot of the Blackbird gave the usual Air Force salute, the middle finger, as he taxied onto the runway. I took a couple of photos. After engine run-up, the SR 71 took off and disappeared at a faster rate than I had ever seen before or would ever see again. As a Marine aviator, I was more embarrassed than I had ever been to date. With two new tires installed, we took off for the Philippines. Baird was very silent the rest of the trip.

The next morning (Friday), I paid the deployed personnel, finishing early. I dismissed my armed MP and had the rest of the day off. I completed my paperwork and headed for the club, where I met up with John Menk. He said a bunch of officers were going into Manila Saturday and asked if I wanted to come along. I said yes. Menk asked if I ever had a pilot shoot movies of a missile shoot from the front cockpit. I said I'd love that. He arranged it with his pilot. I got a take-off and landing, a missile shot and impact, and a simulated run on a tiny island off the coast. (Note: The pilot did not shoot movies with his "free" hand. He mounted the camera to the gun-sight.) My thanks to Menk's pilot was dinner at the club. (Many of my photos and movies were in our twenty-fifth 232 squadron reunion video.)

A dozen of us caught a bus from the base to Manila. Nothing about the big dirty city had changed but I was glad to be part of the group and enjoyed the fraternization. After sightseeing and food and drinks, some of the group wanted to go to a cockfight, something totally legal in the Philippines. I tagged along. It seemed savage at first, but no more so than the bullfighting I'd seen in Mexico. I lost two bets in a row with local Filipinos and decided to quit wasting my money. We headed back to the base. It was the last time I was in the Philippines. Back in Japan, things were looking really good. The fall colors were beautiful and the climate, being similar to that of the United States, was cooling off. Things were slow without the bulk of the squadron. I took advantage of the slack times shopping, writing letters, and sloughed off a little by playing golf. My letter home went like this:

I took a whole roll of movies of the Japanese Islands from the plane the other day and I picked up my first tailor made suit. Wait until you see your well dressed son. [My father is buried in one of those suits] …

Mom, the candy was delicious and I will call you soon. I hope you will forgive my semi, forgetfulness of y'all's anniversary …

For your reference, Iwakuni is about twenty miles south of Hiroshima and on the southern part of the main Island of Honshu …

We are planning another motorcycle trip this weekend …

Dad, who knows about Ho Chi Minh? After all, does the death of our president change the political policy of our country? Not really.

What really counts is how big an influence a president has on his legislature and we all know that sometimes this is very little ...

I am infatuated with this country. The people are industrious, the scenery is beautiful and the architecture is awesome ...

You asked what I want for Christmas: cards, love and peace. I want to be home with my friends and family, enjoying good food and good times.

More soon, Terry

I was working hard for the squadron but had it relatively easy. My weight was about 155 pounds and I was still having problems with the rash I got in Vietnam. After writing home about the limitless items that could be purchased in Japan, I became somewhat of a merchandise catalog for the family. I got myself camera accessories, stereo equipment, and a carved ivory chess set. I had been keeping Jan up on everything with regular calls and letters, telling her all about the beautiful countryside and people. She sounded excited and would be arriving in a week. The final plans for the Marine Corps Ball on November 10 had been ironed out and my gunny would be there for any last-minute details. Fred, Terry, Rusty, and I would be in Tokyo getting laid, which was more important than attending the ball. It was our own ball.

Many wives were already there, including Doug Matzen's wife. Sunday of that weekend, Doug and his wife were drinking at the O Club and decided to have a race home on their bicycles. Doug let her have a head start and the race was on. There were railroad tracks not far beyond the main gate of the base. Tragically, after surviving six months of combat, Doug lost his life when he unsuccessfully tried to beat a train. Even though I was the Admin Officer, I was, thankfully, not directly involved with handling the incident. I had just recently returned from the Philippines and had the weekend off, not resuming my duties until 0600 the next morning. The base chaplain, thank God for him, and the Group HQ handled most of the details. I was deeply saddened by the tragedy.

The next morning, Doug was not the only topic but he commanded most of it. The Japanese authorities took a dim view of delaying their trains. They attempted to sue the U.S. Government one million yen (about $2817 US) per minute that their train was held up. I never knew the outcome of the fine but had a lot of administrative details to attend to and was determined to work through them before heading to Tokyo. Doug and his wife were safely, sadly, and quickly transported back to the States. I got an excellent fitness report for the work I was doing, including the change of command. For the first time, I really didn't care. "What were they going to do, make me a lieutenant and send me to Vietnam?" My thought was, been there, done that, and have the air medals to prove it. I wasn't a career Marine and had no inclination to be one. Fred, Terry, Rusty, and I discussed our wives' imminent arrival at the club. We were ready, anxious, and excited.

Chapter 23

Loving It

The four of us caught a government plane to Atsugi NAS about sixty miles from Tokyo and then took a taxi to the Sanno Hotel, a military-affiliated hotel in Tokyo. After checking in, we had lunch and went to check out the rooms. To our surprise the rooms had twin beds and they could not be changed. That didn't affect anything. Terry's wife was coincidentally named Jan. Both Jans were on the same plane out of Seattle. Their plane was delayed and all four wives arrived within minutes of each other. The two Jans were the first two people off their plane. We all headed back to the hotel. Sex was good but sleeping was cramped. We were all in good spirits the next morning at breakfast. Over the next four days in Tokyo, our group went to the Ginza District during the day and night, ate in the revolving restaurant overlooking the Ginza, attended a Kabuki drama (a stage production in which all parts, male and female, are played by men), visited the Imperial Palace, had lunch at the Tokyo Tower, and visited shrines and a stadium built for the 1964 Olympics.

On Monday, the eight of us went to Kamakura Park, Japanese gardens with a view of Mount Fuji. The main feature of the park was an outdoor Buddha, a twenty-foot tall Diabutsu. The landscaping was phenomenal. After viewing it, Fred and I and our wives, Jan and Paulette, needed to use the restroom. Fred and I entered the men's room and started urinating into the wall-mounted metal urinal trough. We pretty much stopped midstream when eight or so Japanese women walked in using short choppy steps (giggling as they walked) and began using the bathroom stalls. I, for sure, had a befuddled expression on my face and was totally embarrassed. We left as quickly as we could. Later, we found out this was an accepted practice as was peeing in the ditches next to the highways for Japanese men. These ("benjo") ditches were a type of open sewer. There would be other culture shocks while in Japan. Later that day our group took a tour towards Mount Fuji. The view of the snow-covered mountain was fantastic. The mountain, volcanically formed, stood as a stark monolith at 12,388 feet high. Our last night in Tokyo was food and entertainment back in the Ginza.

We boarded the bullet train early that next morning and headed for Iwakuni. The train traveled in excess of 120 miles per hour heading for Osaka. Mount Fuji stayed in view a long time as we passed by. We switched trains at Osaka and even though the site of Expo '70 (under construction) was beautiful, things got ugly for a while. Jan and I sat in front of Fred and Paulette and the girls got tons of attention just because of their bleached blonde hair. Blondes were nonexistent in Japan and all of Asia, actually. Often they were admired up close and personal. Many women we encountered revered them and even touched their hair, treating them somewhat like goddesses. Barely out of the station, two older Japanese men behind Fred and Paulette began being obnoxious. With loud voices, they were antagonistic. Paulette was extremely distraught and had a pained expression on her face. I told her to sit next to Jan and I sat next to Fred.

Fred and I began talking to the inebriated men civilly, in spite of the language barrier. I wasn't afraid of them but was concerned things might escalate. Though Fred, at six-foot-one, towered over Japanese men, collectively they probably could overpower us. It was a little tense at first but as we patiently and calmly talked with the men, they mellowed. It turned out both men worked in the Mitsubishi manufacturing plant and had built Jap Zeros during World War II. Before the train arrived at Iwakuni, Fred and I had formed an odd kinship with them. Though difficult to understand the announcer of the stations, at Iwakuni we got off and headed for our off-base domiciles.

The wives settled into things quickly. Jan and I hired a mamasan for our little house. A delightful Japanese national, Ms. Sako, cooked and cleaned for one dollar (US) per day. All of us who brought our wives to Japan ate on the base together as often as we could. Like us guys, the girls came to love Japan and learned their way around Iwakuni town and the base. Jan teamed up with Jan Foltz and Paulette mostly, but occasionally spent the day at home with Ms. Sako, who taught her things, including Japanese floral arranging. Jan and I often ate at the club and there was frequently live entertainment. We spent as much time exploring and enjoying as much of Japan as possible.

The weekend before Thanksgiving, Fred and I loaded up our wives and headed off on our surprise trip to the mountain chalet. We ended up laughingly referring to it as "the Singing Frog Inn." The four of us motorcycled north toward our destination, sightseeing and eating Japanese food on the way. We checked in and headed to our assigned rooms. It got dark early and was cold, with snow on the ground.

It turned out that it in no way resembled a Western hotel that we were used to in the States. It looked quaint on the outside but it was native. The building was made of concrete and timber and the walls were thick and uninsulated. There was no central heat; in fact, there seemed to be no heat at all. Rather than windows, there were elevated holes in the walls shaped in patterns like a crescent moon and stars. The restrooms down the hall were communal. They were also native style, including the toilets. Toilets were elliptical, porcelain, spoon-shaped affairs which were elevated a few inches off the floor so that one had to squat to do his or her business. We only knew which direction to use it from because the back was slightly elevated over the front. It was difficult to know if you were lined up correctly. Once the girls couldn't hold it any longer, Fred and I stood outside the restroom door making sure no one else came in. As the girls emerged from the restroom, their aggravation and embarrassment were evident.

Dinner at the "Inn" was Japanese fare, fish cooked with the heads on, squid and octopus and vegetables that we didn't recognize. We gingerly ate sparingly and later in the evening were really hungry. Fred and I checked at the front desk for possibilities. We were informed that there were some vending machines and that's all that was available. When we got to the vending machines, all the items were Japanese types of things with Japanese writing. None of the items looked familiar and some didn't look edible. We were in a quandary and had no idea what to pick by the packaging. We now knew our surprise really was a surprise and was turning into a bust. We made our best guess selections and headed back to our gathering place: mine and Jan's room. Each of us made our selection and then proceeded to eat it. Fred, Paulette and Jan ate theirs but really didn't care for them. I bit into one of the two things that resembled a Fig Newton and immediately spit it out. Whatever it was, it was not a cookie. The cake-like item seemed to be filled with a type of bean paste. I trashed them and went hungry.

After "dinner" we explored the Inn. There was an elaborate "hotsy bath" type sauna. It was a large waist deep pool with a dark bottom, large rocks and dim lighting. In Japan there were lots of public bathhouses, most of which were unisex and nude bathing often was the norm. Though this one was on private property, it obviously had the same rules. The girls passed but Fred and I decided to go in, in our underwear. No one saw us enter. But we hadn't been there long before a Japanese man and woman, both nude, came in. Since it was a large area, there was room to remain distant and have relative privacy. The whole situation became emotionally charged with two Caucasian guys seemingly naked in a sauna bath with a Japanese couple whose relationship was unknown, naked and enjoying the romantic atmosphere. As the vapors wisped on and up from the water's surface, the Japanese couple, though curiously eyeing two Marines, began canoodling. Fred and I wanted to leave but wouldn't get out because of our underwear. Finally the couple left and then so did Fred and me.

When we got to our rooms, there was a problem. The bed in Fred and Paulette's room had a curious hump in the middle of it. When the girls pulled back the bedclothes, they were surprised to find a bed warmer frame and semen stains on the bottom sheet. We were all cold in spite of fuming over this revelation and it was pretty much bedtime. The front desk was closed. So far, the "Singing Frog Inn" was a real downer and the night wasn't over yet. We devised a plan as bedtime arrived. Fred and Paulette brought in all the top bedclothes from their futon and we were all going to sleep on ours. We all went to bed dressed, cold, and hungry but optimistic because we were supposed to be served breakfast in our room the next morning. None of us slept that well. It was awkward and chilly. It was unsettling, not because of the movie *Bob and Carol, Ted and Alice* situation, but because of the audible intimate noises that could be heard in other rooms. There was certainly a whole lot of screwing going on, but mine and Fred's plans for intimacy were thwarted.

The next morning we all arose early, changed clothes and freshened up. Going to the bathroom was a frigid affair we all dreaded. All four of us sat around with our stomachs growling waiting for the breakfast that seemed to take forever. Finally we heard someone coming up the stairs. A shy Japanese woman in traditional kimono attire came into the room with two trays containing plates of breakfast food. We all had heard a piece of flatware clang as it hit the floor outside the door and knew she only wiped it off instead of replacing it. As she passed out the plates, Fred ended up with one that had a long black hair in it. The shy woman bowed several times and headed out the door. There was lots of food so we all shared, leaving the fish untouched and then vacated the "Inn" as fast as possible. Fred and I chuckled about that incident long after the wives left to go back the States because we realized we had brought our wives to a brothel and didn't even get lucky. As the four of us headed back to Iwakuni on our motorcycles, we found a restaurant on the main drag and then we went to Miya Jima Park. Our wives loved it.

The next week nearly the whole squadron had Thanksgiving dinner at the club. My thoughts all through dinner were that I had much to be thankful for. Japanese indigenous people ran the club and prepared food which was for the most part a great job, especially eggs Benedict on Sunday mornings. They attempted to cook western and prepare menus that reflected American cuisine. It was an appreciated attempt but often missed the mark. Though some of the dishes tasted good, they often tasted like soy sauce or had other Asian overtones, especially on Italian and Mexican nights. The advantage was that it wasn't bad, it wasn't military, and it wasn't in Vietnam. It was prepared and served by hard-working, gracious, amiable people and when the specialty fare was Japanese, it was fantastic.

I flew just three times in November and stood the hot pad once. The weekend after Thanksgiving, Terry, our two Jans, and I took a train up to Hiroshima. Though it was cold, the gals loved it and were deeply moved. One cannot go to Hiroshima at ground zero and not be moved. Back at work the following Monday, I received, or thought I received, the orders to my next duty station. But when I opened my envelope, instead of orders, I had an offer. I couldn't wait to get home to tell Jan. I rushed home at 1600 hours and after removing my shoes, burst through the door. I told Jan, "I have orders to Hawaii if I am willing to extend my enlistment so I could serve a three-year tour." Jan's answer was immediate and emphatic, not only no, but HELL no. The desire to not spend more time in the Marine Corps was stronger than being stationed in paradise. I declined the offer. Red Devil crony, Captain Castonguay, did accept the offer. Once out of the USMC, I learned that most of the aircrew who accepted these orders had another one-year tour in Vietnam prior to the end of their three-year stint. I also heard that during his tour, Castonguay was shot down near the Cambodian border at dusk. He and his pilot were lucky to be alive and rescued the next morning at dawn. I was doubly thankful I hadn't accepted the orders.

Time was flying by with Jan in Japan. A month had elapsed already. We went to Osaka, Kyoto, and Yanai. We saw the Golden and Silver Pavilions, five-story pagodas, Japanese gardens, and beautifully dressed people. We were in Yanai on December 7, a Japanese holiday and, of course, the anniversary of Pearl Harbor. We did our Christmas shopping and bought tons of household goods and décor for when we got back into our home in Texas. I was also putting in lots of time on Admin work. I had two days' worth of flights called RADEX: radar exercises (intercept work) but was flying very little.

While Jan and I were having fun in Japan, correspondence with my folks revealed my mom's sadness and depression that I wasn't home for the holidays. I wrote and called, trying to lift her spirits. I let her know that we would celebrate Christmas in March when I returned to the States. She was depressed anyway. Many people don't understand the stress and impact that separation has on military families. I did what I could to raise her spirits, not knowing that she was saving every letter I sent home. I wrote regularly, with respect and gratitude. I hoped I honored them by

my service, something that Jan didn't get. My parents understood what
an integral part of the USMC aviation my service was. Most aviators did
"swing with the wing," occasionally being outlandish or outrageous and
sometimes violating protocol and regulations, but the positive effects of
Marine air operations regarding ground Marine forces and other ground
combatant's preservation and protection could never be measured or
minimized. Aviators are their own breed.

Friday morning that week, I felt really frisky and pretty much forced
myself on Jan before going to work. She never did like daytime sex. I was
sure the truth was she really didn't like sex that much at all and deep down
I thought maybe she didn't like sex with me in particular. I had no idea.
And I had no idea that while engaging in some pretty good sexual inter-
course, whether she liked or not, I was missing the weekly all-officers'
meeting, a meeting in which I normally had input. When I got to work,
nothing was said. I didn't care; I was making all the memories that I could
with the time I had.

Christmas happened at the speed of light. I had flights on both
December 23 and Christmas Eve, but did not have duty on New Year's
Eve. On Christmas Eve (Christmas Day in the States), Jan and I called
home to wish each of our parents Merry Christmas. Jan boasted about
the country and scenery. The next day, our Christmas celebration was a
somber affair due to being away from our families and knowing that in
two weeks Jan was heading home. Later that day, after gift exchange, we
had a traditional turkey dinner at the club with our friends. We all talked
of home and the future. Hardly any of my peers were considering careers
in the Marine Corps. We talked about the beauty of Japan and the Japanese
people. The time with Jan and good friends was coming to an end. The gang
was about to be broken up.

New Year's was bittersweet. Everyone looked ahead to the next year, but
not forward to the next week. The freshly packed snow made motorcycling
difficult, almost impossible, but the trains ran. Our foursome took the girls by
train to Hiroshima Airport and we all said our goodbyes amidst lots of tears.
The girls flew via Nippon Airlines to Tokyo, connected to a Japan Airlines
flight to Seattle and my Jan connected back to Dallas. Most of us guys were

depressed for days. I returned to my BOQ and threw myself into my work during the day and listened to recorded music at night. There were still new personnel joining the unit and there was a ton of year-end and year-beginning paperwork. It was January 7, 1970, three years after my first day at OCS. I had two and a half months to go in Japan but didn't know where I was spending my last year in the Corps.

Chapter 24

Sayonara

I wrote a long letter home on the backs of several flight schedules:

Guess who ran out of stationery? Not really, I am at the base, "standing by," so disregard the flight schedules on the back sides of my letter.

… While Jan was here we did and saw lots of things: Kyoto (cultural and religious center of Japan), shrines, pagodas, pavilions, castles, temples, statues and Torii's. We also saw the old Imperial Palace, a deer park called Nara and Expo '70 which is still under construction.

We ate Christmas dinner at the club. The dinner did not compare to yours, Mom, and the gravy didn't come close either. I am looking forward to Christmas in March now.

There is a little bit of Chinese influence here, so out with the chicken and in with the year of the dog later this month. According to them it is supposed to be a good year. Who knows? We'll find out. It will be good to get home for sure.

We spent New Year's at the club partying, but it lacked the enthusiasm of home. It is a new year and I am feeling short. My "short timers" calendar only goes through March 19.

Sorry for my delinquency but, Happy New Year. I'm limiting calls due to the expense.

Love, Terry

My only two flights in January were on the tenth, to Naha, Okinawa. I was scheduled with Baird. By now, both the destination and pilot were routine. I had other flights with Baird but every time I went to Okinawa, Baird was my pilot. I wondered what was up with that. I was getting rusty and losing some of my skills from not flying frequently. I got a weather report for the flight but, to my embarrassment, forgot to file the flight plan. I had to do it while we sat on the apron, ready and waiting to launch. I had never forgotten to file a flight plan before but to my surprise and relief it came through quickly and we boomed up into the sky towards Naha. Baird and I went down to pick up some plane parts and got back after dark. We did not have any tire problems but I vowed to get into the flight schedule a little more often to stay up to speed. The days dragged on in January and my letters home were evidence of it.

With eight weeks left in Japan, I got orders back to El Toro, California. I was ecstatic and had been seriously hoping for this, dreading any other duty station, especially Cherry Point, North Carolina. If I had gone there, I probably would have done one or more Mediterranean (MED) cruises before finishing my time in the Marine Corps. Cruises aboard aircraft carriers lasted anywhere from three to six months. I had never hit the boat and didn't want to. I also didn't think I could manage life aboard a carrier because of my motion sickness. I was sure God was watching over me again. I was pretty sure Jan wanted El Toro too. I headed to Happy Hour at the club.

With obvious glee over my orders, I began drinking rum punches and conversed with my fellow aviators. Harlow and Knudsen had also gotten El Toro, while Foltz, Griffin, and Allen had gotten orders to Cherry Point. We all celebrated. Career pilot Ezell, whom I was very fond of, also got orders to the East Coast. (Sadly, Ezell would die in a plane crash a couple years later.) We kept drinking. Fortunately, the rum punches were small and mostly punch. But after hors d'oeuvres and lots of drinks (totally out of character for me), I suggested we go into Iwakuni town to a strip club and off we went.

In the traditional Japanese custom, we took off our shoes and placed them in plastic bags, before we walked on the tatami mats to sit next to the stage. The strippers weren't that bad and we were all enjoying the show. During the third girl's performance, I felt sick. At the completion of her act, while no one was paying attention to me, I removed my shoes from the plastic bag and threw up in it. I managed to stand up and made it to the restroom just in time to barf again.

Fred came in to check on me and I told him I was going back to the base. I was drunk for the first, and what would be the only, time in my life. I did not like it and was ashamed of myself. After I vomited one more time, Fred and I left. Fred hailed a cab, helped me into it and we headed back to the base. I threw up once out the window of the cab but really didn't feel any better and even though throwing up was sobering, I was not. Fred had the cab stop about a block from the front gate and tipped the driver well. Fred said to me, "You're going to have to get through the main gate, straightaway, on your own." The cold night air helped some. I had my military ID out and walked as straight as I could up to the guard shack. Upon seeing my ID, the corporal guard stood at attention and saluted saying, "Good evening, Sir." To which I replied, "Good evening, corporal, carry on," being sober enough to resist the temptation to return the salute in civilian attire. I retrieved my ID and walked as straight a line as possible along the sidewalk. The further I got from the shack, the more I relaxed. About halfway to my BOQ room, I threw up in the ditch and then it was mostly dry heaves. At my room, I sheepishly viewed myself in the mirror. I looked horrid. I cleaned myself up, thanked Fred,who had followed me to my room after all, and hit the sack.

The next morning, surprisingly, I arose early. Breakfast did not sound good; my head and body ached but I did not let on. I encouraged a group of us to go on a motorcycle outing up into the hills and then led the way. I felt better as the day went on but didn't eat much. Fred and the whole group were surprised that I had the wherewithal to do anything, much less what I was doing. Cold and inclement weather started limiting our motorcycle trips but the snow made the countryside even prettier. I tried to describe the winter beauty in my letters home. I could not disguise my home sickness and did not mention my drunken adventure. I told them about my El Toro orders and two-week leave, then signed it, "Your foreign despondent, Terry."

I flew a bunch of flights in February, mostly intercept work and a night hop with Major Scafe. Our wingman's plane was downed in the chocks so Scafe and I launched solo. It made me nervous because I knew Scafe had a propensity for "hot dogging" and had no idea what he might do with an unrestricted flight. In the end, the flight really didn't amount to more than boring holes in the sky, doing a few aerobatics, and seeing some of the island lights. On a day hop, the same thing happened to me and my pilot Crest. Crest took us out southeast of Honshu and did some loops and rolls and then flew down close to the ocean. After a while, we popped back up and something in the ocean caught my eye. We had gotten a pretty close look at a Japanese submarine. I was pissed because I hadn't brought my camera. "Playtime" like this was rare but rewarding; in fact, this day for me it was fun. I was not aware that my ten flights that February would be my last in the F-4J Phantom. By now I had over 500 hours in that plane and every launch was still a kick in the ass. Two times that month I had two flights in one day and persevered. Due to the training we received in Japan, both 334 and 232 squadrons were attaining a level of aviation prowess they had never attained before—strong adversaries in air combat maneuvering.

Prior to the benefit of this training, there had been weaknesses that were instantly and seriously evidenced in the Vietnam theater, not so much from aircraft design deficiencies and weaponry but mostly due to lack of air-to-air training. The Marine aviation community's superior air-to-ground work was undisputed since most of the training was for the support of ground troops. But Marine F-4 pilots and RIOs were seriously deficient in air-to-air skills and it was communicated up the chain of command in an open letter, which surprisingly was published in the Navy's *Approach* magazine. The letter outlined those deficiencies and boldly declared that the Marine Corps was the worst. Finally, the truth was out. Our stint in Japan was a good but meager beginning; forthcoming were better designed planes and weaponry and a new training program in the Navy called Top Gun. The Air Force would have their equivalent, Red Flag.

On President's Day holiday weekend someone, somehow, with base operations assist, brought dozens of American female schoolteachers to Iwakuni. They taught on military bases in Japan, Guam, and Okinawa. Most of them were relatively unattractive but "round eyes" of the opposite sex were nice to see in a slant-eyed environment. When I arrived at the club, it was a hive of activity. I sat with fellow aircrew eyeing the activity. I thought it was all outrageous until I saw a reasonably cute girl at the bar talking to a Navy pilot and I commented about her. A couple of my peers challenged me to go talk to her. I dismissed the idea and then for some reason, I said, "What the hell. All's fair in love and war." I took off my wedding ring with the tan line still visible, went over and introduced myself. There was an instant attraction both ways. We soon proceeded to our own table and dinner. After a couple more drinks, Sally suggested we go back to her room. Kissing led to some heavy petting and she got up and left the room. It was exciting but totally foreign to me. I had never been in this situation before. She came back dressed in sheer baby doll pajamas and sat on my lap. Things were beginning to heat up and come up as we kissed passionately. She undulated her hips and I cupped and fondled her breasts firmly. At that moment I was instantly overcome with tremendous guilt. I stopped and said, "I can't do this, I'm married." She was in utter shock but said she understood.

I was thirty days from going home. Except for Jan's two months in Japan and our one week in Hawaii, I had been celibate my entire year overseas and I wasn't going to screw it up now. I kissed Sally on the cheek and walked out the door convinced I had done the right and Christian thing. The next night at the club, Rusty got with her. Though a little jealous, I was glad I hadn't succumbed to temptation. It was later rumored that Rusty had gotten an STD. Uncured STDs could keep someone from rotating back to the States.

The next weekend a bunch of us took the train to Osaka, Expo '70, and Kyoto. We were able to be on the grounds of Expo '70, the next World's Fair, even though it was still under construction. I wouldn't be in Japan long enough to see it or the spring cherry blossoms and wished I could. Our time in Japan was coming to an end. We all shipped our stuff to our next duty stations on March 1, including motorcycles of those who wanted to take them back to the States. My bike was shipped in seven wooden crates.

(At El Toro, I received only six of the crates. The engine was missing. When I filed for the loss, the postman delivered it without the crate, with a tag attached to the gear shift pedal.)

A few days later, the 334 squadron main body deployed to Cubi Point in the Philippines for air to ground work again. Only a skeleton crew remained in Japan, including those of us from 232 who were rotating back to the States by the twentieth. I had been replaced as primary Admin Officer and was rear echelon anchor and frequent acting commanding officer during the squadron deployment. There was a lot of messaging back and forth and sometimes calls. One day we received word that Major Noggle, during the deployment in the Philippines, had over-rotated his F-4 on takeoff and he and his RIO safely ejected but the plane nearly destroyed the O Club. I wasn't surprised. At least he didn't kill his RIO. RIO deaths resulting from errant pilot decisions had happened more than once and one time at NAS Dallas where I would eventually join a Marine reserve unit.

The countdown was on for seven of us close-knit RIOs. With the squadron deployed to the Philippines and not due back until the day after we were to leave, it set me to thinking. I was an Admin Officer and acting Commanding Officer; I could change the dates on the orders and get us out early. I disclosed my idea to my peers to see if any of them wanted to leave early. Not one of them said no, so I went to work. I had already gotten orders for my gunnery sergeant and things were coming together. The fact that it was against policy was only a fleeting thought and repercussions never entered my mind, though they were possible and potentially severe. I couldn't fathom what difference a few days would make to anyone and they certainly wouldn't bring any of us back to serve them.

Making the changes turned out to be easy. I got orders written for the seven of us to land in the U.S. ten days early, on March 10. Since leave was authorized, each one of our orders looked a little different but the result was the same: ten days early with the appropriate reporting dates to the next duty station. Viola! I wrote home letting my parents and Jan know when to expect me. I included in my parents' letter, "I have a great deal of anxiety towards the end of this tour now that it is at hand but I can say with pride—I withstood the test; yet not I alone but with the help of those whom

I love, including Him above. I hope I haven't changed too much. A person changes somewhat with every experience, particularly a traumatic one. I am not implying that combat is traumatic, it is for some, but it is unique to say the least. I've never been quite alone as I was in Vietnam. I hope I never am again. I shipped all the items that y'all requested. I look forward to seeing you soon."

I got a little lax about going into work in the mornings. I arrived late in the Admin office two days before my plane was to leave for Okinawa. I had a message to call Captain Gray at the group regarding one of the 334 maintenance jeeps. I got a cup of coffee first and then called Gray, identifying myself as Lieutenant Thorsen, acting commanding officer. The captain was a little snippy but inquired as to why one of our four maintenance jeeps had not been properly dispatched. I responded to the captain that I had no idea but that the bulk of the squadron was deployed and that I would inquire about it and get back to him. He replied, "You see that you do." I instantly sensed this captain was a shithead. The captain's demeanor totally pissed me off. So, I shifted gears and had another cup of coffee as I perused the day's action and regular messages.

I eventually called maintenance and got a hold of the NCO in charge who informed me that he thought that it had been dispatched and that he would check on it. I didn't let him go without telling him I had a captain from the group on my ass and that I needed him to get back to me before lunch and inform me of the status. He replied, "Yes, Sir." He also indicated to me that if it had not been properly dispatched that he would personally see that it was done before the end of the day. The NCO did not get back to me before lunch but Captain Gray did and was pissed. The captain asked if I had found out about the jeep. I reminded him that I was acting commanding officer and I was busy. I told him that I had inquired about the jeep and a maintenance NCO was going to find out and get back to me. I also informed the captain it would be taken care of by the end of the day. He snapped back, "That's not good enough, lieutenant!"

My disdain for this mustang officer unequivocally and instantly came across in the inflection and verbiage of my response: "Captain, I am the ACTING commanding officer and have many duties to attend to besides dispatching your jeep. I said I would attend to it and will before the end of business today. If that is not good enough for you, you can shove the jeep up your ass! I rotate back to the States in two days. There is a skeleton crew here at the present time which I am the commanding officer of, so good fucking luck getting any other action than what I am able to provide," and hung up on him.

Immediately, I knew I had made a mistake. Why couldn't I have held my tongue two more days? I feared that the doctoring of my early departure date might be exposed and my departure might be rescheduled to the correct date or even delayed. But more importantly, there would probably be some sort of disciplinary action. Damn it, I wondered, "Why did God create these assholes?" I picked up the phone and just short of being an asshole myself, got the NCO on the phone and chewed his ass out. I told the NCO in no uncertain terms to expedite his actions and get the jeep dispatched immediately or it would be his ass. I told him that as soon as it was accomplished to bring a copy of the paperwork to me, in Admin, with the date/time stamp on it. After I hung up the phone with the NCO, a thought occurred to me. Some of my Marines were probably joy riding in it the night before. I didn't want to think about that but at least they hadn't been caught in the act or wrecked it. I just wanted the paperwork so I could CYA, cover MY ass. About mid-afternoon, I got a summons to be in the group commander's office at 0900 hours sharp the next morning in my Alpha uniform (greens). There was no doubt what it was regarding.

I had trouble going to sleep, and indeed hardly slept at all that night. A very nervous and practically shaking me, Lieutenant Thorsen, in uniform with paperwork in hand, was outside Group Commanding Officer Colonel Davis's office at 0845 hours. I was scared but determined not to show it. I was prepared to present a good argument, but I would be humble and apologetic for my "insubordination" up front. I prayed things would be okay. The fifteen minutes seemed an eternity during which my stomach growled, my palms sweated profusely, and I wished hard I could be somewhere else at that moment. I hoped for the best and my resolve was to be confident and composed and eventually throw myself on the mercy of the court, Colonel Davis. As my mind wandered and I was trying to compose myself, the adjutant appeared and told me to go in.

I closed the door behind me, stood at attention and said, "Good morning, Colonel." Colonel Davis said, "Sit down lieutenant," and motioned to one of the chairs in front of his desk. The colonel began, "Lieutenant, Captain Gray has brought some pretty serious charges against you, specifically insubordination and conduct unbecoming an officer. How do you respond?"

I explained, "Well Sir, I guess I was a bit insubordinate, but I believe Captain Gray's conduct was more unbecoming than mine. Let me explain," which I did in lengthy detail. I recounted the entire sequence of events and produced a copy of the jeep's status with the date/time stamp on it. I said it was Captain Gray's diatribe that elicited my negative and inappropriate response while I was diligently carrying out a myriad of duties as acting commanding officer of the squadron. I indicated that Gray was not so much unreasonable as he was uncompromising and completely disregarded anything other than what he wanted to hear. I told Colonel Davis I did not comprehend the urgency of the jeep's dispatching in lieu of the fact that the majority of the squadron was deployed. I pleaded my case with remorse, all due candor, calmly, and with conviction and tact. I offered to apologize to Captain Gray but felt that I was due one considering the captain's behavior and my status as acting C. O. I closed my argument by telling Colonel Davis that I had an impeccable record, had been a very capable Administrative Officer, and had performed a very distinguished six months of combat service to my country at the front end of my overseas tour and then, stoically, awaited a response. I didn't have to wait long.

Colonel Davis asked, "Where are you from, Lieutenant?"

"Dallas, Sir," I replied.

"Me too," was the colonel's reply, and we had a nice chat about back home in Texas. So much for the proper and military professional courtesy, I thought, what about the verdict? Colonel Davis said, "I believe you are sincerely remorseful, but, I cannot let this incident go without any action against you." Oh shit I thought, here it comes. The colonel continued, "I will impart your apology to Gray. I am going to put a very brief letter in your jacket in response to Gray's accusations and recommend no action. Thank you for your service Lieutenant. Have a safe trip home."

I couldn't believe it. I told him, "Thank you, Colonel. I deeply appreciate it and hope you have a great tour here." I was dismissed and walked out of Colonel Davis's office with my head up high. The more I thought about it,

I realized that the colonel probably knew that Gray was an asshole. I also knew that I had done well for myself and indeed had saved my own ass or, I was just plain lucky that day. Then I gave the credit to whom it was due and thanked God. I was sure that Captain Gray would be pissed. He deserved some misery.

The next day, my six buddies and I left for Okinawa, where we all passed our physicals and the next day got on a commercial jetliner bound for the USA. The stewardesses were not the best looking but they were Americans and extremely cordial. They welcomed the soldiers back to the United States, many of whom were just back from the war and a few who were on their way to Hawaii for R&R. Once the wheels of the plane were in the wheel well and the plane was heading east for Wake Island, I relaxed. We were home free. On the next leg of the flight, to Hawaii, elation was prevalent in the plane and everyone was in high spirits. As I sat during a moment of silence, I thought ahead to El Toro and then reflected on the war and Japan. Then I thought of Jan. It was going to be awkward to be back together on a daily basis. I had changed but she also seemed different. That is when I withdrew into myself. Instead of setting my mind free, I became absorbed in my thoughts, anxious about the relationship with Jan and wondering if we could get back to "normal."

My thoughts were interrupted by the plane's captain who announced that they were having trouble lowering the landing gear as the plane approached Honolulu. I was not surprised and remained calm. The landing gear were lowered manually and the plane landed safely. I was on Hawaii for the third time within one year. We all got off the plane and waited for another one to take us home. My squadron mates and I went to the bar. We loudly bantered amongst ourselves and got into war stories. Each one of us had our own assortment of stories and flights and yet in many ways they were similar. Everyone around us pricked their ears to hear things ranging from the outrageous and harrowing to the unbelievable. After a few hours, our flight was announced and we took off for Edwards AFB in California. Everyone cheered as the plane lifted off the ground on our final leg back home.

Chapter 25

West Coast Finale

The plane arrived late at Edwards AFB, just before midnight. When I made my way off the plane and stepped onto the tarmac, I side-stepped the group and bent down and kissed the pavement. I was not the only one. All the passengers from the plane were ushered to a staging area in a hangar and searched, not by humans but by sniffer dogs. Our luggage was too. The delay seemed to take forever and I, along with most of the returning warriors, was a little miffed. I wasn't angered about the inconvenience but angered at being treated like suspects rather than veterans. Could anything be more degrading than such an insolent welcome home? I had just completed the most unselfish and patriotic act for my country and fellow countrymen. It was a kick in the teeth and it would not be my only one. The inspection and the delay imposition were finally over in the wee hours of the morning. We were all welcomed home by government officials in a dry and perfunctory ceremony and then issued tickets to our final destinations. We boarded a shuttle to LAX for our commercial connections with our "glorious" arrival in the States overshadowed by abasement.

I called Jan and my parents just before I boarded the plane. During the three-and-a-half-hour flight, I grew more apprehensive the closer I got to Dallas. When we landed I was a ball of nerves, but I managed to beam at everyone as I came down the jet way. I rushed to Jan and hugged her. She was barely hugging back. The cool reception was obvious and noted. I hugged my mom and dad and Jan's mom and dad and then tears welled up. I was home and on leave, such that it was. Jan and I headed to her parents' new home which had been built while I was overseas. We did not have sex that night, and sleep was difficult for me. Sex would not occur for another week. It was bullshit and I was angry. I was a soldier, a combat veteran, and it would take all my strength and tolerance not to show anger or downright explode.

The next night, Jan and I went to my parents' for the belated Christmas celebration. I pretended to have a wonderful time, but inside I was overwhelmed with grief and there was a pit in my stomach that would not go away. I hated Jan for diminishing my mom's special moment. Back at her parents' home, during our private time that evening, I demanded an explanation. She wouldn't reveal anything. I asked if there was someone else. She denied it, but I was certain she was lying. I was unable to sleep again that night. The next several days were agonizing. She was evasive, things were without a resolution, and most of all there was no love. Jan worked every day and I spent most of the daytime at my parents' home visiting with my mom while my dad worked. I had lunch with Jan's best friend hoping for an answer. There was none but I was sure she was sworn to secrecy. I would find out later that the best friend was the one that my sister had seen with Jan and other men out on the town.

As the days passed, a decision about returning to El Toro needed to be made. I was beginning to accept the possibility of going to California alone and in truth it didn't sound that bad. If I was going by myself, I didn't want to waste all of my leave time in Texas. Either way, a car needed to be purchased so we each had one. We went car shopping and ended up with a Corvette hardtop convertible. I again asked Jan if she was going to California. Her answer was, "I don't know."

I replied, "You need to decide soon because I am going as soon as I get things squared away." She was silent. While at my parents' home, my depression was hard to conceal. My mom asked what was wrong. I was vague and told her that I would elaborate later. She knew what I was trying to sort out for myself because my sister had told her about Jan. How ironic, I thought.

I had remained both celibate and faithful the entire year overseas and now almost wished I hadn't. I felt like I was back in hell again.

More revelations due to my overseas combat tour would ultimately come to light. The one for the moment was just that the only people Vietnam veteran status meant anything to were the veterans' families and the military, and in reality, military-wise, only for promotional purposes. The military had gotten what they wanted out of us. The ugly truth was my service; my medals and seventy-five cents would get me a of cup coffee. I could rationalize that away but not my personal dilemma. I abhorred my current emotional state of mind that was a result of Jan's emotional state. I was now ready to move on. I briefly wished I'd died in combat, then dismissed the thought. I hadn't, so "screw her," is exactly what I thought. I knew I deserved better. California was waiting.

The next day, to my surprise, Jan announced that she would go with me with no explanation and we made love that night. The following morning, I told her that I didn't want her to go if she didn't want to. Her slow response was, "I want to go." It would be a bittersweet decision. When I showed off the Corvette to my dad, a practical man, his response was, "Pretty expensive for two bucket seats." I thought it would be the ideal car for Southern California and it was when it was running. We took off in it towing our Plymouth Fury III and got lots of funny looks along the way. The "Vette" was in the shop half the first six months we owned it. It was a lemon.

We got an apartment in the same complex in Tustin and I reported to MAG-33 Admin. I was assigned as the group Classified Material Control Officer (CMCO), I assumed because of my top-secret clearance. I was in charge of all classified material at the Group level. After some missing document issues were resolved, I assumed my duties. I had had my incident with classified material, the Crypto wheel, and wasn't going to let anything bad happen again. Jan and I quickly settled back into Southern California life, much less hectic than before I deployed. I worked 0700 to 1600 hours and left immediately for home.

My billet was an anomaly; my duties were not. I was an extension of Administration but part of S-2, intelligence. I was assigned a Marine lance corporal for assistance and one of his duties was to make coffee in the morning. He was a nice young kid but his coffee fluctuated from brown water to mud you could slice with a knife. I quickly taught him some consistency. One day, while performing my duties and enjoying a cup of coffee, a lieutenant colonel came to my secure Dutch door and wanted to check out a secret document. The lieutenant colonel was not on the access list and my lance corporal appropriately refused to check it out to him. The lieutenant colonel, in a huff, demanded to see me. I wouldn't let him either. The lieutenant colonel became enraged and indignant before I had a chance to tell him how to get on the list. He could be heard bellowing all the way down the hallway of the MAG-33 Admin building. "Here we go again," I thought, as I kept my composure, even though the lieutenant colonel promised to have my ass.

After he settled down, I informed him that once he obtained the credentialed access from the Group Commanding Officer, he could get his document. I informed him that he could initiate the process in the Admin office next door. The lieutenant colonel stomped off really pissed but I wasn't fazed and went back to my coffee. He returned the next day and got his document, rather sheepishly but without any apologies. I added him to the list, fully cognizant that he was one of the things I hated about the Marine Corps and another reason not to make it a career.

Being CMCO turned out not to be such a "cush" job after all, but the hours were great. Harlow was in the F-4B squadron and Knudsen was Embarkation Officer of the Group. Harlow, even with his bunged tailbone, had to fly a lot. Occasionally, I would slip out of the CMCO cubbyhole hole and go down to visit Harlow or Knudsen, both from the Seattle area. The three of us now had less than one year left in the Marine Corps. I didn't know any of the other RIOs in Harlow's squadron and only a few of the pilots. Harlow complained occasionally that his ass was sore but mostly we reminisced, enjoying our status without complaining.

On Friday of that week I got called to come to the X.O.'s office, with no other details. I didn't like starch because it irritated my skin, but that Friday in a freshly starched uniform, I was standing tall in the Executive Officer's vestibule waiting for whatever it was, not knowing if it was good or bad. The X.O. invited me into his office where the Admin Officer and others were assembled. Everyone was congenial and upbeat. The X.O. put me at ease, and said, "On behalf of the Commandant of the Marine Corps, I am honored to bestow upon you the following citation." Then he commenced reading my Bronze Star Award citation. The Executive Officer concluded with, "Congratulations, Lieutenant, sounds like you guys were lucky you didn't get your asses shot off."

My response was, "Yes Sir, thank you." But inside I was bursting with pride. He presented the citation to me and the ceremony was over, such that it was. Not much pomp and circumstance but it was some recognition that, in truth, was confirmation of what I already knew. Many acts of valor and heroism occurred by men and women in all branches of service during the Vietnam War and only the politicians had a conflict calling it a war.

I didn't understand why I wasn't notified ahead of time so Jan could have been there. I took the citation home and read it to her. She expressed her accolades sparingly. I hardly spoke to her the rest the night. I read the citation again, alone, and realized that it was signed by General Buse Jr., FMF Pac Hawaii. He was the general I sat across from at the officer's mess in Vietnam. "Same day, same way," flashed through my mind momentarily. My next day at work, I looked up the flight in my logbook. It was a flight with Lieutenant Colonel Braddon who became my commanding officer in Japan. Was the citation for merit or because of my pilot's rank? I would never know. Was my citation less than Braddon's? I assumed that it was. But I was lucky I didn't get my ass shot off during that mission, now a distant memory—indelible, but distant.

That weekend Jan and I visited Texas friends who lived in Tejunga, California. Don worked for JPL (the Jet Propulsion Lab in Pasadena). Don and I met while we were both students at Arlington State College, now The University of Texas at Arlington. Don had earned a degree in electrical engineering and had worked for Collins Radio, now Texas Instruments. We drove up to their house in our Corvette with the top off. We arrived to see Don and his wife, Karen, standing in the front yard watching their twins play. When we got out of the car, Karen looked at Don and asked, "Why don't you get me a car like that?" Don replied as he looked and then pointed to the two kids, "Yonder is a Mercedes and there's a Cadillac." I laughed out loud and then told Karen the car was crap and that I would never get another one. We grilled steaks and talked about Texas and old times.

We all went to JPL and got to see moon rocks brought back by Apollo astronauts. I told Don I was sad I couldn't see the moon landing. Don gave me digital photos of some of the other planets and their moons. He asked me what I was going to do when I got out of the Marine Corps. I told him I didn't know. He also asked me where we were going to live. Again, I said I didn't know. Essentially, my future was uncertain. Then Don's and my conversation turned to the war. I was surprised to find out that JPL had developed some of the weapons that were used in Vietnam, including a couple dropped by our Phantoms. The next weekend Jan and I headed to Las Vegas in the Corvette and stayed at the Stardust Hotel. We drove up with the top down and got valet parking. I thought Jan was peeved when the car got more looks than her.

I needed flight time in order to maintain flight status and flight pay but decided that I would not set foot in an F-4B, even though I was often tempted and could have any time I wanted. The B model Phantom was older and I didn't feel like having to manage my air sickness. I started getting my monthly minimum flight time in the Base C-117 prop passenger plane. It was a utility plane for cargo, personnel, and mail. On one of those flights back from Yuma, I was seated in the first row just behind the cockpit. I was half asleep when the plane dove abruptly enough to create negative G and pull me up off my seat. Then, just as suddenly, positive G slammed me back down. I grabbed the arm rests and held on as the plane went through this maneuver four or five more times. The plane landed at El Toro a short time later. As I exited the plane, shaken up and probably a little wan, the pilot said, "Whoops, sorry about that. We were having a little trouble getting the gear down and I forgot you were back there." I responded, "No problem, I've been through lots worse," reflecting on the Logan retirement fiasco.

When I got back to my "office," the "Eagle flew," which was military slang for payday. I went to the bank to cash my check on the way home. In uniform, with my ribbons and accomplishments on display, I approached a female teller. As she neared the completion of the transaction, I barely heard her say under her breath, "Baby killer." I was a little shocked and taken aback but did not let the statement go unanswered.

I calmly, simply, replied, "I suppose I am," as the twenty-two-hut village crossed my mind. I turned to leave with my money but turned back adding something like this: "I am not responsible for the policy that engages this country in war, but I think you would think differently if you were there getting your ass shot at in a kill or be killed situation. You don't have a clue sitting there doing your cushy job," and walked out. The farther away from the bank I got, the madder I was. With my ten Air Medals, Bronze Star Award, Combat Action Ribbon, and two Navy Unit Commendations, I didn't have to justify anything to anybody. I stayed angry the rest of the day, even after eating Mexican food. The unmitigated gall of that bitch, I thought. That night, as I lay in bed, I acknowledged the hard truth. I served and fought so that she and everyone else in the United States had the freedom to say whatever they wanted, to whomever they wanted, right or wrong. And then I thought, "you clueless idiot" and drifted off. (To date, that has been my only confrontation with negativism.)

The following Monday I got word that I was going down to the San Diego Naval base to train in classified crypto and ultimately implement the equipment at the squadron level in all MAG-33 units. It was going to be a lot of work. I never shirked any of my responsibilities but really didn't want this one. When I told Jan about the training, she asked me why I had to go and then was pissed with my explanation. I thought she ought to be used to it, plus she could drive there in a couple hours from El Toro if she wanted to. She did not want to and said she would go stay with her relatives. That was fine with me. I was sick of her complaints. She was the worst military wife I knew of. The next week I attended the one-week school at Coronado. It was nice and I really enjoyed the time there. When I got back, I had a week's worth of messages to catch up on. While I was reading them all, I came across an unclassified message that read, "In preparation of a post-Vietnam scale down of personnel, the United States Marine Corps is having a RIF, reduction in force. Any Marine in a non-critical MOS can get as much as a six month early release if he or she is qualified." The qualifications were: not be in a critical MOS, have completed an overseas tour, and have less than a year of service obligation, and others.

I got excited at the prospect. If I submitted my paperwork right away and it was approved within thirty days, I might get out the whole six months early. It was mid-July and my termination date was March 1 of 1971. I called Jan. She was ecstatic. She had a flurry of questions, when will we know? How long will it take? When can we move back home? When will you put in the request? I told her I'd have the paperwork in that afternoon. A little over two hours after reading the message, I had my release request into the Administrative Officer. Less than an hour after that, the X.O. requested my presence in his office. I knew it wasn't a social call, nor another citation and I'd have to defend my request. The X.O. was gruff. He asked, "Why have you made this request?"

"Colonel," I began, "I am not a career Marine. I am ready to end my stint in the Marine Corps and get on with my life. I fully qualify for this and am requesting it."

Then he asked, "Can you delay this request until the crypto project is completed?"

Out of courtesy, I thought a minute. I wasn't sure how long the project would take and I might not get out early at all if there were delays. Besides, I was secretly hoping to avoid it. I replied, "No, Sir. I qualify for this and I am requesting it at this time."

I knew he was pissed but he said, "I will take care of it."

I knew what that meant. If he had been sincere, he'd have said he would submit it or forward it. I was sure it was going in the trash (circular file, or file thirteen as they called it). So, a week later I went up the chain of command and contacted the Third Marine Air Wing Administrative Office and got a hold of Captain White. I asked him if my early release paperwork had come up from the group. The answer was, no. Typical, I thought, fuck you right up until the end and then they wonder why young officers like me didn't want a career in the Corps. I asked the captain if we could meet face-to-face. His response was, "I'll be here until 1600 hours." I went to him and explained the situation. I confided in him that I needed a friend and asked if I prepared a new request and brought it to him, would he forward it to HQMC? The captain said he would. I told him that I would bring it over the next morning and I did. I offered to buy him dinner. The captain declined and then commented to me, "There are some good ones in the Corps."

I said, "Thank you, Captain. I know," and then added, "Like you, I am one of them." It was now into August.

The timing of the crypto installation was getting really close, tense actually. I was stalling as much as I could but knew it would come to a head soon. Eventually the equipment would arrive and personnel at the squadron level would need to be trained and take possession of it, install it, and use it. There were messages almost every day about it. About the time I was ready to give up, I got a call from Captain White at the wing. White asked, "Did you get it?"

"Get what?" I asked.

"Copies of your early release orders," the captain proudly announced.

I replied, "No, Sir. Can I come over and get a copy?"

The captain agreed and said, "I'll be here until 1600 hours."

I exclaimed, "I'm on my way right now!" I could hardly believe it. I thanked the captain profusely and headed back to the group, thanking God on the way. I made a copy of the orders and took one to the Admin Officer. My date of separation was October 1. I was getting out five months early and it was almost September. When I got back to my cubbyhole, my phone was ringing. It was the X.O. My lance corporal heard me say, "Yes Sir, I'll be right there."

I took a copy of my orders and headed to the Executive Officer's office. I knew it would be ugly but I also knew it was over and there was no way I could be hurt. There was nothing anyone in the MAG-33 command could do about it except be an asshole. The X. O. was. When the Executive Officer was done with his tirade, I told him I would do everything I could for my replacement regarding a smooth transition and the crypto project. And I did. Jan and I socialized as much as we could with the Harlows and Knudsens during the next few weeks. Jan drove back to Texas a week before me. One of her aunts went with her and visited relatives before she flew back to California. I had a wisdom tooth extracted on September 30, my last day in the Marine Corps. On October 1, after the movers left, I was ready to drive back to Texas. I contacted the apartment manager to break our one-year lease. He seemed unwilling to accept his obligation until I showed him a copy of my orders and reminded him of a federal law. As I drove away, I was acutely aware that assholes didn't exist solely in the Marine Corps.

Epilogue

During my two-day, twenty-two-hour, drive home, I had plenty of time to think. I was free, owned by no man, authority, or agency. I thought my future looked bright and had no fear of it. I had no regrets when I reflected on my military service. I did not consider myself a hero, even though I had done heroic things. To me, the real heroes of the Vietnam War were those who flew low and slow, controllers, helicopter pilots and their crewmen, and most especially the ground forces who met the enemy face-to-face. I thought not enough praise and honor could be bestowed upon them. And to the families of those who made the ultimate sacrifice, I felt our whole country should show them respect and appreciation for their loss and their sacrifices.

Since returning to the States, I hadn't been praised by anyone outside of my family and that was disappointing. I mulled this injustice over while driving and though it was sobering, I vowed to remain undaunted. I couldn't fathom why public hatred of this war transferred over to military personnel. I had served admirably even though there was never a concise victory or any positive resolution to the "conflict." (Henceforth, this had a profound effect on my politics and my philosophy of war and life.) I recognized that my service was just a small part of all the aviation (USMC, Navy, Army, and Air Force) operations, which killed the enemy and helped all ground forces including the ARVN troops, such that they were.

Then I thought of the bigger picture. The country owed gratitude not to just these veterans but to all soldiers who have served since Revolutionary War times. I now fully understood that the cost of freedom is death for some of our service men and women. I knew my country's liberty could only be preserved through the blood of those who fight for it. As I pondered this, I recalled the Scripture I used in church before I left for Vietnam, John 15:13, "Greater love hath no man than this, that he lay down his life for his friends." I was glad I didn't lose my life in what I considered to be a senseless war but realized I was now part owner of that freedom just like all the others who went before me. I thanked God for seeing me through, not knowing why He did (for I certainly was not worthy), yet knowing full well it was the Almighty's hand.

My nagging question was, had I really accomplished anything? Of that, I had serious reservations. I was convinced that meliorism could not be directly applied to the Vietnam War effort. I was unable to make a viable association and that was depressing. The solace I could and would ultimately claim, that which guaranteed sleep at night, was that I helped, if not saved, an unknown number of friendly ground combatants (Free World Forces) because I had conquered my airsickness and helped put ordnance on target. I also knew that any kills of the enemy from the various ordnances I helped drop prevented a percentage of havoc and death, that those I killed might have wreaked. And I most assuredly knew as long as I lived, I would die in defense of my country at any time, if it were for the right reasons. I endeavored to work in a public service-oriented business with socially redeeming value.

My thoughts turned melancholy when I considered all the members of VMFA-232 and 334 whom I had come to know, most of whom I would probably never see again. Some were friends, some peers, and others were mentors or role models unaware. The majority were Marines but a few were Navy. All contributed directly or indirectly to my military and life experience, an experience I would never forget. "Semper Fidelis and good luck," I whispered aloud. The whole experience gave me a strong sense of patriotism, one that I began noticing was missing in many Americans and I felt it might lead to the downfall of the United States.

I felt more than ever that the whole country needed to vote politicians into office who believed in maintaining a superior national defense. Our country's armed forces' manning levels should be more than adequate for any global scenario and their weaponry and armament should be the best in the world. This means support and fund weapons' research and development. Those same politicians should make sure that any veteran with an emotional or physical need gets whatever he or she requires, at whatever cost, timely, and for as long as he or she needs it. I hoped our future politicians would not engage in another useless, senseless war like 'Nam but was certain that history would repeat itself. I dwelled on the Vietnam War's statistical losses and the cost to taxpayers, thinking it was seemingly for no good reason. To me it was a waste and I hoped families could justify loved ones they lost as a result of our armed forces being there. I could not.

I thought little of Jan until I got close to home. They weren't happy thoughts. Once home, Jan and I moved back into the house we bought before I enlisted. I went to my previous employer and demanded they give me my job back. Reluctantly they did. I hated it. No wonder, I was not yet twenty-seven years old, had flown twice the speed of sound and seen the curvature of the earth from 52,000 feet. I had been in charge of Marine personnel, was a combat veteran having flown 123 combat missions, and been halfway around the world. I thought, what compares to that. After three months back in Texas, I procured a small business loan and bought a photography studio. This became my career for the next twenty years, using my acquired skills to manage personnel and my confidence to accomplish absolutely anything. Yes, the Marine Corps builds men; I was living proof.

When a recession happened after the mid 1980s and my business went bust, I got a job with the Arlington (Texas) Police Department as a crime scene investigator. Being a CSI utilized my science education, my military background, and my photography skills. It was a good marriage. I took to fingerprint work too, becoming a Certified Latent Fingerprint Examiner in addition to being a Certified Crime Scene Investigator (certifications by the International Association for Identification—IAI). While being a criminalist supervisor, I was instrumental in getting the police department I retired from, Plano, Texas, accredited by the American Society of Crime Lab Directors, known by the acronym ASCLD. This was a very prestigious and coveted achievement. Though the accomplishment was very satisfying, nothing can compare to being a Phantom in the Sky.

I truly believed I had one of the better tours of duty the Marine Corps ever gave away but never considered an active duty career. I was promoted to captain in the inactive reserve and seven years later joined the active reserves at NAS Dallas, an environment a whole lot more to my liking, plus I got to fly some in the Phantom. I eventually earned a twenty-year retirement and the rank of major, having been passed over for lieutenant colonel. (I actually received a citation in the mail promoting me to lieutenant colonel, only to receive a letter in the mail thirty days later requesting that I return it because they claimed they made a mistake.) I didn't get that upset, considered the source, and moved on.

Official USMC photo of the author taken for his promotion to lieutenant colonel. The photo was taken while he was attached to MAG-41 at NAS Dallas, Texas, while in the reserves. He was passed over and retired as a major. He was forty-seven years old when the photo was taken.

The photo is of the author's principal pilot Brown, left, who is shown
with VMFA-232 RIOs Devere (center) and Steele, on the right.
The photo was taken by the author at the squadron's 30th reunion in
Gulf Shores, Alabama.

Our VMFA-232 Vietnam complement of personnel began having reun-
ions every five years beginning with the twenty-fifth. I have attended three.
For the twenty-fifth, we jointly met with 334. It is always good to visit with
those peers and was especially nice to see many of my 334 cronies at the first
one, both pilots and RIOs. Many of my photos and movies were incorporated
into a squadron video commemorating our Vietnam tour.

My married-up pilot, Brown, moved to Pensacola after retirement.
We now keep in touch often and always exchange Christmas cards. He ended
up having an illustrious career. He did not deploy with the squadron to Japan
and stayed in Vietnam to finish his tour. He was assigned to 1st MAW
Headquarters and flew with various squadrons while still in Country. He and
his flight earned Distinguished Flying Crosses for one particularly intense
CAS sortie. He wishes I had been in his back seat for it. After his Vietnam
tour, he was transferred to Willow Grove, Pennsylvania, as Operations and
Maintenance Officer and flew F-8s. He next went to Pensacola to become

the VT-4 training squadron's Operations Officer and flew T-2 Buckeyes. Brown went back overseas to the 1st MAW and then to VMFA-115 to become their Executive Officer until he was transferred back to the United States to become the Executive Officer of VMFA-333 at Beaufort, South Carolina, and then commanding officer as a lieutenant colonel.

Brown was assigned to NAAS Whiting Field as Executive Officer and then Commanding Officer of Navy Training Squadron Three. Brown then graduated from the Naval War College and was assigned to the Pentagon to work on the F-18 project. After that, he was the Deputy Director and then Director of the Marine Corps Command and Staff College. He went back to 1st MAW as Chief of Staff and then back to the States to be Chief of Staff at 3rd MAW. His last duty station was as Senior Marine with the Chief of Naval Training Command. He retired as a "bird" Colonel with thirty-one years of service.

My hooch mate, Josh Carpenter, also moved to Pensacola after his stint in the Corps. He became a builder, both commercial and residential, and a remodeler. He bought a boat and named it Whiskey Tango. He had to buy another one when the first one was destroyed by a hurricane. Bob Snyder, incredibly, became a minister after a harrowing flight in a Harrier jet.

One of VMFA-232's F-4J Phantoms is currently on display, complete with markings, in the Smithsonian's Udvar Hazy Air and Space Museum near Dulles International Airport in Washington, D. C. The VMFA-232 Red Devil squadron is the oldest and most decorated squadron in the Marine Corps.

I've come to hate those who disrespect or burn our flag and those individuals who detest our men and women who serve. To me, the Stars and Stripes mean everything, evidence of one's allegiance to this great country. The Stars and Stripes are what every service man and woman serves under, respects, defends, and holds dear, long may it wave. I got angry when I found out about the political involvement in air operations and other ugly truths about the Vietnam War. I still have empathy for veterans who are emotionally scarred, many of whom have never recovered. I also feel sorry for those who have suffered from the effects of Agent Orange. It is an atrocity that their service has cost them dearly.

The white rash I contracted in Vietnam, which reappeared every hot Texas summer for years, eventually went away. After fifteen years of dermatologist treatment, a skin cancer on my forehead, which was probably triggered by my sunbathing in Southeast Asia, had to be surgically removed.

Jan and I had two children, both boys. Neither of them served in the military. Though I made a valiant effort at it for many, many years, our marriage was not good and never got better. Once our relationship was irreconcilable, Jan and I divorced.

Marine Poem

It cannot be inherited,
Nor can it ever be purchased.

You, Nor anyone else alive,
Can buy it at any price.

It is impossible to rent,
It cannot be lent.

You alone and our own
Have earned it
With your sweat, blood and lives.

The Title,
United States Marine

Glossary

Definitions, Acronyms and Combat Slang

AAA: (Triple A), Anti-Aircraft Artillery

ACM: Aerial Combat Maneuvering ("Dog Fighting")

ADI: Attitude, direction indicator

ADIZ: Air Defense Identification Zone

AGL: Actual Ground Level

AOM: All Officers Meeting

AFB: Air Force Base

APC: Area of Positive Control

ARVN: Army of the Republic of Vietnam

ATC: Air Traffic Control

BDA: Bomb Damage Assessment

BARCAP: Barrier Continuous Air Patrol

BNAO: Basic Naval Aviation Orientation ("Banana School")

BOQ: Bachelor Officer's Quarters

CAS: Close Air Support mission

Charlie: Viet Cong Combatants

DMZ: Demilitarized Zone

Echo: In the military phonetic alphabet, letter "E"

FAA: Federal Aviation Administration

FAM (hop): Familiarity flight

FMLP: Field Mirror Landing Practice (touch and goes)

FAC: Forward Air Controller

Friendlies: Friendly Forces (U.S. or ARVN military forces, mercenaries, etc.)

GCA: Ground Control Approach

GCI: Ground Controlled Intercept

GIB: Guy in Back (RIO, etc.)

Grunts: Marine ground forces

GSE: Ground Support Equipment

HE: High explosive (ordnance)

Head: Navy for "latrine" (Restroom)

HQMC: Headquarters Marine Corps

ICS: Intercom system

IFR: Instrument Flight Rules; (on flight schedules) In Flight Refueling

JEST: Jungle Escape and evasion Survival Training

JUDY: Intercept lingo meaning "taking control"

KBMA: Killed By Marine Air

MACH: Speed of sound
MAG: Marine Aircraft Group
MAW: Marine Aircraft Wing
MCAS: Marine Corps Air Station
MEDEVAC: Medical Evacuation
MOS: Military Occupational Specialty
Napes and Snakes: Napalm and cast-iron fragmentary bombs
NAS: Naval Air Station
NATOPS: Naval Aviation Training and Operations Procedures Standardization
NCO: Non-Commissioned Officer
NFO: Naval Flight Officer
OCS: (Marine) Officer Candidates School
OPS: Operations section
PAVN: Peoples' Army of Vietnam
PT: Physical Training
R & D: Research and Development
RAT: Ram Air Turbine
RIO: Radar Intercept Officer
SAM: Surface to Air Missile
SAR: Search and Rescue
SEA hut: Southeast Asia hut
SNAFU: Situation Normal, All Fucked Up
SOP: Standard Operating Procedure
Sortie: One mission or attack by a single plane
TACAN: Tactical Aid to Navigation
TOT: Time on Target
TPQ: Ground Directed Bombing
USMC: United States Marine Corps
VFR: Visual Flight Rules
VIP: Very Important Person, dignitary

Appendix A

USMC History and Mission

The mission of the Marine Corps is as follows: "The Marine Corps shall be organized, trained and equipped to provide Fleet Marine Forces of combined arms, together with supporting air components, for service with the U.S. Fleet in the seizure or defense of advanced naval bases and for the conduct of such land operations as may be essential to the prosecution of a naval campaign; to provide detachments and organizations for service on armed vessels of the Navy, and security detachments for the protection of naval property at naval stations and bases; to develop in connection with the Army, the Navy, and the Air Force, the tactics, technique and equipment employed by landing forces in amphibious operations; to train and equip, as required, Marine forces for airborne operations, in coordination with the Army, the Navy, and the Air Force in accordance with policies and doctrines of the Joint Chiefs of Staff; to develop, in coordination with the Army, the Navy, and the Air Force, doctrines, procedures and equipment of interest to the Marine Corps for airborne operations and which are not provided for by the Army; to be prepared, in accordance with integrated joint mobilization plans, for the expansion of the peacetime components to meet the needs of war."

Semper Fidelis (Always Faithful) was adopted as the Marine Corps Motto in 1888 when John Philip Sousa was the leader of the Marine Corps Band. In the Marines' Hymn, "From the halls of Montezuma" is derived from the Mexican War, and "To the shores of Tripoli" is from the Barbary Wars (even though the chronology is backwards). The Barbary War victory gave birth to the Marine Officer's sword (Mameluke) when Captain Presley O'Bannon, after leading his Marines to victory at Tripoli, was presented a sword by a Mameluke chieftain. The "Devil Dogs" label was applied by German combatants during World War I. One accolade after another came during World War II as Marines took one Pacific island after another. But Iwo Jima stands out because of the raising of the Stars and Stripes on Mount Suribachi both as a Pulitzer Prize-winning photo and then a statue, with one at Quantico and the other at Arlington National Cemetery.

In Korea, the Marines recaptured Seoul and then endured some of the most bitterly cold fighting conditions that any of the U.S. armed forces have ever encountered. Other labels and quotations just as colorful have been applied to the Marines: "Leathernecks," "Gung Ho," "Jarhead," "Esprit de Corps," and even their nickname, "The Few, The Proud." History has also given birth to much of the Marine uniform dress and embellishments, like dress blues with the red stripe on the trousers and the globe and anchor buttons, etc.

Appendix B

VMFA-232 History

VMFA-232, the "Red Devil" squadron, was established by the Marine Corps in 1925 as VF-10. In Navy terminology, the V stands for "fixed wing" and the F for "fighter." VMFA stands for Fixed Wing Marine Fighter Attack (squadron). Without the M it is a Navy unit. The Red Devil insignia has been retained since the squadron's inception. The unit's first overseas action was in China in 1927 during their civil war. Nineteen of the unit's twenty-one planes were destroyed in the Japanese attack on Pearl Harbor. A detachment of the unit's personnel were sent to Wake Island in the Pacific where they served in the final defense of the island. All were captured or killed there after a long fight for the Red Devils. They supported the battle of Guadalcanal, then Bougainville, Cape Esperance, New Georgia, Bismarck, Archipelago, Okinawa, and the Solomon Islands.

After World War II, the unit was a training squadron at El Toro during the Korean War and in 1954, it moved to MCAS Kanehoe Bay on Oahu, Hawaii. The unit was one of the first to fly the FJ jet aircraft and deployed to Atsugi, Japan, in 1958. In 1959 the squadron received the Vought F-8 Crusader jet and the awards rolled in over several years. The squadron was called the "Finest Fighter Squadron in Naval Aviation." They received "Top Gun" honors two years running. The squadron received the coveted Commandant's Aviation Efficiency Trophy (awarded for highest excellence in the performance of its designated mission) and the CNO (Chief of Naval Operations) "Aviation Safety Award."

In 1965, the squadron entered the Vietnam Theater as VMF/AW, the AW meaning "all weather," and flew 290 consecutive days of operations, flying sorties in virtually every Marine operation during this period. The squadron returned to El Toro in 1967 and traded their worn-out F-8 Crusaders for brand-new, straight from McDonnell Douglas, F-4J Phantoms. The squadron was re-designated VMFA-232.

Appendix C

McDonnell Douglas F-4J Phantom II Aircraft Statistical Data

The F-4 Phantom aircraft was designed for intermediate and long-range high altitude interceptions using missiles as the principal armament and for intermediate or long-range attack missions to deliver airborne weapons/stores. It was powered by two single-rotor, axial flow, variable stator turbo jet General Electric J79-10 engines with afterburner. The engines produced 11,870 pounds each of static thrust at sea level, and 17,900 pounds of thrust each with afterburner (the aircraft was not considered to be thrust limited). The aircraft featured a low mounted swept-back wing with anhedral at the wing tips, and a one-piece stabilator with cathedral, mounted low on the aft fuselage. The wings had hydraulically operated leading edge and trailing edge flaps, ailerons, spoilers, and speed brakes. The dimensions, statistics, and capacities of this mean-looking plane were:

Wing span (spread)—38 feet 5 inches; folded—27 feet 7 inches

Length—58 feet, 3 inches

Height (to top of fin)—16 feet, 6 inches

Weight (clean, empty)—29,500 lbs

Fuel capacity (internal)—13,587 lbs (JP5 fuel is 6.8 pounds per gallon @ 60 degrees F)

Maximum Gross Takeoff weight (fuel and ordnance)—56,000 lbs

The Phantom is equipped to carry and deliver an assortment of air-to-air missiles, air-to-ground missiles, rockets, bombs, land mines, leaflet dispensers, and airborne weapons/stores. The aircraft is also equipped with gunnery capabilities with the addition of the MK-4 (Hughes) gun pod on the centerline station—a two-barrel, Gatling-style, machine gun capable of delivering 6,000 rounds of 20mm ammo per minute. Note: The F-4J's maximum gross takeoff weight of 56,000 pounds was exceeded by 1,000 pounds prior to takeoff when it was fully loaded with gas, including external fuel of 5,000 pounds in either a centerline tank or two wing tanks, and 6,000 pounds of ordnance. One thousand pounds of fuel was consumed during takeoff, resulting in the plane being exactly at the maximum gross takeoff weight as the plane's nose gear rotated off the runway.

Appendix D

VMFA-334 History

Marine Fighter Attack Squadron (VMFA) 334 was activated on August 1, 1943, as Marine Scout Bomber Squadron 334, flying SBD Dauntless aircraft and assigned to MAG-33, 3rd MAW, FMFPAC.

Throughout World War II, the squadron remained stateside operating from MCAS El Toro, California, and deploying for intensive Anti-Submarine Warfare Training to MCAS Cherry Point, North Carolina, NAAS Boca Chica, Florida, MCARF Kingston, North Carolina, and MCARF Newport, Arkansas. The squadron was not committed to combat operations and deactivated on October 10, 1944.

In May 1952, re-designated as Marine Attack Squadron, VMA-334 was reactivated and resumed flight operations utilizing the F6F-5 Hellcat. During the winter months of 1952–53, the squadron transitioned to the F-4U Corsair and in May 1953, to the Grumman F-9F Panther Jet Fighter.

In the early summer of 1954, the squadron was re-designated Marine Fighter Attack Squadron 334 and received the FJ-2 Fury. The FJ-3s replaced the FJ-2s in 1956 and during the closing months of the year the squadron received the FJ-4.

In January of 1957, VMF-334 deployed to NAS Atsugi, Japan, and joined MAG-11, 1st MAW, Air, FMFPAC. Rotating to rejoin MAG-33, 3rd MAW in February 1958, the unit became the first West Coast Marine Fighter Squadron to be equipped with the supersonic F8U-1 Crusader in April 1958. The unit was re-designated as Marine All Weather Fighter Squadron 334. During the succeeding nine years, the squadron was equipped with the F8U-1, 2 and 2N.

On June 6, 1967, 334 received the all-new, highly sophisticated F-4J Phantom and was re-designated VMFA-334. 334 was the first Marine squadron to receive the F-4J.

In mid-1968, VMFA-334 began preparations for deployment to the Far East to participate in the Vietnam War. On August 20, the squadron joined MAG-11, 1st MAW, at Da Nang AB, RVN, to assume the air-to-air and air-to-ground role in support of Free World Forces.

January 1969, VMFA-334 changed its home to "Fighter Town" when the squadron joined MAG-13. In doing so, the squadron became the first F-4J squadron to permanently operate out of the Chu Lai Air Base. From that point forward, the "Falcons" performed an in-Country role of close air support of troops in contact and interdiction of enemy supply routes in the I-Corps Tactical Zone as well as supporting the U.S. 7th Fleet with air-to-air capability in the Gulf of Tonkin.

During the first nine months of operations in the Republic of Vietnam, the Falcons flew over 5,000 combat sorties and expended over 10,000 tons of ordnance on Communist forces.

Appendix E

MAG-13 History

Marine Aircraft Group-13 was activated March 1, 1942, at San Diego, California, and participated in the Marshall Islands Campaign during World War II. It was deactivated at the close of the war.

Reformed in April 1951, the Group moved to Kanehoe Bay, Hawaii, in early 1952 with only two fighter squadrons and Marine Air Control Squadron-2. Aviation units based at El Toro, California, were rotated to Kanehoe Bay every six months for training until April 1954.

On May 1, 1956, the First Marine Brigade assumed its title in lieu of the 1st Provisional Marine Air-Ground Task Force designation. MAG-13 gained air support for this unique organization.

At this time MAG-13 gained the distinction of being the only Composite Marine Aircraft Group. Comprised of Fighter, Attack, and Helicopter Squadrons support and ground arm of the 1st Marine Brigade. The squadrons then comprising MAG-13 were: Marine Fighter Attack Squadron 214, the famous "Black Sheep" of Medal of Honor winner Colonel Gregory "Pappy" Boyington, the "Red Devils" of Marine All Weather Fighter Squadron 232, the "Lancers" of Marine All Weather Squadron 121 and the "Work Horse" squadron, Marine Medium Helicopter Squadron 161, the first Marine helicopter squadron to be activated.

In mid-1964, MAG-13 first began to become involved in the planning of Operation Silver Lance. During the period of 1–8 February 1965, MAG-13 embarked aboard one APA and eight LSTs. On February 16, MAG-13 arrived at San Clemente Island and commenced to offload. At 2300 hours of the same date, MAG-13 was ordered to commence back-loading and was phased out of Operation Silver Lance along with the rest of the 1st Marine Brigade. By the evening of February 17, MAG-13 was en route back to Pearl Harbor and arrived on February 29. Here, the Group remained loaded and in a ready status until March 11 when MAG-13 departed for Okinawa. Upon arrival, on March 31, MAG-13 unloaded and set up operations at MCAF (Marine Corps Air Field), Futema, Okinawa. On April 1, all tactical Squadrons were phased out and assigned to the 1st MAW.

At this time, MAG-13 was assigned to MCAS Iwakuni, Japan. On May 26, the advanced party arrived at Iwakuni marking the beginning of a gradual relocation of personnel and equipment, which was completed on June 30. MAG-13 operated from this location until October 1966.

At the time, the squadrons that comprised MAG-13 were H&MS (Headquarters and Maintenance Squadron, referred to as "Hams") 13, MABS (Marine Air Base Squadron) 13, VMFA 211, joined on June 6, 1965, by Marine All Weather Fighter Squadron (VMF/AW) 312. VMFA 115 joined on June 26, 1965. VMFA 314 joined on July 4, 1965 and VMFA 223 on 15 September 15, 1965.

MAG-13 was deployed to Chu Lai, Republic of Vietnam, during October 1966 comprised of the following squadrons: H&MS-13, MABS-13, VMFA-115, VMFA-122, VMFA-232, VMFA-314, VMFA-323 and VMFA-334.

Endnotes

1. "Muhammad Ali and Vietnam," *Atlantic Daily* (Washington D.C.), June 4, 2016.

2. Details on USMC history are from the *Guidebook for Marines*, 11th ed., published by *Leatherneck Magazine* (Washington D.C.: Marine Corps Association, 1966).

3. Details on USMC mission are from the *Guidebook for Marines*, 11th ed., published by *Leatherneck Magazine* (Washington D.C.: Marine Corps Association, 1966).

4. Information on the M-14 rifle is from *Guidebook for Marines*, 11th ed., published by *Leatherneck Magazine* (Washington D.C.: Marine Corps Association, 1966).

5. NAS Pensacola history is found on the website: www.cnic.navy.mil

6. Information on Payne Stewart's death is found on his Wikipedia page.

7. Information on the Navy UC-45J Beechcraft "Expeditor" trainer aircraft, is from the website of the Naval Aviation Museum, Barber's Point: http://www.nambp.org/beechcraft-uc-45j-expeditor

8. Information on the Navy T-33 "Shooting Star" jet trainer is from the website https://www.militaryfactory.com/aircraft/detail.asp?aircraft_id=726

9. Information on the Navy F9F Grumman "Panther" jet trainer, is from the Wikipedia page.

10. Information on the Navy T-39 North American "Sabreliner" jet, is from the Wikipedia page.

11. Details on the MCAS El Toro patch and logo can be found at www.irvinecitynews.com, California, accessed June 1, 2017.

12. The MCAS El Toro history is from the website: www.navy.mil

13. The VMFA -232 history is from the website: www.marines.mil

14. Details on the McDonnell Douglas F-4 Phantom II jet can be found in the *F4J NATOPS Manual*.

15. Aviator poem "High Flight," by John Magee, USAF/RCAF.

16. VMFA-232 Phantoms tanking, photo from page 155 of *Vietnam: The War in the Air* by Rene J. Francillon.

17. Details on the Chu Lai Base and airfield are from the *Seabee Magazine* article titled "The Sands of Chu Lai," found at www.seabeemagazine.navylive.dodlive.mil

18. Cruise Book photo of the author, from 1969 *VMFA-232 Cruise Book.*
19. Details on the Battle of Khe Sanh are found at www.history.com
20. Information on the Rockpile, Vietnam, is from the Marine Corps Association article "In the Shadow of the Rockpile," found at www. mca-marines.org

Bibliography

Books

Guidebook for Marines. Washington D. C.: The Leatherneck Association, 1966.

Francillon, Rene J. *Vietnam: The War in the Air*. New York: Arch Cape Press, 1987.

VMFA-232 Cruisebook. Tokyo, Japan: Daito Art Printing Co., Ltd, 1969

VMFA-334 Cruisebook. Tokyo, Japan: Daito Art Printing Co., Ltd, 1969

Magazine Articles

Bartlett, Tom. "In the Shadow of the Rockpile." *Leatherneck Magazine*, Washington D.C.: Marine Corps Association, 1991.

Blazich, Frank A., Jr. "Sands of Chu Lai." *Seabee Magazine*, Washington D. C., 2015.

Manuals

Roberts, Michael L. *U.S. Navy F4J NATOPS Flight Manual*. Atglen, PA: Schiffer Publishing Ltd, 1995.

Newspapers

"Disney Goes to War at the Great Park." *Irvine City News* (California), June 1, 2017.

"Muhammad Ali and Vietnam." *Atlantic Daily* (Washington D. C.), June 4, 2016.

Websites

www.cnic.navy.mil

www.history.com

www.marines.mil

www.militaryfactory.com

www.nambp.com

www.navy.mil

www.nnam.org

www.ntsb.gov

Index

Page numbers in italics indicate photos

A